Listening to Earth

Other readers featured in the "Longman Topics" series include:

Translating Tradition
Karen E. Beardslee

Reading City Life
Patrick Bruch and Richard Marback

Citizenship Now
Jon Ford and Marjorie Ford

Issues of Gender
Ellen Friedman and Jennifer Marshall

The Counterculture Reader
E. A. Swingrover

Music and Culture
Anna Tomasino

Ethics in the 21st Century
Mary Alice Trent

Considering Cultural Difference
Pauline Uchmanowicz

Language and Prejudice
Tamara M. Valentine

CyberReader (Abridged Edition)
Victor J. Vitanza

Listening to Earth

CHRISTOPHER HALLOWELL
Baruch College, City University of New York

WALTER LEVY
Pace University

New York   San Francisco   Boston
London   Toronto   Sydney   Tokyo   Singapore   Madrid
Mexico City   Munich   Paris   Cape Town   Hong Kong   Montreal

Senior Vice President and Publisher: Joseph Opiela
Senior Acquisitions Editor: Lynn M. Huddon
Marketing Manager: Wendy Albert
Production Manager: Eric Jorgensen
Project Coordination, Text Design, and Electronic Page Makeup:
   Sunflower Publishing Services, Inc.
Cover Designer/Manager: Wendy Ann Fredericks
Cover Photo: ©Mark E. Gibson
Senior Manufacturing Buyer: Alfred C. Dorsey
Printer and Binder: Courier Corporation
Cover Printer: Coral Graphic Services

For permission to use copyrighted material, grateful acknowledge-
ment is made to the copyright holders on pp. 239–241, which are
hereby made part of this copyright page.

Library of Congress Cataloging-in-Publication Data

Listening to earth / [edited by] Christopher Hallowell, Walter Levy.
   p. cm.— (A Longman topics reader)
   ISBN 0-321-19515-9
   1. Human ecology in literature. 2. Geographical perception in literature. I. Hallowell, Christopher. II. Levy, Walter. III. Longman
topics.

PN48.L57 2005
810.9'3556—dc22   2004053384

Visit us at http://www.ablongman.com

ISBN 0-321-19515-9

2345678910-CRS-070605

CONTENTS

Historical Chronology and Context   *ix*

Introduction   **1**

CHAPTER 1   Value of the Land   **5**

John Muir, The American Forests   7

John Muir believed that nature was God's temple and its
destruction sacrilegious. Muir's central question is: "Why
should man value himself as more than a small part of the
one great unit of creation?"

Mary Austin, My Neighbor's Field   13

Mary Austin, naturalist and feminist, embraced the
Southwest—its spaces, vegetation, native peoples, and the
bravado of white settlers. In "My Neighbor's Field," she
takes pleasure in land she does not own and admires it as
it slowly goes wild.

Aldo Leopold, The Land Ethic   18

The land ethic simply enlarges the boundaries of
community to include soils, waters, plants, animals, or
collectively—the land.

Margaret L. Knox, The World According
to Cushman   31

Chuck Cushman, disillusioned environmentalist, argues that
property owners must defend themselves against the governments depriving citizens of their land and property rights.

Barry Lopez, Caring for the Woods   35

Taking care of the land is a powerful way of taking care of
oneself.

Thinking and Writing About Chapter 1   42
Additional Resources   42

CHAPTER 2   Urban Vision, Rural Reflections   **43**

Henry David Thoreau, Walking   44

A rhapsody on the need for "wildness" as a restorative for
the human spirit, a restorative that Thoreau believes
cannot be found in the town or city.

v

Peter Huber, How Cities Green the Planet   53

Ironically, the growth of cities may turn out to be
necessary to the protection of the environment.

Marie Winn, The Regulars   63

New York City's Central Park has become an unintended
haven for birds and other wild animals, and for the
people who observe and listen to them.

Tara Hulen, Dispatch from Toxic Town   73

Anniston, Alabama, once a Model City, is now suffering
the effects of years of toxic dumping. What are its people
to do?

Thinking and Writing About Chapter 2   78

Additional Resources   78

CHAPTER 3   Local Landscapes   79

Sarah Orne Jewett, A White Heron   81

A nine-year-old girl in this short story is tempted by the
beauty of a wild thing, a white heron, and the ten
dollars, a princely sum, she will receive from an
ornithologist/hunter for disclosing its whereabouts.

Sue Hubbell, Winter   90

The author's calm life in rural Arkansas is set in turmoil
when locals collide over damming a river.

Joy Williams, One Acre: On Devaluing
Real Estate to Keep Land Priceless   95

Even an acre of land can maintain its natural integrity if
its owners can maintain theirs.

Rebecca Solnit, The Orbits of Earthly Bodies   105

As much as Rebecca Solnit loves the wilderness and
wildlife, she must have urban excitement.

Thinking and Writing About Chapter 3   109

Additional Resources   109

CHAPTER 4   The Human Price   111

Rachel Carson, The Human Price   113

The chemical control of nature and indiscriminate use of
pesticides may benefit us immensely before the
devastating effects become apparent.

Terry Tempest Williams, The Clan of
One-Breasted Women   122

When radiation fall-out drifted over their homes in the
Salt Lake region of Utah, the women in the Williams's
family suffered an increase of breast cancer, but the
government would not listen.

Michael Pollan, Behind the Organic-
Industrial Complex   130

As organic foods have become big agribusiness, the
meaning of organic has become mired in legislation and
slick labeling.

Darcy Frey, How Green Is BP?   149

BP, the world's second largest oil company, is having a
hard time reinventing itself as environmentally friendly
when its bottom line remains oil and profit.

Thinking and Writing About Chapter 4   162

Additional Resources   162

CHAPTER 5   Personal Views   163

Edward Abbey, The First Morning   165

While entranced by the natural beauty of Moab National
Monument in Utah, the author wonders why people do
not take the time to appreciate what is in front of them.

Leslie Marmon Silko, Landscape, History,
and the Pueblo Imagination   171

For some Native Americans, every plant, every rock, every
arroyo establishes a link between character and place.

Sallie Bingham, A Woman's Land   183

Turning the sexist tradition of society and property rights
topsy-turvy, Bingham wonders if developing ideas and
practices for land use are gender-related.

Steve Chapple, Bugz   188

An off-the-cuff look at bothersome insects eventually
recognizes that their onerousness has nothing to do with
us, and everything to do with the wonders of nature.

Thinking and Writing About Chapter 5   193

Additional Resources   193

CHAPTER 6   Prospects for the Future   195

Edward O. Wilson, The Environmental Ethic   198

If we lose our connection with nature and the totality of
biodiversity, the consequences will be catastrophic.

Linda Hogan, Walking   207

Learning to listen to the earth may help find a language
that heals the universal soul.

*Paul Hawken, Amory Lovins, and L. Hunter
Lovins,* Once Upon a Planet   210

The challenge to business in the future is to understand
how ecosystems work and to operate within nature's
rules—which are not society's rules.

Christopher Hallowell, Coming to Terms   224

The disappearance of South Louisiana's coastal wetlands
due to lackadaisical environmental considerations has
marked a shift in the attitudes and ways of local
fishermen and bayou dwellers.

Thinking and Writing About Chapter 6   238

Additional Resources   238

Credits   239

HISTORICAL CHRONOLOGY AND CONTEXT

1861–1865	American Civil War.
1862	Homestead Act, opens western lands for settlement.
1864	U.S. Congress grants Yosemite Valley to California for use as a state park.
1867	Alaska purchased from Russia.
1869	Completion of the Transcontinental Railroad.
1872	Yellowstone is the first national park created by Congress.
1878	Timber Culture Act, allows logging on public lands by residents of western states.
1879	U.S. Geological Survey established.
1892	John Muir founds the Sierra Club.
1893	Frederick Jackson Turner, historian, contends that the west is no longer a frontier.
1897	Forest Management Act, allows authorized commercial use of public forests.
1902	Reclamation Act, finances federal irrigation projects.
1903	Orville and Wilbur Wright fly the first airplane.
1906	U.S. Forest Service created.
1908	National Bison Range established to protect this vanishing species.
1911	Weeks Act, expands public forest reserves by purchase of private lands.
1914–1918	World War I.
1916	National Park Service Act passed.
1918	Migratory Bird Treaty with Canada, restricts hunting of migratory species.
	Save-the-Redwoods League founded.

1920	Mineral Leasing Act, regulates mining on federal lands.
1929	Congress passes the Migratory Bird Conservation Act.
1933	Both the Civilian Conservation Corp (CCC) and Tennessee Valley Authority (TVA) established.
1934	Taylor Grazing Act, regulates grazing on public lands.
1935	Soil Conservation Act passed. Soil Conservation Service becomes part of Department of Agriculture.
1935	Wilderness Society formed.
1939–1945	World War II.
1946	U.S. Bureau of Land Management created to oversee use of public lands.
1948	Federal Water Pollution Control Act established.
1949	Aldo Leopold's *A Sand County Almanac* published posthumously. First Sierra Club Biennial Wilderness Conference held.
1950–1953	Korean War.
1955	World's automobile population surpasses one hundred million.
1960	World population tops three billion.
1962	Rachel Carson's *Silent Spring* published. Endangered Species Preservation Act passed.
1964	National Wilderness Preservation System passed by Congress.
1965–1975	Vietnam War. The Water Quality Act, Noise Control Act, and Solid Waste Disposal Act all passed. The green revolution begins.
1968	Wild and Scenic Rivers Act passed.
1969	National Environmental Policy Act passed.
1970	Environmental Protection Agency established. First Earth Day celebrated.
1972	Clean Water Act passed. Marine Mammal Protection Act passed. United Nations Conference on the Human Environment in Stockholm.

1973	Endangered Species Act passed.
1974	Safe Drinking Water Act passed.
1975	World population tops four billion.
1976	Federal Land Policy and Management Act, Whale Conservation and Protective Study Act, and National Forest Management Act all passed.
1977	U.S. Department of Energy created. Both the Soil and Water Conservation Act and Surface Mining and Reclamation Act passed.
1978	Toxic waste in Love Canal, New York, causes entire neighborhood to be abandoned. *Amoco Cadiz* runs aground off France, spilling over 8 million gallons of crude oil.
1979	Three Mile Island, Pennsylvania, nuclear power plant nearly melts down.
1980	Liability (Superfund) Act requires polluters to clean up major contamination sites.
1982	Both the Coastal Barrier Resources Act and Nuclear Waste Policy Act passed.
1986	Chernobyl, Ukraine, nuclear power plant explodes.
1985	Automobile population tops five hundred million.
1989	The *Exxon Valdez*, a supertanker, strikes reef in Prince William Sound, Alaska, releasing 11 million gallons of oil.
1990	Twentieth anniversary of Earth Day and 140 countries celebrate; Gallup Poll finds that 76 percent of Americans call themselves environmentalists. World population tops five billion.
1992	United Nations Earth Summit Conference meets in Rio de Janeiro. Supertanker *Braer* runs aground in the Hebrides and leaks 26 million gallons of crude oil.
1993	Moratorium placed on toxic waste incineration. Ozone layer is reported to be decreasing.
1995	Long-term trends suggest global climate warming.
1998	About half the world's population lives in urban areas.
2001	President George W. Bush seeks to allow oil and gas drilling in the Arctic National Wildlife Refuge. President Bush forms an energy task force to de-

velop a national energy policy; chaired by Vice President Dick Cheney, it accepts recommendations primarily from utility companies and the oil, gas, coal, and nuclear energy industries.

United States declines to ratify the Kyoto Protocol.

2002   President Bush announces his "Clear Skies" initiative, purportedly to reduce power plant pollution but that would in fact allow older power plants to avoid installing pollution controls as they modernize facilities.

Senate authorizes a nuclear waste storage facility for Yucca Mountain, Nevada.

2003   A federal appeals court rules that the Bush administration's practice of allowing coal mining companies to remove mountaintops does not violate the Clean Water Act.

2004   The Interior Department rejects a petition that would prevent the hunting of wolves from airplanes in Alaska.

The Bush administration proposes to reduce funding to prevent lead poisoning.

The White House is accused of watering down a report on the risks of mercury poisoning.

This land is your land, This land is my land,
From California to the New York island;
From the redwood forest to the Gulf Stream waters:
This land was made for you and me.

After two centuries, Americans remain in flux over their relationship with the land and natural bounty. We cherish America's vastness and marvel at its snow-clad peaks that we assume reflect the grandeur of our civilization. We cluster about ocean, lake, and river shores enjoying the aesthetics of clean water. We explore old-growth forests and trek miraculous deserts. We boast of seemingly unlimited natural resources. We take pleasure in landscapes and gaze rapturously at natural wonders from the Grand Canyon to Maine's bedrock islets. At the same time, we tear tops off mountains to expose coal seams and clear-cut forests. Housing subdivisions spring up overnight like giant fungi. We are surprised and act helpless in the knowledge that fewer songbirds wake us at dawn or serenade us in the evening. We watch valuable estuaries and wetlands die from agricultural runoff. We empty human and industrial waste into rivers, making them unsafe for drinking or water sports. Nevertheless, there is no disagreement about whether we love our land; polls, surveys, and literature affirm common consent on one issue: what we have is special. So there is great irony in the fact that so many actions point to our relentless use and abuse of the land to suit our myriad purposes.

The American environmental movement owes its existence to such long-sputtering contradictions. In the mid-nineteenth century, the forests of New England and New York were ravaged so severely that exposed land could not hold water. Topsoil literally washed off farms; rivers silted up and could not be navigated. The land and water that formed the basis of the region's economy were jeopardized. People such as George Perkins Marsh, a Vermont lawyer; John Muir, a naturalist (and the father of environmental preservation); and President Theodore Roosevelt, a practi-

1

cal politician and naturalist, raised their voices, writing and speaking about the inherent dangers of waste and the misuse of the land, water, and other natural resources. Among the eventual results of their efforts were the formation of Yellowstone National Park (1872), the Sierra Club (1892), and the U.S. Forest Service (1906) to protect and manage natural resources. But while the voices of these individuals formed the vanguard in an on-going struggle between the conservationists and preservationists and the users and exploiters, that same battle is still being fought today. By the late nineteenth century, as America began to expand its role as a powerful industrial nation on an international scale, some feared that we would achieve greatness at the cost of an unhealthy environment, foul air, polluted water, and diminished species diversity. Our high standard of living might be achieved at a hidden cost.

We are perhaps fortunate for the contradictions and longstanding arguments. They have at least provided us with context and perspective. It would be interesting to speculate what the American landscape would now look like if only one side or the other had had its way. Would any redwoods remain if the timber industry had a free hand? Would there be *any* wolves in the wild? Or bald eagles? Or think of a more immediate problem—that 90 percent of the world's fish stocks have been depleted due to powerful pro-industrial fishing lobbies and the difficulty of regulation. Whether once abundant species such as cod, grouper, and snapper will ever be able to recover is a subject of sharp debate in management and scientific circles. On the other hand, if preservationists had their way, we would have been deprived of redwoods—their beauty and their utility—as a functional building material. An entire segment of the timber industry would never have developed. Coal is another example of a natural resource used and abused. This country is blessed with more coal reserves than any other region of the world, and burning it powers our lights and factories. Extracting it, however, not only decapitates mountains but also scars vast stretches of the country. The balance between reaping the bounty of fuel and preserving the bounty of natural beauty that cloaks its seams remains elusive. One thing is certain, though—if we had not exploited the coal, our industrial power and quality of life (for good or bad) would not be what it is today.

Attempts at balancing human influence are difficult because our natural heritage is constantly being compromised by economic, political, and recreational forces championing one cause or another: Ranchers want to exterminate coyotes; pork barrel interests sink millions of dollars into a questionable navigation canal here or an unneeded road there; skimobiles distress the landscape in national parks; and old-growth forests in the Pacific Northwest are being cut for lumber.

It is tempting to argue the merits of leaving well enough alone. We must recognize the inevitability of change; some species survive over time, others die off. Real estate developers build subdivisions and malls, after all, because people need housing and stores. Forests are cut to provide lumber for the subdivisions and to furnish them. Of course, it may be argued that not *all* forests are cut, and that many forested regions are well-protected in national and state parks and monuments.

This ceaseless flux of pros and cons is the organizing principle of *Listening to Earth*. Our purpose is to present essays, reportage, and fiction that probe the contradictions suggestive of the environmental dilemma facing the United States. In all fairness to the reader, the authors acknowledge a bias toward nature and environmental preservation. We advocate for nature, but this does not mean we are hands-off preservationists. We enjoy our electric conveniences and wooden decks as well as the next fellow. Enjoying the comforts of civilization makes it all the more difficult to recognize that progress is not achieved without cost and irreparable damage.

Americans are far too passionate, argumentative, equally selfish and altruistic, and deeply caring to let things just happen—to let nature take its course—to permit users and exploiters to have their way. It is just not the American way, at least not without a debate. Some Americans might wish to control nature; others argue that nature cannot be controlled. Whatever the case, the American environment has changed and will continue to change and *Listening to Earth* presents the arguments for using, conserving, preserving, and finding pleasure, beauty, and spirituality in our land.

ACKNOWLEDGMENTS

This book is dedicated to protectors of the environment and lovers of the natural world. We gratefully acknowledge the criticism and suggestions of Jonathan Ausubel, Chaffey College; James Countryman, University of Minnesota–Twin Cities; Susan Hanson, Texas State University–San Marcos; Ashton Nichols, Dickinson College; Catherine Schutz, University of Central

Florida; and John L. Wallin, III, University of Massachusetts–Dartmouth. We thank our colleagues and friends who made useful comments and suggestions for readings. We owe much to Lynn Huddon, our editor at Longman, for her thoughtfulness and professionalism. *Listening to Earth* also owes a debt to our respective spouses: Willa Zakin Hallowell and Gene L. Moncrief. We have enjoyed collaborating on this book, and we hope that our enthusiasm is evident to our readers.

CHRISTOPHER HALLOWELL
WALTER LEVY

CHAPTER 1

Value of the Land

John Muir, often considered the founder of this country's environmental movement, stakes out the preservationist claim and
scolds humans for being contrary. At the outset of "The American
Forests," a chapter from *Our National Parks* (1901), Muir boast-
fully and humbly reminds us that God "planted" the forests and
"they were the best he ever planted." He argues that while the
clearing of land and the felling of trees were necessary as the country moved westward, the settlers "waged interminable forest wars;
chips flew thick and fast; trees in their beauty fell crashing by the
millions." Enough is enough, Muir pleads when he witnesses the
carnage of the land, forest, and waters. He is frustrated by un-
abated exploitation in the name of progress, and he beseeches the
government to intervene: "God has cared for these trees, saved
them from drought, disease, avalanches, and a thousand straining,
leveling tempests and floods; but he can not save them from
fools—only Uncle Sam can do that."

Although Uncle Sam can save some fools from destroying the
ecological integrity of the land, a democracy allows anyone to argue an opposing opinion and shape the final decision. A democracy also encourages private ownership, which introduces the
slippery slope inherent in property rights. If you own property, is
it not yours to do with as you wish? Mary Austin's essay "My
Neighbor's Field" from *Land of Little Rain* (1903) shows the influence various owners have had on an overgrown field. Austin sub-
tly suggests human impact has not made a significant change in
the land or improved it in any material sense. Though Austin cov-
ets the land, she knows from careful observation that it is better
to enjoy than to own. Esthetic ownership does not demand improvements.

The major concern of both Muir and Austin is not ownership; it is the fate of the land. While the land, whether in forest or field, is in many respects more enduring than any individual, it is people who are able to dominate the land, to pillage it, at least in the short term. Muir's early twentieth-century hands-off idealism would be hard put to the test of practicality today, as is evident in the controversy surrounding even such an isolated place as the Artic National Wildlife Refuge in Alaska.

So how can we use land and risk altering the face of nature as a result? How can we preserve the land but possibly not benefit from its resources? Aldo Leopold is the grand counselor in this rolling argument. In "The Land Ethic" (1933), a speech later published in his influential collection of essays *A Sand County Almanac and Sketches Here and There* (1949), Leopold looks to the larger community and redefines its boundaries to include soils, waters, plants, animals, or collectively—the land. He asserts that people must act responsibly and ethically when it comes to using the land. We are in control of our environmental destiny, he says, when we act as stewards rather than users. When first presented, "The Land Ethic" was a radical notion, and it lay dormant until the 1960s when environmental activists recognized his arguments as powerful rebuttals against the unmitigated use of natural resources. Leopold took Henry David Thoreau's concept of man in nature as expressed in *Walden* (1854) and in his essay "Walking" (1862) and placed it in a more modern political and environmental context. Like *Walden*, *A Sand County Almanac* has become a standard, and it is an especially key document in the argument concerning the use and preservation of land and natural resources.

Arguments for and against land ownership and land use are far from settled, as Margaret L. Knox's "The World According to Cushman" (1993) demonstrates. Knox offers a look at the question through the deliberations of Chuck Cushman, a professional lobbyist, who argues against any federal controls of land use, environmental protection, or easements. Cushman claims to be for property rights, loosely meaning that an owner can do anything with his or her property. Knox portrays Cushman as a disillusioned youthful environmentalist now advocating an end to any federal regulation of land and natural resources. Although Cushman is a glib speaker whose radical argument is more emotional than factual, his attack on federal authority, while not physical, is an effort to permit landowners to do what they will with their land. In Knox's view, the question remains whether the federal government has the moral right to lock up land in preservation or to develop it according to its self-proclaimed guidelines.

The questionable right of an individual landowner to do what he or she wishes with private property has produced a quagmire of moral and ethical uncertainty. In "Caring for the Woods" (1995), Barry Lopez puts the issue in a perspective, discussing his 35 acres of forest in Oregon. For Lopez, like Muir, such a place is sacred. But Lopez is well-enough attuned to the material greed of others and the diminishing wildlife that frequent his land to realize that it is not enough just to extol its majesty. Action must be taken to protect it from the influences of people and places far away. Thus, rather than owning their land, Lopez and his wife are land-wardens, guarding their terrain as best as they can from civilization.

The American Forests
JOHN MUIR

John Muir (1838–1914) believes that nature is God's temple and abusing it is sacrilegious. Muir sees trees, mountains, glaciers, and wildlife as belonging to God. Human beings, he complains, do not see fit to be part of this scheme. Muir's central question is, "Why should man value himself as more than a small part of the one great unit of creation?" Muir was born in Scotland and immigrated with his family to the wilderness of central Wisconsin when he was eleven. Though he married well and lived in a mansion, Muir periodically escaped to backpack in the wild country. In 1871, he led a crusade to preserve the Yosemite Valley. He began a campaign to achieve this end: first by founding the Sierra Club as a publicity vehicle, and second, by gaining the support of President Theodore Roosevelt, who was a staunch naturalist. Under Roosevelt's auspices, legislation in 1916 created the National Park Service. Muir's other works include: The Mountains of California *(1894),* My First Summer in the Sierra *(1911),* Yosemite *(1912),* Travels in Alaska *(1915),* A Thousand Mile Walk to the Gulf of Mexico *(1916), and* Steep Trails *(1918).*

---------------- ✦ ----------------

The forests of America, however slighted by man, must have been a great delight to God; for they were the best he ever planted. The whole continent was a garden, and from the beginning it seemed to be favored above all the other wild parks and gardens of the globe. To prepare the ground, it was rolled and sifted in seas with infinite loving deliberation and forethought, lifted into the light, submerged and warmed over and over again, pressed and crumpled into folds and ridges, mountains, and hills, subsoiled with heaving volcanic fires, ploughed and ground and sculptured into scenery and soil with glaciers and rivers,—every feature growing and changing from beauty to beauty, higher and higher. And in the fullness of time it was planted in groves, and belts, and broad, exuberant, mantling forests, with the largest, most varied, most fruitful, and most beautiful trees in the world. Bright seas made its border, with wave embroidery and icebergs; gray deserts were outspread in the middle of it, mossy tundras on the north, savannas on the south, and blooming prairies and plains; while lakes and rivers shone through all the vast forests and openings, and happy birds and beasts gave delightful animation. Everywhere, everywhere over all the blessed continent, there were beauty and melody and kindly, wholesome, foodful abundance.

These forests were composed of about five hundred species of trees, all of them in some way useful to man, ranging in size from twenty-five feet in height and less than one foot in diameter at the ground to four hundred feet in height and more than twenty feet in diameter,—lordly monarchs proclaiming the gospel of beauty like apostles. For many a century after the ice-ploughs were melted, nature fed them and dressed them every day,—working like a man, a loving, devoted, painstaking gardener; fingering every leaf and flower and mossy furrowed bole; bending, trimming, modeling, balancing; painting them with the loveliest colors; bringing over them now clouds with cooling shadows and showers, now sunshine; fanning them with gentle winds and rustling their leaves; exercising them in every fibre with storms, and pruning them; loading them with flowers and fruit, loading them with snow, and ever making them more beautiful as the years rolled by. Wide-branching oak and elm in endless variety, walnut and maple, chestnut and beech, ilex and locust, touching limb to limb, spread a leafy translucent canopy along the coast of the Atlantic over the wrinkled folds and ridges of the Alleghanies,—a green billowy sea in summer, golden and purple in autumn, pearly gray like a steadfast frozen mist of interlacing branches and sprays in leafless, restful winter.

To the southward stretched dark, level-topped cypresses in knobby, tangled swamps, grassy savannas in the midst of them like lakes of light, groves of gay, sparkling spice-trees, magnolias and palms, glossy-leaved and blooming and shining continually. To the northward, over Maine and Ottawa, rose hosts of spiry, rosiny evergreens,—white pine and spruce, hemlock and cedar, shoulder to shoulder, laden with purple cones, their myriad needles sparkling and shimmering, covering hills and swamps, rocky headlands and domes, ever bravely aspiring and seeking the sky; the ground in their shade now snow-clad and frozen, now mossy and flowery; beaver meadows here and there, full of lilies and grass; lakes gleaming like eyes, and a silvery embroidery of rivers and creeks watering and brightening all the vast glad wilderness.

Thence westward were oak and elm, hickory and tupelo, gum and liriodendron, sassafras and ash, linden and laurel, spreading on ever wider in glorious exuberance over the great fertile basin of the Mississippi, over damp level bottoms, low dimpling hollows, and round dotting hills, embosoming sunny prairies and cheery park openings, half sunshine, half shade; while a dark wilderness of pines covered the region around the Great Lakes. Thence still westward swept the forests to right and left around grassy plains and deserts a thousand miles wide: irrepressible hosts of spruce and pine, aspen and willow, nut-pine and juniper, cactus and yucca, caring nothing for drought, extending undaunted from mountain to mountain, over mesa and desert, to join the darkening multitudes of pines that covered the high Rocky ranges and the glorious forests along the coast of the moist and balmy Pacific, where new species of pine, giant cedars and spruces, silver firs and Sequoias, kings of their race, growing close together like grass in a meadow, poised their brave domes and spires in the sky, three hundred feet above the ferns and the lilies that enameled the ground; towering serene through the long centuries, preaching God's forestry fresh from heaven.

Here the forests reached their highest development. Hence 5 they went wavering northward over icy Alaska, brave spruce and fir, poplar and birch, by the coasts and the rivers, to within sight of the Arctic Ocean. American forests! the glory of the world! Surveyed thus from the east to the west, from the north to the south, they are rich beyond thought, immortal, immeasurable, enough and to spare for every feeding, sheltering beast and bird, insect and son of Adam; and nobody need have cared had there been no pines in Norway, no cedars and deodars on Lebanon and the Himalayas, no vine-clad selvas in the basin of the Amazon. With such variety, harmony, and triumphant exuberance, even nature, it would seem, might have rested content with the forests of North America, and planted no more.

So they appeared a few centuries ago when they were rejoicing in wildness. The Indians with stone axes could do them no more harm than could gnawing beavers and browsing moose. Even the fires of the Indians and the fierce shattering lightning seemed to work together only for good in clearing spots here and there for smooth garden prairies, and openings for sunflowers seeking the light. But when the steel axe of the white man rang out on the startled air their doom was sealed. Every tree heard the bodeful sound, and pillars of smoke gave the sign in the sky.

I suppose we need not go mourning the buffaloes. In the nature of things they had to give place to better cattle, though the change might have been made without barbarous wickedness. Likewise many of nature's five hundred kinds of wild trees had to make way for orchards and cornfields. In the settlement and civilization of the country, bread more than timber or beauty was wanted; and in the blindness of hunger, the early settlers, claiming Heaven as their guide, regarded God's trees as only a larger kind of pernicious weeds, extremely hard to get rid of. Accordingly, with no eye to the future, these pious destroyers waged interminable forest wars; chips flew thick and fast; trees in their beauty fell crashing by millions, smashed to confusion, and the smoke of their burning has been rising to heaven more than two hundred years. After the Atlantic coast from Maine to Georgia had been mostly cleared and scorched into melancholy ruins, the overflowing multitude of bread and money seekers poured over the Alleghanies into the fertile middle West, spreading ruthless devastation ever wider and farther over the rich valley of the Mississippi and the vast shadowy pine region about the Great Lakes. Thence still westward, the invading horde of destroyers called settlers made its fiery way over the broad Rocky Mountains, felling and burning more fiercely than ever, until at last it has reached the wild side of the continent, and entered the last of the great aboriginal forests on the shores of the Pacific.

Surely, then, it should not be wondered at that lovers of their country, bewailing its baldness, are now crying aloud, "Save what is left of the forests!" Clearing has surely now gone far enough; soon timber will be scarce, and not a grove will be left to rest in or pray in. The remnant protected will yield plenty of timber, a

perennial harvest for every right use, without further diminution
of its area, and will continue to cover the springs of the rivers that
rise in the mountains and give irrigating waters to the dry valleys
at their feet, prevent wasting floods and be a blessing to everybody forever.

. . . An exception would seem to be found in the case of our
forests, which have been mismanaged rather long, and now come
desperately near being like smashed eggs and spilt milk. Still, in
the long run the world does not move backward. The wonderful
advance made in the last few years, in creating four national
parks in the West, and thirty forest reservations embracing nearly
forty million acres; and in the planting of the borders of streets
and highways and spacious parks in all the great cities, to satisfy
the natural taste and hunger for landscape beauty and righteous-
ness that God has put, in some measure, into every human being
and animal, shows the trend of awakening public opinion. The
making of the far-famed New York Central Park was opposed by
even good men, with misguided pluck, perseverance, and ingenu-
ity; but straight right won its way, and now that park is appreci-
ated. So we confidently believe it will be with our great national
parks and forest reservations. There will be a period of indiffer-
ence on the part of the rich, sleepy with wealth, and of the toiling
millions, sleepy with poverty, most of whom never saw a forest; a
period of screaming protest and objection from the plunderers,
who are as unconscionable and enterprising as Satan. But light is
surely coming, and the friends of destruction will preach and be-
wail in vain.

The United States government has always been proud of the
welcome it has extended to good men of every nation, seeking
freedom and homes and bread. Let them be welcomed still as
nature welcomes them, to the woods as well as to the prairies
and plains. No place is too good for good men, and still there is
room. They are invited to heaven, and may well be allowed in
America. Every place is made better by them. Let them be as
free to pick gold and gems from the hills, to cut and hew, dig
and plant, for homes and bread, as the birds are to pick berries
from the wild bushes, and moss and leaves for nests. The
ground will be glad to feed them, and the pines will come down
from the mountains for their homes as willingly as the cedars
came from Lebanon for Solomon's temple. Nor will the woods
be the worse for this use, or their benign influences be diminished any more than the sun is diminished by shining. Mere de-

10

stroyers, however, tree-killers, wool and mutton men, spreading death and confusion in the fairest groves and gardens ever planted,—let the government hasten to cast them out and make an end of them. For it must be told again and again, and be burningly borne in mind, that just now, while protective measures are being deliberated languidly, destruction and use are speeding on faster and farther every day. The axe and saw are insanely busy, chips are flying thick as snowflakes, and every summer thousands of acres of priceless forests, with their underbrush, soil, springs, climate, scenery, and religion, are vanishing away in clouds of smoke, while except in the national parks, not one forest guard is employed.

All sorts of local laws and regulations have been tried and found wanting, and the costly lessons of our own experience, as well as that of every civilized nation, show conclusively that the fate of the remnant of our forests is in the hands of the federal government, and that if the remnant is to be saved at all, it must be saved quickly.

Any fool can destroy trees. They cannot run away; and if they could, they would still be destroyed,—chased and hunted down as long as fun or a dollar could be got out of their bark hides, branching horns, or magnificent bole backbones. Few that fell trees plant them; nor would planting avail much towards getting back anything like the noble primeval forests. During a man's life only saplings can be grown, in the place of the old trees—tens of centuries old—that have been destroyed. It took more than three thousand years to make some of the trees in these Western woods,—trees that are still standing in perfect strength and beauty, waving and singing in the mighty forests of the Sierra. Through all the wonderful, eventful centuries since Christ's time—and long before that—God has cared for these trees, saved them from drought, disease, avalanches, and a thousand straining, leveling tempests and floods; but he cannot save them from fools,—only Uncle Sam can do that.

1901

Discussion

1. When you walk in the forest or woods, describe how you feel about the trees around you.

2. How does Muir's contention that "any fool can destroy trees" compare with his belief that trees must be felled in order for the country to progress?

3. Consider the irony of the necessity of cutting trees and Muir's argument that "God has cared for these trees, saved them from drought, disease, avalanches, and a thousand straining, leveling tempests and floods."
4. Are there any areas in this country that you know about where Muir's argument for preservation could still be applied?
5. Compare Muir's reference to God's creation of forests as a "garden" with Mary Austin's attitude toward the field in "My Neighbor's Field" (see below).

My Neighbor's Field
MARY AUSTIN

Mary Austin (1868–1934), a naturalist and feminist, was attracted to the physical and spiritual aspects of nature. Especially in her first and most memorable work, The Land of Little Rain *(1903, in which the following essay appears), she embraced the southwest— its spaces, vegetation, native peoples, and the bravado of white settlers. In "My Neighbor's Field," she takes pleasure in land she does not own and admires it as it slowly goes wild. Austin was born in Illinois and moved to southern California with her mother and brothers when she was twenty. From there she expanded her range to the Southwest where she worked as a naturalist and befriended local Native Americans. "My Neighbor's Field" is typical of Austin's essay structure, combining the human history of the place with its natural history. Austin's marriage to Wallace Stafford Austin was volatile and ultimately failed, but it stimulated her writing, and she published regularly in magazines such as* Harper's, The Atlantic Monthly, *and* Century, *and wrote twenty-seven books, among them* The Basket Women *(1904),* Isidro *(1905),* The Flock *(1906),* The Green Bough *(1913),* The Ford *(1917),* The Young Woman Citizen *(1918),* Starry Adventure *(1931), and her autobiography* Earth Horizon *(1932).*

--------------- ✦ ---------------

It is one of those places God must have meant for a field from all time, lying very level at the foot of the slope that crowds up against Kearsarge, falling slightly toward the town. North and south it is fenced by low old glacial ridges, boulder strewn and untenable. Eastward it butts on orchard closes and the village gardens, brimming over into them by wild brier and creeping grass. The village street, with its double row of unlike houses, breaks off abruptly at the edge of the field in a footpath that goes up the streamside, beyond it, to the source of waters.

The field is not greatly esteemed of the town, not being put to the plough nor affording firewood, but breeding all manner of wild seeds that go down in the irrigating ditches to come up as weeds in the gardens and grass plots. But when I had no more than seen it in the charm of its spring smiling, I knew I should have no peace until I had bought ground and built me a house beside it, with a little wicket to go in and out at all hours, as afterward came about.

Edswick, Roeder, Connor, and Ruffin owned the field before it fell to my neighbor. But before that the Paiutes, mesne lords of the soil, made a campoodie by the rill of Pine Creek; and after, contesting the soil with them, cattle-men, who found its foodful pastures greatly to their advantage; and bands of blethering flocks shepherded by wild, hairy men of little speech, who attested their rights to the feeding ground with their long staves upon each other's skulls. Edswick homesteaded the field about the time the wild tide of mining life was roaring and rioting up Kearsarge, and where the village now stands built a stone hut, with loopholes to make good his claim against cattle-men or Indians. But Edswick died and Roeder became master of the field. Roeder owned cattle on a thousand hills, and made it a recruiting ground for his bellowing herds before beginning the long drive to market across a shifty desert. He kept the field fifteen years, and afterward falling into difficulties, put it out as security against certain sums. Connor, who held the securities, was cleverer than Roeder and not so busy. The money fell due the winter of the Big Snow, when all the trails were forty feet under drifts, and Roeder was away in San Francisco selling his cattle. At the set time Connor took the law by the forelock and was adjudged possession of the field. Eighteen days later Roeder arrived on snowshoes, both feet frozen, and the money in his pack. In the long suit at law ensuing, the field fell to Ruffin, that clever one-armed lawyer with the tongue to wile a bird out of the bush, Connor's counsel, and was sold by him to my neighbor, whom from envying his possession I call Naboth.

Curiously, all this human occupancy of greed and mischief left no mark on the field, but the Indians did, and the unthinking sheep. Round its corners children pick up chipped arrow points of obsidian, scattered through it are kitchen middens and pits of old sweat-houses. By the south corner, where the campoodie stood, is a single shrub of "hoopee" (*Lycium Andersonii*), maintaining itself hardly among alien shrubs, and near by, three low rakish trees of hackberry, so far from home that no prying of mine has been able to find another in any cañon east or west. But the berries of both were food for the Paiutes, eagerly sought and traded for as far south as Shoshone Land. By the fork of the creek where the shepherds camp is a single clump of mesquite of the variety called "screw bean." The seed must have shaken there from some sheep's coat, for this is not the habitat of mesquite, and except for other single shrubs at sheep camps, none grows freely for a hundred and fifty miles south or east.

Naboth has put a fence about the best of the field, but neither the Indians nor the shepherds can quite forego it. They make camp and build their wattled huts about the borders of it, and no doubt they have some sense of home in its familiar aspect. 5

As I have said, it is a low-lying field, between the mesa and the town, with no hillocks in it, but a gentle swale where the waste water of the creek goes down to certain farms, and the hackberry-trees, of which the tallest might be three times the height of a man, are the tallest things in it. A mile up from the water gate that turns the creek into supply pipes for the town, begins a row of long-leaved pines, threading the watercourse to the foot of Kearsarge. These are the pines that puzzle the local botanist, not easily determined, and unrelated to other conifers of the Sierra slope; the same pines of which the Indians relate a legend mixed of brotherliness and the retribution of God. Once the pines possessed the field, as the worn stumps of them along the streamside show, and it would seem their secret purpose to regain their old footing. Now and then some seedling escapes the devastating sheep a rod or two down-stream. Since I came to live by the field one of these has tiptoed above the gully of the creek, beckoning the procession from the hills, as if in fact they would make back toward that skyward-pointing finger of granite on the opposite range, from which, according to the legend, when they were bad Indians and it a great chief, they ran away. This year the summer floods brought the round, brown, fruitful cones to my very door, and I look, if I live long enough, to see them come up greenly in my neighbor's field.

It is interesting to watch this retaking of old ground by the wild plants, banished by human use. Since Naboth drew his fence about the field and restricted it to a few wild-eyed steers, halting between the hills and the shambles, many old habitués of the field have come back to their haunts. The willow and brown birch, long ago cut off by the Indians for wattles, have come back to the streamside, slender and virginal in their spring greenness, and leaving long stretches of the brown water open to the sky. In stony places where no grass grows, wild olives sprawl; close-twigged, blue-gray patches in winter, more translucent greenish gold in spring than any aureole. Along with willow and birch and brier, the clematis, that shyest plant of water borders, slips down season by season to within a hundred yards of the village street. Convinced after three years that it would come no nearer, we spent time fruitlessly pulling up roots to plant in the garden. All this while, when no coaxing or care prevailed upon any trans-planted slip to grow, one was coming up silently outside the fence near the wicket, coiling so secretly in the rabbit-brush that its presence was never suspected until it flowered delicately along its twining length. The horehound comes through the fence and un-der it, shouldering the pickets off the railings; the brier rose mines under the horehound; and no care, though I own I am not a close weeder, keeps the small pale moons of the primrose from rising to the night moth under my apple-trees. The first summer in the new place, a clump of cypripediums came up by the irrigat-ing ditch at the bottom of the lawn. But the clematis will not come inside, nor the wild almond.

I have forgotten to find out, though I meant to, whether the wild almond grew in that country where Moses kept the flocks of his father-in-law, but if so one can account for the burning bush. It comes upon one with a flame-burst as of revelation; little hard red buds on leafless twigs, swelling unnoticeably, then one, two, or three strong suns, and from tip to tip one soft fiery glow, whis-pering with bees as a singing flame. A twig of finger size will be furred to the thickness of one's wrist by pink five-petaled bloom, so close that only the blunt-faced wild bees find their way in it. In this latitude late frosts cut off the hope of fruit too often for the wild almond to multiply greatly, but the spiny, tap-rooted shrubs are resistant to most plant evils.

It is not easy always to be attentive to the maturing of wild fruit. Plants are so unobtrusive in their material processes, and always at the significant moment some other bloom has reached its perfect hour. One can never fix the precise moment when the rosy tint the field has from the wild almond passes into the inspir-ing blue of lupines. One notices here and there a spike of bloom, and a day later the whole field royal and ruffling lightly to the wind. Part of the charm of the lupine is the continual stir of its plumes to airs not suspected otherwhere. Go and stand by any crown of bloom and the tall stalks do but rock a little as for drowsiness, but look off across the field, and on the stillest days there is always a trepidation in the purple patches.

From midsummer until frost the prevailing note of the field is   10
clear gold, passing into the rusty tone of bigelovia going into a de-
cline, a succession of color schemes more admirably managed than the transformation scene at the theatre. Under my window a colony of cleome made a soft web of bloom that drew me every morning for a long still time; and one day I discovered that I was looking into a rare fretwork of fawn and straw colored twigs from which both bloom and leaf had gone, and I could not say if it had been for a matter of weeks or days. The time to plant cucumbers and set out cabbages may be set down in the almanac, but never seed-time nor blossom in Naboth's field.

Certain winged and mailed denizens of the field seem to reach their heyday along with the plants they most affect. In June the leaning towers of the white milkweed are jeweled over with red and gold beetles, climbing dizzily. This is that milkweed from whose stems the Indians flayed fibre to make snares for small game, but what use the beetles put it to except for a displaying ground for their gay coats, I could never discover. The white but-terfly crop comes on with the bigelovia bloom, and on warm mornings makes an airy twinkling all across the field. In September young linnets grow out of the rabbit-brush in the night. All the nests discoverable in the neighboring orchards will not account for the numbers of them. Somewhere, by the same secret process by which the field matures a million more seeds than it needs, it is maturing red-hooded linnets for their devour-ing. All the purlieus of bigelovia and artemisia are noisy with them for a month. Suddenly as they come as suddenly go the fly-by-nights, that pitch and toss on dusky barred wings above the field of summer twilights. Never one of these nighthawks will you see after linnet time, though the hurtle of their wings makes a pleasant sound across the dusk in their season.

For two summers a great red-tailed hawk has visited the field every afternoon between three and four o'clock, swooping and soaring with the airs of a gentleman adventurer. What he finds there is chiefly conjectured, so secretive are the little people of Naboth's field. Only when leaves fall and the light is low and slant, one sees the long clean flanks of the jackrabbits, leaping like small deer, and of late afternoons little cotton-tails scamper in the runways. But the most one sees of the burrowers, gophers and mice is the fresh earthwork of their newly opened doors, or the pitiful small shreds the butcher-bird hangs on spiny shrubs.

It is a still field, this of my neighbor's, though so busy, and admirably compounded for variety and pleasantness,—a little sand, a little loam, a grassy plot, a stony rise or two, a full brown stream, a little touch of humanness, a footpath trodden out by moccasins. Naboth expects to make town lots of it and his fortune in one and the same day; but when I take the trail to talk with old Seyavi at the campoodie, it occurs to me that though the field may serve a good turn in those days it will hardly be happier. No, certainly not happier.

1903

Discussion

1. Do you think it is "right" of Austin to covet her neighbor's field? How can a person really own a piece of the earth?
2. What is the natural and social history of the field belonging to Austin's neighbor?
3. When you see a vacant field, do you think of it as the site of a potential home or do you think some vacant lots should be maintained as such or turned into planned parks?
4. Why is Austin content not to own the field, but to have a house built beside it? Explain what she means at end of her essay when she states that the field "will hardly be happier."
5. Describe the process by which nature is reclaiming the field. How does this demonstrate both Austin's knowledge as a naturalist and her understanding of the aesthetic aspects of the ecological succession of life?

The Land Ethic

ALDO LEOPOLD

Aldo Leopold (1887–1948), born in Iowa, was educated at Yale and studied at the Yale School of Forestry, where Gifford Pinchot, environmental conservationist, influenced him. He joined the U.S. Forest Service, and served in Arizona and New Mexico. During this time, he argued for the establishment of game refuges in which predators should be wiped out. Later, he shifted his argument and advocated the need for a balance best achieved by nature. Beginning in 1933, Leopold taught at the University of Wisconsin, Madison, in the Department of Game Management. It was at this time that he presented "The Land Ethic" before the American Association for the Advancement of Science. Among Leopold's most enduring works is a prairie in Wisconsin that he began to restore to its original natural condition. He died in 1948 and A Sand County Almanac and Sketches Here and There *(the book in which this essay appears) was published posthumously. Leopold was a voice of reason in the controversy between land use and conservation.*

———————— ✦ ————————

When god-like Odysseus returned from the wars in Troy, he hanged all on one rope a dozen slave-girls of his house-hold whom he suspected of misbehavior during his absence.

This hanging involved no question of propriety. The girls were property. The disposal of property was then, as now, a matter of expediency, not of right and wrong.

Concepts of right and wrong were not lacking from Odysseus' Greece: witness the fidelity of his wife through the long years before at last his black-prowed galleys clove the wine-dark seas for home. The ethical structure of that day covered wives, but had not yet been extended to human chattels. During the three thousand years which have since elapsed, ethical criteria have been extended to many fields of conduct, with corresponding shrinkages in those judged by expediency only.

THE ETHICAL SEQUENCE

This extension of ethics, so far studied only by philosophers, is actually a process in ecological evolution. Its sequences may be described in ecological as well as in philosophical terms. An ethic, ecologically, is a limitation on freedom of action in the struggle for existence. An ethic, philosophically, is a differentiation of social from anti-social conduct. These are two definitions of one thing. The thing has its origin in the tendency of interdependent individuals or groups to evolve modes of co-operation. The ecologist calls these symbioses. Politics and economics are advanced symbioses in which the original free-for-all competition has been replaced, in part, by co-operative mechanisms with an ethical content.

The complexity of co-operative mechanisms has increased 5 with population density, and with the efficiency of tools. It was simpler, for example, to define the anti-social uses of sticks and stones in the days of the mastodons than of bullets and billboards in the age of motors.

The first ethics dealt with the relation between individuals; the Mosaic Decalogue is an example. Later accretions dealt with the relation between the individual and society. The Golden Rule tries to integrate the individual to society; democracy to integrate social organization to the individual.

There is as yet no ethic dealing with man's relation to land and to the animals and plants which grow upon it. Land, like Odysseus' slave-girls, is still property. The land-relation is still strictly economic, entailing privileges but not obligations.

The extension of ethics to this third element in human environment is, if I read the evidence correctly, an evolutionary possibility and an ecological necessity. It is the third step in a sequence. The first two have already been taken. Individual thinkers since the days of Ezekiel and Isaiah have asserted that the despoliation of land is not only inexpedient but wrong. Society, however, has not yet affirmed their belief. I regard the present conservation movement as the embryo of such an affirmation.

An ethic may be regarded as a mode of guidance for meeting ecological situations so new or intricate, or involving such deferred reactions, that the path of social expediency is not discernible to the average individual. Animal instincts are modes of guidance for the individual in meeting such situations. Ethics are possibly a kind of community instinct in-the-making.

THE COMMUNITY CONCEPT

10   All ethics so far evolved rest upon a single premise: that the individual is a member of a community of interdependent parts. His instincts prompt him to compete for his place in that community, but his ethics prompt him also to co-operate (perhaps in order that there may be a place to compete for).

The land ethic simply enlarges the boundaries of the community to include soils, waters, plants, and animals, or collectively: the land.

This sounds simple: do we not already sing our love for and obligation to the land of the free and the home of the brave? Yes, but just what and whom do we love? Certainly not the soil, which we are sending helter-skelter downriver. Certainly not the waters, which we assume have no function except to turn turbines, float barges, and carry off sewage. Certainly not the plants, of which we exterminate whole communities without batting an eye. Certainly not the animals, of which we have already extirpated many of the largest and most beautiful species. A land ethic of course cannot prevent the alteration, management, and use of these 'resources,' but it does affirm their right to continued existence, and, at least in spots, their continued existence in a natural state.

In short, a land ethic changes the role of *Homo sapiens* from conqueror of the land-community to plain member and citizen of it. It implies respect for his fellow-members, and also respect for the community as such.

In human history, we have learned (I hope) that the conqueror role is eventually self-defeating. Why? Because it is implicit in such a role that the conqueror knows, *ex cathedra*, just what makes the community clock tick, and just what and who is valuable, and what and who is worthless, in community life. It always turns out that he knows neither, and this is why his conquests eventually defeat themselves.

In the biotic community, a parallel situation exists. Abraham   15 knew exactly what the land was for: it was to drip milk and honey into Abraham's mouth. At the present moment, the assurance with which we regard this assumption is inverse to the degree of our education.

The ordinary citizen today assumes that science knows what makes the community clock tick; the scientist is equally sure that he does not. He knows that the biotic mechanism is so complex that its workings may never be fully understood.

That man is, in fact, only a member of a biotic team is shown by an ecological interpretation of history. Many historical events, hitherto explained solely in terms of human enterprise, were actually biotic interactions between people and land. The characteristics of the land determined the facts quite as potently as the characteristics of the men who lived on it.

Consider, for example, the settlement of the Mississippi valley. In the years following the Revolution, three groups were contending for its control: the native Indian, the French and English traders, and the American settlers. Historians wonder what would have happened if the English at Detroit had thrown a little more weight into the Indian side of those tipsy scales which decided the outcome of the colonial migration into the cane-lands of Kentucky. It is time now to ponder the fact that the cane-lands, when subjected to the particular mixture of forces represented by the cow, plow, fire, and axe of the pioneer, became bluegrass. What if the plant succession inherent in this dark and bloody ground had, under the impact of these forces, given us some worthless sedge, shrub, or weed? Would Boone and Kenton have held out? Would there have been any overflow into Ohio, Indiana, Illinois, and Missouri? Any Louisiana Purchase? Any transcontinental union of new states? Any Civil War?

Kentucky was one sentence in the drama of history. We are commonly told what the human actors in this drama tried to do, but we are seldom told that their success, or the lack of it, hung in large degree on the reaction of particular soils to the impact of the particular forces exerted by their occupancy. In the case of Kentucky, we do not even know where the bluegrass came from— whether it is a native species, or a stowaway from Europe.

20   Contrast the cane-lands with what hindsight tells us about the Southwest, where the pioneers were equally brave, resourceful, and persevering. The impact of occupancy here brought no bluegrass, or other plant fitted to withstand the bumps and buffetings of hard use. This region, when grazed by livestock, reverted through a series of more and more worthless grasses, shrubs, and weeds to a condition of unstable equilibrium. Each recession of plant types bred erosion; each increment to erosion bred a further recession of plants. The result today is a progressive and mutual deterioration, not only of plants and soils, but of the animal community subsisting thereon. The early settlers did not expect this: on the ciénegas of New Mexico some even cut ditches to hasten it. So subtle has been its progress that few residents of the region are aware of it. It is quite invisible to the tourist who finds this wrecked landscape colorful and charming (as indeed it is, but it bears scant resemblance to what it was in 1848).

This same landscape was 'developed' once before, but with quite different results. The Pueblo Indians settled the Southwest in pre-Columbian times, but they happened *not* to be equipped with range livestock. Their civilization expired, but not because their land expired.

In India, regions devoid of any sod-forming grass have been settled, apparently without wrecking the land, by the simple expedient of carrying the grass to the cow, rather than vice versa. (Was this the result of some deep wisdom, or was it just good luck? I do not know.)

In short, the plant succession steered the course of history; the pioneer simply demonstrated, for good or ill, what successions inhered in the land. Is history taught in this spirit? It will be, once the concept of land as a community really penetrates our intellectual life.

THE ECOLOGICAL CONSCIENCE

Conservation is a state of harmony between men and land. Despite nearly a century of propaganda, conservation still proceeds at a snail's pace; progress still consists largely of letterhead pieties and convention oratory. On the back forty we still slip two steps backward for each forward stride.

The usual answer to this dilemma is 'more conservation education.' No one will debate this, but is it certain that only the *volume* of education needs stepping up? Is something lacking in the *content* as well?

It is difficult to give a fair summary of its content in brief form, but, as I understand it, the content is substantially this: obey the law, vote right, join some organizations, and practice what conservation is profitable on your own land; the government will do the rest.

Is not this formula too easy to accomplish anything worthwhile? It defines no right or wrong, assigns no obligation, calls for no sacrifice, implies no change in the current philosophy of values. In respect of land-use, it urges only enlightened self-interest. Just how far will such education take us? An example will perhaps yield a partial answer.

By 1930 it had become clear to all except the ecologically blind that southwestern Wisconsin's topsoil was slipping seaward. In 1933 the farmers were told that if they would adopt certain remedial practices for five years, the public would donate CCC labor to install them, plus the necessary machinery and materials. The offer was widely accepted, but the practices were widely forgotten when the five-year contract period was up. The farmers continued only those practices that yielded an immediate and visible economic gain for themselves.

This led to the idea that maybe farmers would learn more quickly if they themselves wrote the rules. Accordingly the Wisconsin Legislature in 1937 passed the Soil Conservation District Law. This said to farmers, in effect: *We, the public, will furnish you free technical service and loan you specialized machinery, if you will write your own rules for land-use. Each county may*

25

write its own rules, and these will have the force of law. Nearly all the counties promptly organized to accept the proferred help, but after a decade of operation, *no county has yet written a single rule.* There has been visible progress in such practices as strip-cropping, pasture renovation, and soil liming, but none in fencing woodlots against grazing, and none in excluding plow and cow from steep slopes. The farmers, in short, have selected those remedial practices which were profitable anyhow, and ignored those which were profitable to the community, but not clearly profitable to themselves.

30   When one asks why no rules have been written, one is told that the community is not yet ready to support them; education must precede rules. But the education actually in progress makes no mention of obligations to land over and above those dictated by self-interest. The net result is that we have more education but less soil, fewer healthy woods, and as many floods as in 1937.

The puzzling aspect of such situations is that the existence of obligations over and above self-interest is taken for granted in such rural community enterprises as the betterment of roads, schools, churches, and baseball teams. Their existence is not taken for granted, nor as yet seriously discussed, in bettering the behavior of the water that falls on the land, or in the preserving of the beauty or diversity of the farm landscape. Land-use ethics are still governed wholly by economic self-interest, just as social ethics were a century ago.

To sum up: we asked the farmer to do what he conveniently could to save his soil, and he has done just that, and only that. The farmer who clears the woods off a 75 per cent slope, turns his cows into the clearing, and dumps its rainfall, rocks, and soil into the community creek, is still (if otherwise decent) a respected member of society. If he puts lime on his fields and plants his crops on contour, he is still entitled to all the privileges and emoluments of his Soil Conservation District. The District is a beautiful piece of social machinery, but it is coughing along on two cylinders because we have been too timid, and too anxious for quick success, to tell the farmer the true magnitude of his obligations. Obligations have no meaning without conscience, and the problem we face is the extension of the social conscience from people to land.

No important change in ethics was ever accomplished without an internal change in our intellectual emphasis, loyalties, affections, and convictions. The proof that conservation has not yet touched these foundations of conduct lies in the fact that philosophy and religion have not yet heard of it. In our attempt to make conservation easy, we have made it trivial.

SUBSTITUTES FOR A LAND ETHIC

When the logic of history hungers for bread and we hand out a stone, we are at pains to explain how much the stone resembles bread. I now describe some of the stones which serve in lieu of a land ethic.

One basic weakness in a conservation system based wholly   35
on economic motives is that most members of the land community have no economic value. Wildflowers and songbirds are examples. Of the 22,000 higher plants and animals native to Wisconsin, it is doubtful whether more than 5 per cent can be sold, fed, eaten, or otherwise put to economic use. Yet these creatures are members of the biotic community, and if (as I believe) its stability depends on its integrity, they are entitled to continuance.

When one of these non-economic categories is threatened, and if we happen to love it, we invent subterfuges to give it economic importance. At the beginning of the century songbirds were supposed to be disappearing. Ornithologists jumped to the rescue with some distinctly shaky evidence to the effect that insects would eat us up if birds failed to control them. The evidence had to be economic in order to be valid.

It is painful to read these circumlocutions today. We have no land ethic yet, but we have at least drawn nearer the point of admitting that birds should continue as a matter of biotic right, regardless of the presence or absence of economic advantage to us.

A parallel situation exists in respect of predatory mammals, raptorial birds, and fish-eating birds. Time was when biologists somewhat overworked the evidence that these creatures preserve the health of game by killing weaklings, or that they control rodents for the farmer, or that they prey only on 'worthless' species. Here again, the evidence had to be economic in order to be valid. It is only in recent years that we hear the more honest argument that predators are members of the community, and that no special interest has the right to exterminate them for the sake of a benefit, real or fancied, to itself. Unfortunately this enlightened view is still in the talk stage. In the field the extermination of predators goes merrily on: witness the impending erasure of the timber wolf by fiat of Congress, the Conservation Bureaus, and many state legislatures.

Some species of trees have been 'read out of the party' by economics-minded foresters because they grow too slowly, or have too low a sale value to pay as timber crops: white cedar, tamarack, cypress, beech, and hemlock are examples. In Europe, where forestry is ecologically more advanced, the non-commercial tree species are recognized as members of the native forest community, to be preserved as such, within reason. Moreover some (like beech) have been found to have a valuable function in building up soil fertility. The interdependence of the forest and its constituent tree species, ground flora, and fauna is taken for granted.

40   Lack of economic value is sometimes a character not only of species or groups, but of entire biotic communities: marshes, bogs, dunes, and 'deserts' are examples. Our formula in such cases is to relegate their conservation to government as refuges, monuments, or parks. The difficulty is that these communities are usually interspersed with more valuable private lands; the government cannot possibly own or control such scattered parcels. The net effect is that we have relegated some of them to ultimate extinction over large areas. If the private owner were ecologically minded, he would be proud to be the custodian of a reasonable proportion of such areas, which add diversity and beauty to his farm and to his community.

In some instances, the assumed lack of profit in these 'waste' areas has proved to be wrong, but only after most of them had been done away with. The present scramble to reflood muskrat marshes is a case in point.

There is a clear tendency in American conservation to relegate to government all necessary jobs that private landowners fail to perform. Government ownership, operation, subsidy, or regulation is now widely prevalent in forestry, range management, soil and watershed management, park and wilderness conservation, fisheries management, and migratory bird management, with more to come. Most of this growth in governmental conservation is proper and logical, some of it is inevitable. That I imply no disapproval of it is implicit in the fact that I have spent most of my life working for it. Nevertheless the question arises: What is the ultimate magnitude of the enterprise? Will the tax base carry its eventual ramifications? At what point will governmental conservation, like the mastodon, become handicapped by its own dimensions? The answer, if there is any, seems to be in a land ethic, or some other force which assigns more obligation to the private landowner.

Industrial landowners and users, especially lumbermen and stockmen, are inclined to wail long and loudly about the extension of government ownership and regulation to land, but (with notable exceptions) they show little disposition to develop the only visible alternative: the voluntary practice of conservation on their own lands.

When the private landowner is asked to perform some unprofitable act for the good of the community, he today assents only with outstretched palm. If the act costs him cash this is fair and proper, but when it costs only forethought, open-mindedness, or time, the issue is at least debatable. The overwhelming growth of land-use subsidies in recent years must be ascribed, in large part, to the government's own agencies for conservation education: the land bureaus, the agricultural colleges, and the extension services. As far as I can detect, no ethical obligation toward land is taught in these institutions.

To sum up: a system of conservation based solely on economic self-interest is hopelessly lopsided. It tends to ignore, and thus eventually to eliminate, many elements in the land community that lack commercial value, but that are (as far as we know) essential to its healthy functioning. It assumes, falsely, I think, that the economic parts of the biotic clock will function without the uneconomic parts. It tends to relegate to government many functions eventually too large, too complex, or too widely dispersed to be performed by government.   45

An ethical obligation on the part of the private owner is the only visible remedy for these situations.

***

LAND HEALTH AND THE A-B CLEAVAGE

A land ethic, then, reflects the existence of an ecological conscience, and this in turn reflects a conviction of individual responsibility for the health of the land. Health is the capacity of the land for self-renewal. Conservation is our effort to understand and preserve this capacity.

Conservationists are notorious for their dissensions. Superficially these seem to add up to mere confusion, but a more careful scrutiny reveals a single plane of cleavage common to many specialized fields. In each field one group (A) regards the land as soil, and its function as commodity-production; another group (B) regards the land as a biota, and its function as something broader. How much broader is admittedly in a state of doubt and confusion.

In my own field, forestry, group A is quite content to grow trees like cabbages, with cellulose as the basic forest commodity. It feels no inhibition against violence; its ideology is agronomic. Group B, on the other hand, sees forestry as fundamentally different from agronomy because it employs natural species, and manages a natural environment rather than creating an artificial one. Group B prefers natural reproduction on principle. It worries on biotic as well as economic grounds about the loss of species like chestnut, and the threatened loss of the white pines. It worries about a whole series of secondary forest functions: wildlife, recreation, watersheds, wilderness areas. To my mind, Group B feels the stirrings of an ecological conscience.

50   In the wildlife field, a parallel cleavage exists. For Group A the basic commodities are sport and meat; the yardsticks of production are ciphers of take in pheasants and trout. Artificial propagation is acceptable as a permanent as well as a temporary recourse—if its unit costs permit. Group B, on the other hand, worries about a whole series of biotic side-issues. What is the cost in predators of producing a game crop? Should we have further recourse to exotics? How can management restore the shrinking species, like prairie grouse, already hopeless as shootable game? How can management restore the threatened rarities, like trumpeter swan and whooping crane? Can management principles be extended to wildflowers? Here again it is clear to me that we have the same A-B cleavage as in forestry.

In the larger field of agriculture I am less competent to speak, but there seem to be somewhat parallel cleavages. Scientific agriculture was actively developing before ecology was born, hence a slower penetration of ecological concepts might be expected. Moreover the farmer, by the very nature of his techniques, must modify the biota more radically than the forester or the wildlife manager. Nevertheless, there are many discontents in agriculture which seem to add up to a new vision of 'biotic farming.'

Perhaps the most important of these is the new evidence that poundage or tonnage is no measure of the food-value of farm crops; the products of fertile soil may be qualitatively as well as quantitatively superior. We can bolster poundage from depleted soils by pouring on imported fertility, but we are not necessarily bolstering food-value. The possible ultimate ramifications of this idea are so immense that I must leave their exposition to abler pens.

The discontent that labels itself 'organic farming,' while bearing some of the earmarks of a cult, it is nevertheless biotic in its direction, particularly in its insistence on the importance of soil flora and fauna.

The ecological fundamentals of agriculture are just as poorly known to the public as in other fields of land-use. For example, few educated people realize that the marvelous advances in technique made during recent decades are improvements in the pump, rather than the well. Acre for acre, they have barely sufficed to offset the sinking level of fertility.

In all of these cleavages, we see repeated the same basic paradoxes: man the conqueror *versus* man the biotic citizen; science the sharpener of his sword *versus* science the searchlight on his universe; land the slave and servant *versus* land the collective organism. Robinson's injunction to Tristram may well be applied, at this juncture, to *Homo sapiens* as a species in geological time:

> Whether you will or not
> You are a King, Tristram, for you are one
> Of the time-tested few that leave the world,
> When they are gone, not the same place it was.
> Mark what you leave.

THE OUTLOOK

It is inconceivable to me that an ethical relation to land can exist without love, respect, and admiration for land, and a high regard for its value. By value, I of course mean something far broader than mere economic value; I mean value in the philosophical sense.

Perhaps the most serious obstacle impeding the evolution of a land ethic is the fact that our educational and economic system is headed away from, rather than toward, an intense consciousness of land. Your true modern is separated from the land by many middlemen, and by innumerable physical gadgets. He has no vital relation to it; to him it is the space between cities on which crops grow. Turn him loose for a day on the land, and if the spot does not happen to be a golf links or a 'scenic' area, he is bored stiff. If crops could be raised by hydroponics instead of farming, it would suit him very well. Synthetic substitutes for wood, leather, wool, and other natural land products suit him better than the originals. In short, land is something he has 'outgrown.'

Almost equally serious as an obstacle to a land ethic is the attitude of the farmer for whom the land is still an adversary, or a taskmaster that keeps him in slavery. Theoretically, the mechanization of farming ought to cut the farmer's chains, but whether it really does is debatable.

One of the requisites for an ecological comprehension of land is an understanding of ecology, and this is by no means coextensive with 'education'; in fact, much higher education seems deliberately to avoid ecological concepts. An understanding of ecology does not necessarily originate in courses bearing ecological labels; it is quite as likely to be labeled geography, botany, agronomy, history, or economics. This is as it should be, but whatever the label, ecological training is scarce.

60 The case for a land ethic would appear hopeless but for the minority which is in obvious revolt against these 'modern' trends.

The 'key-log' which must be moved to release the evolutionary process for an ethic is simply this: quit thinking about decent land-use as solely an economic problem. Examine each question in terms of what is ethically and esthetically right, as well as what is economically expedient. A thing is right when it tends to preserve the integrity, stability, and beauty of the biotic community. It is wrong when it tends otherwise.

It of course goes without saying that economic feasibility limits the tether of what can or cannot be done for land. It always has and it always will. The fallacy the economic determinists have tied around our collective neck, and which we now need to cast off, is the belief that economics determines *all* land-use. This is simply not true. An innumerable host of actions and attitudes, comprising perhaps the bulk of all land relations, is determined by the land-users' tastes and predilections, rather than by his purse. The bulk of all land relations hinges on investments of time, forethought, skill, and faith rather than on investments of cash. As a land-user thinketh, so is he.

I have purposely presented the land ethic as a product of social evolution because nothing so important as an ethic is ever 'written.' Only the most superficial student of history supposes that Moses 'wrote' the Decalogue; it evolved in the minds of a thinking community, and Moses wrote a tentative summary of it for a 'seminar.' I say tentative because evolution never stops.

The evolution of a land ethic is an intellectual as well as emotional process. Conservation is paved with good intentions which prove to be futile, or even dangerous, because they are devoid of critical understanding either of the land, or of economic land-use. I think it is a truism that as the ethical frontier advances from the individual to the community, its intellectual content increases.

The mechanism of operation is the same for any ethic: social   65
approbation for right actions: social disapproval for wrong actions.

By and large, our present problem is one of attitudes and im-
plements. We are remodeling the Alhambra with a steam-shovel,
and we are proud of our yardage. We shall hardly relinquish the
shovel, which after all has many good points, but we are in need
of gentler and more objective criteria for its successful use.

1933

Discussion

1. What does Leopold mean by an "ecological conscience"? Do you think the people in your neighborhood have an ecological conscience?
2. How does Leopold use his thesis that the land is a fountain of energy as a platform on which to build a new definition of conservation?
3. What is Leopold's land ethic, and does it seem unusual to have an ethical relationship with the land, one which is not human?
4. Why do you think Leopold maintains that humans resist understanding the environment and that conservation represents more than an economic problem?
5. Discuss Leopold's contention that the evidence of history and ecology support the theory that the fewest changes to any environment is to be desired.

The World According to Cushman
Margaret L. Knox

Margaret L. Knox is a freelance journalist who writes frequently about environmental issues from her home in Missoula, Montana. Her work has appeared in Smithsonian, Mother Jones, Sierra, Environmental Journal, *and many newspapers. She grew up in California but has lived in many places including Zimbabwe, where she and her husband were both journalists. Knox is currently on the board of directors of the Montana Committee for the Humanities. Because of its great size and small population, Missoula, Montana, is an excellent location for Knox to report from. The clash between the federal government and property owners is tangible in a state in which the federal government, the biggest landowner in the west, seeks to purchase more land for parks, national monuments, and wildlife refuges. By profiling Cushman, a lobbyist advocating property rights since the 1970s, Knox is able to capture the attention of landowners who fear that they will lose control of their land and their heritage. Knox is particularly keen on revealing Cushman's exaggerations, a tendency endemic to most lobbyists.*

---------------- ◆ ----------------

Big Chuck Cushman paces the stage like the huggable host of a kiddie TV show. "I generally just like to have a good time with people," he booms, spreading his hands and rocking back on his heels with a gravelly laugh. "I'm not trying to *scaaaaare* you." This is the Captain Kangaroo of the movement against public lands: he's having a good time, and wants you to feel good, too! He jokes about how long you'll have to sit on your "fanny" tonight. He cocks his head and glances at you sideways. Then he pushes away the pesky podium, scratches his beard with a hand the size of a catcher's mitt, and leans forward, all 270-jean-clad-towering pounds of him oozing sincerity. "You know what a willing seller is for the U.S. Government?" Cushman puts a finger pistol-fashion to his temple. "Right?" He pauses, smiles. A hush falls over the audience of thirty or so golf-shirted businessmen and Sacramento Delta farmers. This is getting serious now. "A 44 caliber willing seller. Right?"

For nearly twenty years Cushman has made a living putting a name to the vague fears of small-town, recession-bound America. The name is the federal government, whose different land-managing agencies are "all the same." A table-full of fill-in-the-blank bumper stickers and posters at the back of the room make Cushman's favorite point. "If You Like the IRS, You'll Love ___." In this case the blank has been filled in with the U.S. Fish and Wildlife Service, the villain that aims to manage the Stone Lakes National Wildlife Refuge near Walnut Grove, California.

As I punch the remote control and scroll back and forth through the video of this August, 1991, speech in Walnut Grove, it occurs to me how simple is the pitch Cushman throws again and again from Mentone, Alabama, to Sitka, Alaska. In the world according to Cushman, the federal government is one big land-grabbing, tax-base-eating bogeyman. And the government's henchmen are the "preservationists." That's a word Cushman teaches people to use. "Most of *you* are environmentalists," he tells his rural audiences. The "preservationists," on the other hand, are the sharpster urban attorneys and their bleeding-heart, nature-loving clients, the kind of people Cushman's friends refer to in this post-Cold War era as "watermelons": green on the outside, red on the inside.

Cushman has fanned his brand of anti-government anger into three fiery political organizations, all of which, without non-profit status, are highly personalized and secretive fiefdoms. He founded the National Inholders Association in 1978 to fight the regulation of private land within national parks and other federal preserves. A decade later, he was in on the launching of the so-called Wise Use Movement, and created his own Multiple Use Land Alliance to prod conservative farmers, loggers, miners, ranchers, inholders, and off-road motorists to yelp in chorus for less protection and more access to federal lands. And now when private-property rights is becoming a buzzword phrase, Cushman is on stage again with the League of Private Property Voters—antitrope of the League of Conservation Voters—which he launched in 1991 to keep track of congressional votes on policies the Wise Use Movement abhors, like wetlands conservation, growth management, wilderness designation, and the protection of endangered species. "This issue is not about clean water," Cushman tells the Walnut Grove crowd. "It's not about pollution." He pauses, and his next words ring off the far walls. "This is a LAND USE CONTROL ISSUE!"

Like just about every other star of the Wise Use Movement,   5 Cushman has a story of youthful environmental idealism gone sour. There's the story of Cushman as a young Boy Scout rowing Audubon Society members through the surf to Anacapa Island for bird-watching. There's Cushman as a Student Conservation Corps volunteer and an earnest Sierra Club member. And then there's the turning point, when Cushman, the cabin-owner in Yosemite National Park, is riled by a Park Service that wants to tell him what he can do with his own private property. But none of that explains how he came to be so good—and he is good—at selling the anti-green agenda.

Cushman, 49, grew up in the suburbs of Los Angeles, where as a young man he dogged his way up from peanut vendor at Dodger stadium through a few real estate deals with a fellow peanut vendor to become, by the early 1970s, an award-winning insurance salesman for Mutual of New York. To understand the rest, you have to look at the efforts of the late Congressman

Phillip Burton to strengthen national park protection in the late 1970s.

Amendments that Burton offered to the Omnibus National Parks Act of 1978 would have directed the National Park Service to buy, within four years if funds were available, the private in-holdings in most of the old wilderness parks, including Yosemite. The idea behind his proposals was that logging, strip-mining, junk yards, and subdivisions—often smack in the middle of prime scenery—were fast undermining the intended purposes of the National Park System.

The amendments were rejected, but Burton's campaign in-censed cabin-owner Cushman, who organized a group of neighbors in and around Yosemite to file a lawsuit against the National Park Service. The lawsuit challenged current national parkland acquisitions, defended commercial development inside the parks, and went so far as to suggest that Yosemite should sell off the land it already owned. The lawsuit failed, but Cushman's new career was launched. He left his insurance job, obtained the names of more than 30,000 owners of property and permits within the national parks, and founded what would become the National Inholders Association. He has since been enormously successful at playing the politics of resentment in small-town America, painting the government in Washington as a pawn of entrenched and all-powerful conservation groups. Cushman's lobbying, lawsuits, and rural organizing have reduced and de-feated parks and monuments, preserves and wild rivers from Big Sur to the Adirondacks. He doesn't always win, but wherever he shows up, he at least makes it a lot more time-consuming and ex-pensive to protect green space, control growth, stem pollution, restrict logging, or manage grazing. Estimates of how much he has cost the conservation community in recent years range as high as $10 million. He can claim responsibility for lost conser-vation measures on thousands—some say millions—of acres of public lands.

Cushman is also known for shattering hard-fought compro-mises at the local level. "We had 90 percent of a good wetlands or-dinance agreed upon," says John Karpinski of the Clark County Natural Resources Council in Vancouver, Washington. Karpinski, an attorney, had negotiated for months with real estate develop-ers, county planners, and environmental groups to come up with a draft. "Then Cushman came in and incited people to near riots at all his workshops."

1993

Discussion

1. Do you think Knox is fair to Cushman in her depiction of him?
2. Whom do you respect more: Cushman for his efforts to explain his skepticism of the government to landowners, or Knox for writing about Cushman's actions?
3. Do you think the arguments against the federal government and its land management policies that Cushman offers his audiences are fair and logical?
4. Discuss the idea of setting aside land for public enjoyment versus individual property owners losing the rights to their land.
5. Do you agree with the premise that if a person buys land, he or she should be able to do anything with it?
6. Relate Cushman's ideas about land and land use to Mary Austin's argument for land use in "My Neighbor's Field" (p. 13).

Caring for the Woods
BARRY LOPEZ

Barry Lopez (1945–) believes that culture is infused with nature just as are individuals. Born in Southern California, he moved to New York City when he was eleven. He was educated at the University of Notre Dame, in South Bend, Indiana. Lopez is known for his books on natural history and the environment, such as Of Wolves and Men *(1978),* Arctic Dreams: Imagination and Desire in a Northern Landscape *(1986, for which he won a National Book Award),* Crossing Open Ground *(1988), and* About This Life *(1998). His fiction includes* Desert Notes: Reflections in the Eye of a Raven *(1976),* River Notes: The Dance of Herons *(1979),* Winter Count *(1981), and* Light Action in the Caribbean *(2000). Other works include* Giving Birth to Thunder, Sleeping with His Daughter *(1977). His writing appears regularly in* Harper's, The Paris Review, Orion, *and* The Georgia Review. *Lopez lives in western Oregon.*

———————————— ✦ ————————————

M y family has been in the Americas for almost five centuries. Marín López, a shipwright on my father's side, was in the Caribbean with Cortés in 1511. My mother's English and German ancestors began farming on the Pennsylvania side of the Delaware River valley in the 1650s. A scion of that group later moved to Virginia (where the Holston River still bears the family name); his progeny moved into the Carolinas and eastern Alabama, where my mother was born on a plantation in 1914. One relative in that clan moved on to New Mexico at the close of the 19th century and then dropped from sight. He is recalled as a man obsessed with killing Indians.

My father's family, originally tobacco farmers in Cuba, eventually came to St. Louis and New York as tobacco merchants, though they maintained close ties with Asturias, their homeland in northern Spain. Neither the Romans nor the Moors, my father is still proud to say, ever conquered Asturias. He traces his lineage there back to Rodrigo Díaz de Vivar—El Cid. In her last years my mother followed her own path back as far, to a baron of Somerset who ratified the Magna Carta at Runnymede.

All these centuries later, the wandering, the buying up, the clearing, the planting, and the harvesting of land in my single branch of the family has come down to a parcel in Oregon: 35 acres of mixed old-growth forest, rising quickly into the foothills of the Cascade Mountains from the north bank of the McKenzie River. These woods harbor Roosevelt elk and mountain lion, suites of riparian and mixed-forest birds, and an assortment of insects, wildflowers, and mushrooms that trails off into a thousand species.

I understand the desire to own the land, the dream of material wealth that brought each of my lines of descent to the Americas. I respect the determination, the tenacity, and the uses to which the land-profit was put—formal education, for example. But I've come to believe, at the age of 49, that sacrificing the biological integrity of land to abet human progress is a practice my generation must end. If we do not, I believe the Americas will finally wash into the sea like Haiti, leaving behind a social nightmare.

5   My wife, Sandra, and I have lived on the right bank of the river for 24 years. We want to keep this single wooded slope of land in the West undeveloped and uncut. We want to pass it on like a well-read book, not the leavings of someone's meal.

The enormous trees and the river, because of their scale, dominate what we see here, but the interstices of this landscape are jammed with life: hummingbirds, spiders, butterflies, cutthroat trout, wild ginger, skinks, the cascading blossoms of wild rhododendron. In the1940s some of the larger trees—Douglas fir, western hemlock, and western red cedar, four to six feet in diameter—were selectively logged. The selective logging and a fire that burned a long stretch of the north bank of the McKenzie in 1855 created a forest with a few tall, rotting stumps; dense patches of younger Douglas fir; and several dozen massive, isolated, towering trees, 300 to 400 years old, all standing among many fewer Pacific yew, chinquapin, bigleaf maple, red alder, Pacific dogwood, California hazel, and the odd Pacific madrone.

In 1989 a neighbor who owned this slope put 32 acres of it up for sale. Timber companies that intended to clear-cut the property were the most active bidders, and Sandra and I were forced to match money and wits with them. But in 1990 we were able to add these acres to three we'd bought in 1976. We then completed a legal arrangement to prevent the land from being either logged or developed after we passed away. Good intention toward an individual stretch of land has now become well-meaning of another kind in my family.

We did not set out to preserve these woods. From the start we felt it a privilege, also a kind of wonder, to live here. Twenty-inch spring chinook spawn on a redd in front of the house in September every year. Wild bleeding heart, yellow violets, white flowers such as trillium and wood sorrel, and the red flowers of coralroot are brilliant in the deep, green woods in April and May. I find bear scat, beaver-clipped willows, and black-tailed deer prints regularly on my walks. On the same night we've listened to northern spotted owls, western screech owls, and northern saw-whet owls call. Spotted skunks and a short-tail weasel have tried to take up residence in the house. On summer nights, when we leave the windows open, bats fly through.

From a certain perspective, this wooded hill with its unnamed creek and marvelous creatures—I nearly stepped on a rubber boa one morning on the way to the toolshed—is still relatively unmanipulated; but I try not to let myself be fooled by the thought. The number of songbirds returning each spring I would guess to be half what it was a decade ago. The number of chinook on the redd, though it fluctuates, has also fallen off in recent years. And I've taken hundreds of dead animals off the road along the river—raccoon, brush rabbit, even Steller's jay and mink. People new to the area are apt to log the few Douglas firs left on their property, to roll out fresh lawns and plant ornamental trees in their place. Their house cats leave shrews, white-footed mice, and young birds strewn in the woods like so much litter.

10   Driftnets that snag salmon in the far-off Pacific, industrial logging in Central America that eliminates migratory-bird habitat, speeding trucks and automobiles, attractive prices for timber—all of it directly affects these acres. There is no way to fence it out.

The historical detail that might make vivid what, precisely, occurred in the McKenzie River valley after its location in 1812 by Donald MacKenzie—a trapper and kinsman of the Canadian explorer Alexander MacKenzie—is hard to come by, but the story is similar to those told of a hundred other valleys in the West. Beaver trappers were the first whites to sleep in these woods. (Molala and Kalapuya Indians, from the east and west side of the Cascades respectively, apparently camped along the McKenzie in summer, when salmon were running and openings in the heavily forested mountains were crowded with ripening blue and red huckleberries, soft thimbleberries, strawberries, orange salmonberries, blue and red elderberries, and trailing blackberries.) When the free trappers and the company trappers were gone, gold and silver miners filtered in. Toward the end of the 19th century some homestead settlement followed small-scale logging operations along the river, though steep mountains and dense forests made farming and grazing in the area impractical. Clearcutting in modern times, with its complicated attendant problems—siltation smothering salmon redds,"predator control" programs directed against black bears—has turned the road between our house and Eugene, 40 miles downriver, into as butchered a landscape as any I know in the Cascades.

        In the 1980s, when the price of Douglas fir reached $300 for 1,000 board feet, some small-property owners succumbed—two or three trees might bring them $2,500. The resulting harvest has grown to look like mange on the hills. Hand in hand with that has come real estate promotion, the hundreds of FOR SALE signs along the road a sort of Muzak.

        I am not a cynical man, but watching the quick spread of suburban logging and seeing the same house put up for sale every few years—with a little more landscaping, a higher fence, and another $30,000 to $40,000 added to the price—pushes me closer to it than anything else I know. A long-term commitment to the place, knowledge of its biological limits, or concern for the valley's fate—these do not appear to be a part of the transactions. The hacking away at natural growth, the incessant prettifying with rosebushes and trimmed hedges, and the imposition of incongruous antebellum architecture look like a scatter of bad marriages—reigning husbands with presentable wives.

If I had answers to these problems, or if I felt exempt in this mess, I would be angry about it more often than I am. As it is, Sandra and I pace ourselves. We work on initiatives to control real estate development and rein in logging along the river. We provide a place for the release of rehabilitated raptors, including spotted owls. We work amicably with the state highway department and the Bonneville Power Administration (BPA), which maintain corridors across the land we occupy. We have had to threaten a lawsuit to curb the recklessness of the highway department with chainsaws and heavy equipment, and we have had to insist through an attorney that the BPA not capriciously fall "danger trees"along its power-line right-of-way.

But these agencies, whose land-management philosophies   15
differ so strikingly from our own, have slowly accommodated us. Instead of flooding the roadside with herbicides and flailing at it with oversize brush cutters, the highway department now permits us (and others along the river) to trim back by hand what brush actually threatens motor traffic. And the regional director of the BPA wrote into a recent contract that I could accompany his fallers, to be certain no felled tree was sent crashing needlessly into other trees.

Sandra and I ourselves, of course, have not left the place untouched. In January 1991 two windstorms felled about 30 trees. We logged them out with horses and put the money toward the land payment. I have felled standing dead trees that threatened the house. We compost our kitchen waste, laundry lint, and woodstove ashes in the woods. We've planted gardens and built outbuildings. But it is our habit to disturb these acres very little and to look after them in a way only humans can: by discouraging or preventing the destruction other humans bring. I've asked my neighbors to stop dumping refuse on our place. (They had done it for years because it was only "the woods," a sort of warehouse for timber, deer, and fish, and a dumping ground for whatever one wanted to abandon—cars, bedsprings, fuel drums, mall packaging.) I've asked another neighbor's children not to shoot at birds or chop down trees. I've asked unwitting fishermen not to walk through the salmon redd. And, reluctantly, I've gated and posted the land to keep out wanton hunters and people in four-wheel-drives looking for something to break down or climb over.

We know we cannot fence off the endangered chinook redd without attracting curious passersby. Neither I nor anyone can outlaw the product advertising (or foolish popular history) that contributes to images of men taming a violent West. Neither I nor anyone, I fear, can soon change human sentiment to put lands that are unharvested, unhunted, unroaded, or untenanted on the same footing with lands that are domesticated or industrialized. So the birds and animals, the fish and spiders, the wild orchids and other flowers will not have these shields.

Piece by piece, however, as a citizen and as a writer, I want to contest the obsessions that I believe imperil American landscapes—the view that they are principally sources of material wealth or scenic backdrops for a more important human drama. I want to consider the anomalies that lie at the heart of our incessant desire to do good. And I want to see how to sidestep despair, by placing my faith in something larger than my own ideas.

Sandra and I know we do not own these 35 acres. The Oregon ash trees by the river, in whose limbs I have seen flocks of 100 Audubon's warblers, belong also to the families in Guatemala in whose forests these birds winter. The bereavement I feel at the diminishment of life around me is also a bereavement felt by men and women and children I don't know, living in cities I've never visited. And the exhilaration I experience seeing fresh cougar tracks in mud by a creek is an emotion known to any person in love who hears the one-who-is-loved speak.

20   There is more mystery to be contemplated, there are more lessons to be absorbed, on these 35 acres than all the people in my lineage going back to Runnymede and medieval Asturias could manage, should the study be pursued another 1,000 years. My generation's task, I believe, is to change the direction of Western civilization in order to make such a regard practicable.

When I rise in the morning I often walk down to the riverbank. If it's summer I'm likely to see mergansers, tree swallows, and osprey. I see first light brightly reflected on alder twigs stripped by beaver. I feel the night movement of cool air downriver and see deer-head orchid and blue gilia blooming in the dark-green salal and horsetail rushes.

I am acutely aware, winter or summer, that these waters have come from farther east in the mountains, that in a few days they will cross the bar at the mouth of the Columbia and become part of the Pacific. The ancient history alone of this river, this animate and elusive business of rain and snow and gravity, gives me hope.

Walking back to the house in this serene frame of mind, I know that to love life, to swear an allegiance to what is alive, is the essence of what I am after. I'm moved to forgive whoever does not find in these acres what I do. I glance into the moving picket of trees and shadow, alert for what I've never noticed before, in a woods I'm trying to take care of—as in its very complicated way it is taking care of me.

1995

Discussion

1. What seems to be the point of Lopez's recitation of his family's lineage and the history of the McKenzie River Valley where he has lived for thirty-five years?
2. What makes Lopez feel the urgency of maintaining the biological integrity of the land?
3. What is Lopez's complaint about the biological integrity of his immediate neighborhood along the McKenzie River?
4. Discuss the measures by which Lopez and his wife Sandra have tried to forestall the process by which his rural neighborhood is becoming suburban.
5. Explain why Lopez put up gates on access routes to his property.
6. Compare Lopez's view of the urgency of maintaining his woodland with Joy Williams's suburban experience in "One Acre: On Devaluing Real Estate to Keep Land Priceless" (p. 95).
7. Compare Lopez's attitudes toward the diversity and beauty of his landscape with Edward Abbey's sentiments in "The First Morning" (p. 165).

Thinking and Writing About Chapter 1

1. When you see a scene in nature that deeply impresses you, how do you respond to it?
2. What do you think people can learn from being in or visiting preserved wilderness areas?
3. Discuss the ethics of land use based on the readings in this chapter.
4. If mankind is only a part of nature, rather than its dominating influence, is it man's responsibility to care for the environment and by doing so perhaps compromise the benefit gained from it?
5. Former Vice President Spiro Agnew once famously said: "If you have seen one tree, you have seen all of them." Do you think there is any sense in preserving entire forests? Considering the size of our national and state parks, do you think we have preserved enough "nature" in this country.
6. Discuss the pros and cons of accommodating both industrial development and environmental protection. Give an example of a business or industry in your community that has embraced environmental preservation.
7. Discuss the pros and cons of the argument that change in the environment due to human action and needs is inevitable and should not be discouraged.
8. Do you think John Muir ("The American Forests," p. 7) and Aldo Leopold ("The Land Ethic," p. 18) would have had a friendly conversation? Discuss how they might have agreed or disagreed with each other.

Additional Resources

Film
The Grapes of Wrath (1940), directed by John Ford

Fiction
Frank Norris, The Octopus (1901)
John Steinbeck, The Grapes of Wrath (1939)

Essays
Henry David Thoreau, Walden (1854)
George Perkins Marsh, Man and Nature (1864)
Bill McKibben, The End of Nature (1989)

CHAPTER 2

Urban Vision,
Rural Reflections

The clash of country and city life is ingrained in the American character. Think about the never-ceasing deprecatory attitudes: "country bumpkin" versus "city slicker." Once America was a wilderness, and once most Americans were engaged in farming and agriculture, but this is no longer the case. By the 1850s, after two centuries of concentrated agricultural settlement along the eastern seaboard, Henry David Thoreau, a resident of the small town of Concord, Massachusetts, felt hemmed in by the pace of town life, the drive for income, the rush to own material things, and most of all the lessening of his contact with nature. "Walking" (1862) is Thoreau's rhapsody on the need for wildness as a restorative for the human spirit. He says, "I seek the darkest wood, the thickest and most interminable and, to the citizen, most dismal swamp" which he enters as a "sacred place." Thoreau had to leave his town to find nature, a common contemporary complaint of city dwellers who seek solace, rest, and relaxation. For Thoreau, heading west was both the real escape from the town as well as the symbolic imaginative vision of freedom from servility.

Paradoxically, Marie Winn found nature in the heart of New York City over a century later. In "The Regulars" (1998), a story of bird-watching in Central Park, Winn reminds us that wildlife exists and follows its own patterns of behavior even in the middle of a city of eight million. As an unforeseen consequence of the genius of Frederick Law Olmsted and Calvert Vaux, landscape architects and builders of Central Park, this 640-acre swath of parkland in Manhattan has become an unintended haven for birds and other wild animals, and for the people who observe and listen to them.

Contrary to Thoreau's idea of finding freedom in rural nature, Peter Huber aggravates the split between the rural and the urban by arguing that the development of cities is an essential means of saving the countryside. In "How Cities Green the Planet" (2000), he claims that efforts by disciples of the green movement to halt urban organic growth and curtail sprawl are wrong. He writes: "The rise and spread of the metropolis has brought about a magnificent renaissance of green." Huber looks at land and cities as economic entities. His bottom-line argument concludes that if the growth of cities is stymied, the result will be a loss of progress and wealth.

Huber suggests that the Greens are misguided and on the verge of doing more harm than good for our civilization and the vitality of life. However, Tara Hulen's "Dispatch from Toxic Town" (2003) suggests that urban prosperity may be short-lived. Her report on Anniston, Alabama (population 24,000) shows how the base of Anniston's economic well-being has destroyed the city: The ironworks left a residue of lead waste and a chemical plant dumped PCBs into the water supply. The people of Anniston love their city, but feel strongly that they have nearly lost it and now have nowhere else to go. Implicit in Hulen's dispatch is the idea that the threat of pollution is often underreported regardless of urban or rural location. The important question that she raises, which economists and big business often disregard, is what can local citizens do to protect their health and quality of life. When there is no "west" in Thoreau's sense of the word and cities are polluted, what can a person do?

Walking

HENRY DAVID THOREAU

Henry David Thoreau (1817–1862) was a life-long resident of Concord, Massachusetts, a small town from which he seldom traveled far. Thoreau, a Harvard College graduate, never had a steady career, but is chiefly remembered for his account of living in a cabin that he built for himself at Walden Pond, a short walk from Concord, in an effort to prove that one could live happily in a state of rustic simplicity. Walden (1854) is the journal he kept during the year and a half in his cabin. Ironically, "Walking," his final publica-

tion before dying of tuberculosis, was completed while he was confined to bed. Thoreau's prose and poetry were virtually unknown to the reading public during his lifetime; it was not until the 1880s, two decades after his death, that his writings became popular and respected for their unconventional logic and accurate observations on life and nature. As an apostle of self-reliance and natural spirituality, Thoreau attempted to show that a person could come to terms with nature by living in its midst and taking the time to understand it. He is now considered by many to be the preeminent American nature writer and the inspiration for Aldo Leopold's "The Land Ethic" (1949).

———————— ✦ ————————

I wish to speak a word for Nature, for absolute freedom and wildness, as contrasted with a freedom and culture merely civil—to regard man as an inhabitant, or a part and parcel of Nature, rather than a member of society. I wish to make an extreme statement, if so I may make an emphatic one, for there are enough champions of civilization: the minister and the school committee and every one of you will take care of that.

I think that I cannot preserve my health and spirits, unless I spend four hours a day at least—and it is commonly more than that—sauntering through the woods and over the hills and fields, absolutely free from all worldly engagements. You may safely say, A penny for your thoughts, or a thousand pounds. When sometimes I am reminded that the mechanics and shopkeepers stay in their shops not only all the forenoon, but all the afternoon too, sitting with crossed legs, so many of them—as if the legs were made to sit upon, and not to stand or walk upon—I think that they deserve some credit for not having all committed suicide long ago.

No doubt temperament, and, above all, age, have a good deal to do with it. As a man grows older, his ability to sit still and follow indoor occupations increases. He grows vespertinal in his habits as the evening of life approaches, till at last he comes forth only just before sundown, and gets all the walk that he requires in half an hour.

But the walking of which I speak has nothing in it akin to taking exercise, as it is called, as the sick take medicine at stated hours—as the Swinging of dumbbells or chairs; but is itself the enterprise and adventure of the day. If you would get exercise, go in search of the springs of life. Think of a man's swinging dumb-bells for his health, when those springs are bubbling up in far-off pastures unsought by him! . . .

5   Living much out of doors, in the sun and wind, will no doubt produce a certain roughness of character—will cause a thicker cuticle to grow over some of the finer qualities of our nature, as on the face and hands, or as severe manual labor robs the hands of some of their delicacy of touch. So staying in the house, on the other hand, may produce a softness and smoothness, not to say thinness of skin, accompanied by an increased sensibility to certain impressions. Perhaps we should be more susceptible to some influences important to our intellectual and moral growth, if the sun had shone and the wind blown on us a little less; and no doubt it is a nice matter to proportion rightly the thick and thin skin. But methinks that is a scurf that will fall off fast enough—that the natural remedy is to be found in the proportion which the night bears to the day, the winter to the summer, thought to experience. There will be so much the more air and sunshine in our thoughts. The callous palms of the laborer are conversant with finer tissues of self-respect and heroism, whose touch thrills the heart, than the languid fingers of idleness. That is mere sentimentality that lies abed by day and thinks itself white, far from the tan and callus of experience.

When we walk, we naturally go to the fields and woods: what would become of us, if we walked only in a garden or a mall? Even some sects of philosophers have felt the necessity of importing the woods to themselves, since they did not go to the woods. "They planted groves and walks of Platanes," where they took subdiales ambulationes in porticos open to the air. Of course it is of no use to direct our steps to the woods, if they do not carry us thither. I am alarmed when it happens that I have walked a mile into the woods bodily, without getting there in spirit. In my afternoon walk I would fain forget all my morning occupations and my obligations to Society. But it sometimes happens that I cannot easily shake off the village. The thought of some work will run in my head and I am not where my body is—I am out of my senses. In my walks I would fain return to my senses. What business have I in the woods, if I am thinking of something out of the woods? I suspect myself, and cannot help a shudder when I find myself so implicated even in what are called good works—for this may sometimes happen.

My vicinity affords many good walks; and though for so many years I have walked almost every day, and sometimes for several days together, I have not yet exhausted them. An absolutely new prospect is a great happiness, and I can still get this any afternoon. Two or three hours' walking will carry me to as strange a country as I expect ever to see. A single farmhouse which I had not seen before is sometimes as good as the dominions of the King of Dahomey. There is in fact a sort of harmony discoverable between the capabilities of the landscape within a circle of ten miles' radius, or the limits of an afternoon walk, and the threescore years and ten of human life. It will never become quite familiar to you.

Nowadays almost all man's improvements, so called, as the building of houses and the cutting down of the forest and of all large trees, simply deform the landscape, and make it more and more tame and cheap. A people who would begin by burning the fences and let the forest stand! I saw the fences half consumed, their ends lost in the middle of the prairie, and some worldly miser with a surveyor looking after his bounds, while heaven had taken place around him, and he did not see the angels going to and fro, but was looking for an old post-hole in the midst of paradise. I looked again, and saw him standing in the middle of a boggy Stygian fen, surrounded by devils, and he had found his bounds without a doubt, three little stones, where a stake had been driven, and looking nearer, I saw that the Prince of Darkness was his surveyor. . . .

At present, in this vicinity, the best part of the land is not private property; the landscape is not owned, and the walker enjoys comparative freedom. But possibly the day will come when it will be partitioned off into so-called pleasure-grounds, in which a few will take a narrow and exclusive pleasure only—when fences shall be multiplied, and man-traps and other engines invented to confine men to the PUBLIC road, and walking over the surface of God's earth shall be construed to mean trespassing on some gentleman's grounds. To enjoy a thing exclusively is commonly to exclude yourself from the true enjoyment of it. Let us improve our opportunities, then, before the evil days come.

What is it that makes it so hard sometimes to determine   10
whither we will walk? I believe that there is a subtle magnetism in Nature, which, if we unconsciously yield to it, will direct us aright. It is not indifferent to us which way we walk. There is a right way; but we are very liable from heedlessness and stupidity to take the wrong one. We would fain take that walk, never yet taken by us through this actual world, which is perfectly symbolical of the path which we love to travel in the interior and ideal

world; and sometimes, no doubt, we find it difficult to choose our direction, because it does not yet exist distinctly in our idea.

When I go out of the house for a walk, uncertain as yet whither I will bend my steps, and submit myself to my instinct to decide for me, I find, strange and whimsical as it may seem, that I finally and inevitably settle southwest, toward some particular wood or meadow or deserted pasture or hill in that direction. My needle is slow to settle,—varies a few degrees, and does not always point due southwest, it is true, and it has good authority for this variation, but it always settles between west and south-southwest. The future lies that way to me, and the earth seems more unexhausted and richer on that side. The outline which would bound my walks would be, not a circle, but a parabola, or rather like one of those cometary orbits which have been thought to be non-returning curves, in this case opening westward, in which my house occupies the place of the sun. I turn round and round irresolute sometimes for a quarter of an hour, until I decide, for a thousandth time, that I will walk into the southwest or west. Eastward I go only by force; but westward I go free. Thither no business leads me. It is hard for me to believe that I shall find fair landscapes or sufficient wildness and freedom behind the eastern horizon. I am not excited by the prospect of a walk thither; but I believe that the forest which I see in the western horizon stretches uninterruptedly toward the setting sun, and there are no towns nor cities in it of enough consequence to disturb me. Let me live where I will, on this side is the city, on that the wilderness, and ever I am leaving the city more and more, and withdrawing into the wilderness. I should not lay so much stress on this fact, if I did not believe that something like this is the prevailing tendency of my countrymen. I must walk toward Oregon, and not toward Europe. And that way the nation is moving, and I may say that mankind progress from east to west. Within a few years we have witnessed the phenomenon of a southeastward migration, in the settlement of Australia; but this affects us as a retrograde movement, and, judging from the moral and physical character of the first generation of Australians, has not yet proved a successful experiment. The eastern Tartars think that there is nothing west beyond Thibet. "The world ends there," say they; "beyond there is nothing but a shoreless sea." It is unmitigated East where they live.

We go eastward to realize history and study the works of art and literature, retracing the steps of the race; we go westward as into the future, with a spirit of enterprise and adventure. The

Atlantic is a Lethean stream, in our passage over which we have had an opportunity to forget the Old World and its institutions. If we do not succeed this time, there is perhaps one more chance for the race left before it arrives on the banks of the Styx; and that is in the Lethe of the Pacific, which is three times as wide.

The West of which I speak is but another name for the Wild; and what I have been preparing to say is, that in Wildness is the preservation of the World. Every tree sends its fibers forth in search of the Wild. The cities import it at any price. Men plow and sail for it. From the forest and wilderness come the tonics and barks which brace mankind. Our ancestors were savages. The story of Romulus and Remus being suckled by a wolf is not a meaningless fable. The founders of every state which has risen to eminence have drawn their nourishment and vigor from a similar wild source. It was because the children of the Empire were not suckled by the wolf that they were conquered and displaced by the children of the northern forests who were.

I believe in the forest, and in the meadow, and in the night in which the corn grows. We require an infusion of hemlock, spruce or arbor vitae in our tea. There is a difference between eating and drinking for strength and from mere gluttony. The Hottentots eagerly devour the marrow of the koodoo and other antelopes raw, as a matter of course. Some of our northern Indians eat raw the marrow of the Arctic reindeer, as well as various other parts, including the summits of the antlers, as long as they are soft. And herein, perchance, they have stolen a march on the cooks of Paris. They get what usually goes to feed the fire. This is probably better than stall-fed beef and slaughterhouse pork to make a man of. Give me a wildness whose glance no civilization can endure— as if we lived on the marrow of koodoos devoured raw.

There are some intervals which border the strain of the wood 15
thrush, to which I would migrate—wild lands where no settler has squatted; to which, methinks, I am already acclimated.

Life consists with wildness. The most alive is the wildest. Not yet subdued to man, its presence refreshes him. One who pressed forward incessantly and never rested from his labors, who grew fast and made infinite demands on life, would always find himself in a new country or wilderness, and surrounded by the raw material of life. He would be climbing over the prostrate stems of primitive forest trees.

Hope and the future for me are not in lawns and cultivated fields, not in towns and cities, but in the impervious and quaking swamps. When, formerly, I have analyzed my partiality for some farm which I had contemplated purchasing, I have frequently found that I was attracted solely by a few square rods of impermeable and unfathomable bog—a natural sink in one corner of it. That was the jewel which dazzled me. I derive more of my subsistence from the swamps which surround my native town than from the cultivated gardens in the village. There are no richer parterres to my eyes than the dense beds of dwarf andromeda (*Cassandra calyculata*) which cover these tender places on the earth's surface. Botany cannot go farther than tell me the names of the shrubs which grow there—the high blueberry, panicled andromeda, lambkill, azalea, and rhodora—all standing in the quaking sphagnum. I often think that I should like to have my house front on this mass of dull red bushes, omitting other flower plots and borders, transplanted spruce and trim box, even graveled walks—to have this fertile spot under my windows, not a few imported barrowfuls of soil only to cover the sand which was thrown out in digging the cellar. Why not put my house, my parlor, behind this plot, instead of behind that meager assemblage of curiosities, that poor apology for a Nature and Art, which I call my front yard? It is an effort to clear up and make a decent appearance when the carpenter and mason have departed, though done as much for the passer-by as the dweller within. The most tasteful front-yard fence was never an agreeable object of study to me; the most elaborate ornaments, acorn tops, or what not, soon wearied and disgusted me. Bring your sills up to the very edge of the swamp, then (though it may not be the best place for a dry cellar), so that there be no access on that side to citizens. Front yards are not made to walk in, but, at most, through, and you could go in the back way.

Yes, though you may think me perverse, if it were proposed to me to dwell in the neighborhood of the most beautiful garden that ever human art contrived, or else of a Dismal Swamp, I should certainly decide for the swamp. How vain, then, have been all your labors, citizens, for me!

My spirits infallibly rise in proportion to the outward dreariness. Give me the ocean, the desert, or the wilderness! In the desert, pure air and solitude compensate for want of moisture and fertility. The traveler Burton says of it—"Your MORALE improves; you become frank and cordial, hospitable and single-minded. . . . In the desert, spirituous liquors excite only disgust. There is a keen enjoyment in a mere animal existence." They who have been traveling long on the steppes of Tartary say, "On re-entering cultivated lands, the agitation, perplexity, and turmoil of civilization oppressed and suffocated us; the air seemed to fail us, and we felt every moment as if about to die of asphyxia." When I would recreate myself, I seek the darkest wood, the thickest and most interminable and, to the citizen, most dismal swamp. I enter a swamp as a sacred place,—a sanctum sanctorum. There is the strength, the marrow, of Nature. The wildwood covers the virgin mould,—and the same soil is good for men and for trees. A man's health requires as many acres of meadow to his prospect as his farm does loads of muck. There are the strong meats on which he feeds. A town is saved, not more by the righteous men in it than by the woods and swamps that surround it. A township where one primitive forest waves above while another primitive forest rots below—such a town is fitted to raise not only corn and potatoes, but poets and philosophers for the coming ages. In such a soil grew Homer and Confucius and the rest, and out of such a wilderness comes the Reformer eating locusts and wild honey.

To preserve wild animals implies generally the creation of a   20 forest for them to dwell in or resort to. So it is with man. A hundred years ago they sold bark in our streets peeled from our own woods. In the very aspect of those primitive and rugged trees there was, methinks, a tanning principle which hardened and consolidated the fibers of men's thoughts. Ah! already I shudder for these comparatively degenerate days of my native village, when you cannot collect a load of bark of good thickness, and we no longer produce tar and turpentine.

It is said to be the task of the American "to work the virgin soil," and that "agriculture here already assumes proportions unknown everywhere else." I think that the farmer displaces the Indian even because he redeems the meadow, and so makes himself stronger and in some respects more natural. I was surveying for a man the other day a single straight line one hundred and thirty-two rods long, through a swamp at whose entrance might have been written the words which Dante read over the entrance to the infernal regions,—"Leave all hope, ye that enter"—that is, of ever getting out again; where at one time I saw my employer actually up to his neck and swimming for his life in his property, though it was still winter. He had another similar swamp which I could not survey at all, because it was completely under water, and nevertheless, with regard to a third swamp, which I did SURVEY from a distance, he remarked to me, true to his instincts, that he would not part with it for any consideration, on account of the mud which it contained. And that man intends to put a girdling ditch round the whole in the course of forty months, and so redeem it by the magic of his spade. I refer to him only as the type of a class.

The weapons with which we have gained our most important victories, which should be handed down as heirlooms from father to son, are not the sword and the lance, but the bushwhack, the turf-cutter, the spade, and the bog hoe, rusted with the blood of many a meadow, and begrimed with the dust of many a hard-fought field. The very winds blew the Indian's cornfield into the meadow, and pointed out the way which he had not the skill to follow. He had no better implement with which to intrench himself in the land than a clam-shell. But the farmer is armed with plow and spade.

In short, all good things are wild and free. There is something in a strain of music, whether produced by an instrument or by the human voice—take the sound of a bugle in a summer night, for instance—which by its wildness, to speak without satire, reminds me of the cries emitted by wild beasts in their native forests. It is so much of their wildness as I can understand. Give me for my friends and neighbors wild men, not tame ones. The wildness of the savage is but a faint symbol of the awful ferity with which good men and lovers meet.

For my part, I feel that with regard to Nature I live a sort of border life, on the confines of a world into which I make occasional and transient forays only, and my patriotism and allegiance to the state into whose territories I seem to retreat are those of a moss-trooper. Unto a life which I call natural I would gladly follow even a will-o'-the-wisp through bogs and sloughs unimaginable, but no moon nor firefly has shown me the causeway to it. Nature is a personality so vast and universal that we have never seen one of her features. The walker in the familiar fields which stretch around my native town sometimes finds himself in another land than is described in their owners' deeds, as it were in some faraway field on the confines of the actual Concord, where her jurisdiction ceases, and the idea which the word Concord suggests ceases to be suggested. These farms which I have myself surveyed, these bounds which I have set up, appear dimly still as through a mist; but they have no chemistry to fix them; they fade from the surface of the glass, and the picture which the painter painted stands out dimly from beneath. The world with which we are commonly acquainted leaves no trace, and it will have no anniversary. . . .

So we saunter toward the Holy Land, till one day the sun   25
shall shine more brightly than ever he has done, shall perchance shine into our minds and hearts, and light up our whole lives with a great awakening light, as warm and serene and golden as on a bankside in autumn.

1862

Discussion

1. What is the imaginative and environmental significance of the direction that Thoreau prefers to walk?
2. What does Thoreau suggest about the urban and the rural when he says, "Hope and the future for me are not in lawns and cultivated fields, not in towns and cities, but in the impervious and quaking swamps"?
3. Why does Thoreau say, "I believe in the forest, and in the meadow, and in the night in which the corn grows"?
4. How prophetic and ironic is Thoreau's notion that the Prince of Darkness is the surveyor for "almost all man's improvements, so called, as the building of houses and the cutting down of the forest and of all large trees"?
5. Discuss three meanings of Thoreau's use of the word "wild" in this essay. How many of his connotations of wild still apply to our contemporary environment?

How Cities Green the Planet
PETER HUBER

Peter Huber is a lawyer with a doctorate in mechanical engineering from M.I.T. He is a senior fellow at the Manhattan Institute for Policy Research. His books include Hard Green: Saving the Environment from the Environmentalists *(2000),* Law and Disorder in Cyberspace: Abolish the FCC and Let Common Law Rule the Telecosm *(1997),* Orwell's Revenge *(1994),* Galileo's Revenge: Junk in the Courtroom *(1991), and* Sandra Day O'Connor: A Biography *(1990). He writes often about telecommunications and is a regular columnist for* Forbes Magazine.

———————— ✦ ————————

Think of the skyscraper as America's great green gift to the planet. It packs more people onto less land, which leaves more wilderness undisturbed in other places, where the people aren't. The city gets Wall Street, Saks, the Met, and the Times Square crowds, which leaves more flyover country for bison and cougars. It's Saul Steinberg's celebrated *New Yorker* cover, painted green.

Among all the various metrics of green, land is by far the most important and, in today's debate, the most often overlooked. As traditional conservationists have always recognized, land—broadly defined to include streams, rivers, and coastal waters—is critical, because that's where the wild things are. The less real estate we occupy for economic gain, the more we leave undisturbed as wilderness. And the city, though profligate in its consumption of most everything else, is very frugal with land. The one thing your average New Yorker does *not* occupy is 40 acres and a mule.

As it grows—or, as the Sierra Club sees it, as it sprawls—a city does indeed seize land. In 1800, Manhattan ended at about City Hall Park; farms and unsettled wilderness occupied everything north of Chambers Street. In 1811, when the Commissioners' Plan laid out the New York City grid, it extended only to 155th Street—the Commissioners not being able to imagine that the city would extend beyond that point "for centuries to come." Even as the twentieth century opened, Vincenzo Bendetto was still farming his family acres at Broadway and 213th Street. Today's seamless Manhattan spread of tarmac, concrete, and high-rise is just yesterday's sprawl come of age.

The sprawling hasn't stopped, around New York or any other major city. Nationwide, cities, suburbs, and local roads cover about 27 million acres, and highways cover as much again. This 54-million-acre total is well over double the area occupied in 1920. Thousands of acres of farmland and forest are developed every day in the environs of cities and towns. One projection foresees 60 megacities in America by 2050, with over 10 million people each—a total of city dwellers that is more than double the population of the entire nation today. These cities, one should then expect, would doubtless cover something like twice their current area.

This is what so alarms the greens, and they're determined to stop it. "This time the enemy isn't the Soviets, but sprawl," declares New Jersey governor Christine Todd Whitman. It's "a virus eating us from the inside out," says the Sierra Club. In January 1999, Vice President Gore proposed a $10 billion program of "Better America

Bonds" to help cities contain themselves. The idea is to halt the city's organic growth with collars of development-free green. And by containing the city we will . . . well, what exactly *will* we achieve?

Just the opposite of what the sprawl police suppose. Collaring the city will culminate in less wilderness, not more. The natural growth of the city is the best thing going for the wilderness. The rise and spread of the metropolis has brought about a magnificent renaissance of green.

Sure, our cities are big, but the country is a lot bigger. Cities, suburbs, roads, and all the highways cover under 3 percent—yes, only 3 percent—of the 2 billion acres of land that constitute the lower 48 states. If that percentage seems implausibly low, it's because our casual impressions are so biased. Some 80 percent of us live in the cities or their immediate suburbs, and we spend almost all our time there.

That's today. In 1790, the demographics were reversed: the U.S. population was 80 percent rural. What brought about such a remarkable shift? Technology, mainly: relentless improvements in agricultural productivity have enabled us to feed more Americans and more of the rest of the world, too, using less land. The farmers stopped farming; their children moved to the city.

The city has had a second, equally powerful environmental impact: it has lowered fecundity. Cities grow not because the people living in them have a lot of children, but because the people in the country do. Absent continuous immigration, the population of cities would shrink. Population growth in the city represents, in large part, population decline out in the sticks.

People come to the city in search of money; and money, it appears, induces them to have fewer children once they get there. This much is clear: where wealth rises, fertility falls. Rural versus urban figures confirm that fact, so do developed-world versus developing-world statistics, and so do the historical trends. Developed-world fertility has been falling quite steadily for two centuries. In the United States, it dropped from eight children per woman to two.

Parents recognize, it seems, that wealth permits them to raise fewer, more robust, children, and, given the chance, that is what they choose to do. When people get rich enough, lifetime fecundity falls to the point of zero population growth, or below. This takes a while, of course. At first, more resources, more wealth, make possible more life. Richer people live longer. More women

10

grow to adulthood to bear children of their own. Population rises, just as Malthus said it would—with just one critical correction: the lowering of fertility. Wealth concentrates in the city, and it is there that fertility drops the furthest. So far as the wilderness is concerned, the green case for the city can be as simple as that. The city is a population sink. To put it another way, the view from Wall Street is the greenest on earth.

For America as a whole, wealth and city overtook poverty and country sometime around 1920. Until about that time, the effects of immigration, an increasing life span, and a rising demand for food outweighed the effects of rising agricultural productivity and declining fertility. As a result, forests contracted. But around 1920, the balance shifted, and forests began to expand once again.

The upshot has been a truly remarkable, if little noted, environmental reversal: the steady reforestation of the American continent. When Europeans first arrived—after millennia of deforestation by fire, promoted by American Indians—the area now represented by the lower 48 states had about 950 million acres of forest. That area shrank steadily until about 1920, to a low of 600 million acres. It has been rising ever since. Just how fast is hard to pin down: the continent is large, most of the land is privately owned, and definitional debates rage. But all analyses show more, not less, forest land in America. And all agree that roughly 80 million more acres of cropland were harvested 60 years ago than are harvested today. Most of this land is on its way to being reforested, too. At least 10 million acres have been reforested since 1987 alone. Thus, for the first time in history, a Western nation has halted, and is now rapidly reversing, the decline of its woodlands.

Why do so many of us believe just the opposite? We've been spun, that's why. Green activists and their political friends publicize only half of the environmental ledger and play a shell game with definitions. They're engaged in a great green fraud, and a very harmful one, too.

15 Definitions first. The anti-sprawl activists often count as "developed land" some 90 million acres of farmsteads, field windbreaks, barren land, and marshland. This rural land has nothing to do with any reasonable definition of urban sprawl or even of "development," and to count it as such is to conflate Trump Tower with a stand of poplar trees grown by a farmer as a windbreak. But the activists need these 90 million acres, because if

they admitted that cities and their suburbs covered only a tiny 3 percent of the continental U.S., who could take their fear of sprawl seriously? That extra 90 million acres makes it seem as if the "sprawling city" covers 150 million acres, more than double the real number. This begins to sound like quite a lot, though it is still only 8 percent of the 48 contiguous states.

Now, the ledger. Some 25 million acres of land have given way to new development of one kind or another in the past three decades; perhaps half that area was farmland that gave way to suburbs at the periphery of cities. The expansion of the city largely replaced one human use of land—agriculture—with a second—dwellings. Where we used to house corn and cattle, we now house ourselves. No great loss for wilderness there, but that's the half-story we hear about. What we don't hear is that, during exactly the same period, 95 million acres of agricultural land even farther from the city returned to wilderness or began the process of doing so, now that farmers no longer cultivate them. In other words, far more land is being relinquished by agriculture to wilderness than is being converted from agriculture to suburbs. A fair estimate of the net gain for wilderness: some 70 million acres in the last quarter century. The loss of agricultural land to the city has meant a loss in greenish vistas for (mostly wealthier) people living at the periphery of the suburbs but almost no loss of true wilderness. The simultaneous, and much larger, return of agricultural land to wilderness farther out was just that—an enormous gain for the wild.

The city curtails not only its own Malthusian propensities but the country's, too. The city plants no taters or cotton, but it's very good at cultivating two things greener still: capital and knowledge.

For at least a century now, the average American has eaten more food and consumed more energy, even as the American farmer has plowed fewer acres and cut less wood. We accomplished that by learning to live in three dimensions, not just two, taking less from the living surface of the planet and more from its sterile depths. Cement, steel, and synthetic plastics displace hardwoods in our ships, dwellings, and furniture, leaving the wood itself to the forest. Fossil and nuclear fuels displace wood in our residential and industrial furnaces. Fertilizers, pesticides, factory farms, and high-yield crops from the laboratory substitute, at the margin, for some three-quarters of the acres once needed to produce equivalent amounts of food. It is by extending human enterprise into the third dimension that we painlessly retreat from the two-dimensional surface, where the rest of life dwells. Cities expand skyward and extract their building materials and fuels from the depths of the earth: they exert their pressure on the planet vertically, not horizontally.

Moving our economy into the third dimension has required one input above all others: capital. It takes vast amounts of it to extract oil from two miles beneath Alaskan ice or Saudi sand, or to process the oil into plastics that then displace teak and ivory, or to reconfigure the genes that quadruple yields on the farm. From wood to coal to oil to uranium, the higher the technology, the more capital it requires to burn it, and the less natural resource. And you don't raise capital down on the farm, alongside the hogs. You raise it on Wall Street, among the bulls.

20   The second crucial input to the three-dimensional economy has been knowledge. Oil two miles beneath Alaskan ice or Saudi sand is not "wealth" at all. It doesn't belong to anyone, least of all to "the world." We call such things "resources" by convention, but the "resource" is not the stuff itself; it's knowing how to get it. Anyone can gather wood and burn it—man has been doing that successfully for tens of thousands of years. Gathering and burning uranium is very much harder, but a tiny volume of it, prepared just so, can heat and light an entire city.

And it takes more of the same—knowledge—to convert oil into solar-power-enhancing additives: fertilizers and pesticides, both of which help us use less sun to put more food on the table. It takes still more knowledge to breed and bioengineer high-yield crops, develop growth hormones for our livestock, use better preservatives, package in spoilage-retarding plastic, and irradiate our food—which all promote the same efficiency: more usable food from less sun. These are the technologies, in other words, that have so dramatically increased the useful yield of each acre of farm or range. And overwhelmingly, they have emerged from the great centers of learning—established, of course, in the metropolis.

The city itself is all the more kind to the environment, because it has so completely rejected the policies that the green establishment holds dearest. It shuns "renewables." The city isn't animal or vegetable; it's mineral.

Start with construction. The city certainly favors nonrenewable resources here, and about that, at least, the green establishment remains silent, as it should. America currently harvests about 240 million tons of wood off the land each year, almost all of it for construction. The city, however, prefers to build with the three-dimensional resources, steel and concrete. Those materials can hold up a skyscraper; renewable wood can't. Even if it could, nobody imagines that it would be greener to build with materials harvested from the living surface, no matter where the trees grew, no matter how delicately they might be harvested. The way we build things now, a comparatively tiny area of land yields, from far beneath its surface, all the mineral resources that it takes to build a city. You can't get any greener than that.

The energy picture looks much the same. There's no way the city could ever adopt the green establishment's "renewable" path to energy. Manhattan is never going to heat its buildings or power its computers with rooftop solar cells, biomass, or windmills. There's nowhere near enough rooftop or wind, and no biomass to speak of, other than the mass of the people. Live on a good-size spread in the country, and harvest it aggressively, and you can plausibly imagine living off the renewable sources of energy the greens so strongly favor. Live in the city, and you can't, not on your own acres. You have no acres. Nevertheless, you have tremendous energy efficiency when your energy comes from an oil well and a refinery and gets delivered by a tanker: the supplies are highly concentrated to begin with, and it takes relatively little energy to deliver them to a highly concentrated point of use, like a city.

Cities have become environment-friendly by rejecting the   25
greens' food policies, too—the policies that emphasize organic farming, free of bioengineered seeds and man-made fertilizers and pesticides. When food is grown or raised in the agricultural counterpart to the oil well—the mammoth factory farm, outfitted with every high-tech innovation—it takes relatively little land to produce it in the first place, and it takes little additional energy to deliver it to the tightly packed city.

Three-dimensional resources perfectly complement the three-dimensional city: they are as concentrated in their production as the city is in its consumption. The city is green not only because its residents occupy little land, but because its non-green sources of building materials, fuel, and food—and their delivery systems—can be frugal with land, too. Adopt the greens' energy policies and we'd be blanketing the rest of the state with solar cells and cornfields just to fuel New York City.

As steel-for-wood trade-offs make clear, the city isn't green because it uses little stuff overall, but because it uses little of the stuff that must be culled from the surface of the land outside the city. The Sierra Club labors to convince itself that city dwellers actually use less of a whole grab bag of "resources": copper pipe, heating fuel, postal delivery, and personal cars, for example—an endless catalog of things said to be scarce, dangerous, prone to pollute, or otherwise hostile to the planet. But this kind of accounting is a distraction. If performed honestly, it inevitably leads to the environmentally ruinous conclusion that living in the country is greener, all in all, than living in the city.

   To begin with, any honest accounting of copper, fuel, and such must surely allow for the serious inefficiencies that congestion causes. The city may be efficient as long as you are sitting still, but the moment you try to move—yourself to the Met, or a sofa to your apartment—you find that the city is not efficient at all. A city at rest (an utterly oxymoronic notion, of course) may be frugal with its resources, but a city in motion never can be, because the friction is so high. Driving a car fewer miles is no great virtue in city traffic; ten cars idling in gridlock can burn fuel quite as fast as a single car does cruising down a wide-open highway. Green bookkeepers count efficiency as a very serious credit in almost all other contexts, so why not give green credit to the "efficient" country over the city, too, for its free-flowing traffic?

   It gets worse. Being the center of capital and knowledge that it is, the city makes its inhabitants much richer than their country cousins. And when all the accounts are finally in, richer people invariably consume more of just about everything. If you're not spending your extra wealth to heat your apartment on the Upper East Side, then you're probably spending it to vacation in the snow farther west, in Aspen. If you don't drive a car much in the city, you probably fly more planes out of it. Moreover, you may not consume much copper and fuel yourself, but Saks and the Met consume some on your behalf; so do taxi drivers and delivery trucks and airplanes. To find out how much you and your neighbors consume in this indirect way, you don't have to whip out a tape to measure copper pipes. Just measure spending. And city dwellers spend more, because they have more to spend.

30   The only thing they evidently don't get with their higher wealth is more land. Rich as they are, they can't afford to. A rather small area of virtual land 12 stories above the edge of Central Park costs far more than a farm and 100 acres in Vermont. Life in the city is incontestably frugal with the one thing that should eclipse all others in environmental discourse: land.

   By building the city up out of non-renewable resources, by heating and lighting it with non-renewable fuels, and by feeding it with non-organic foods preserved with chemicals or plastic packaging, the city returns acre upon acre of land in the country to wilderness, the greenest accomplishment of all. And in doing that, the hard city and its hard fuels take care of a lot of pollution, too. Nature has enormous power to cleanse and restore; freeing up 95 million acres to be reclaimed by watershed and forest has surely done more to clean water and protect birds than the curtailing of pesticides ever achieved. The best estimates at hand likewise indicate that forest regrowth in America currently recaptures all the carbon and then some that America releases into the air in burning fossil fuels.

With food and fuel, the greens keep trying to spread things back out again—that's the whole thrust of the food and energy policies they so tirelessly promote. It's a mistake. But, contradictorily, their plan to improve on the city is to pile it up all the higher—by collaring and quarantining the metropolis and choking off suburban sprawl. That's a mistake, too.

The organic growth of the city is what has made possible the greening of the country. Manhattan itself would be greener today if its sprawl had been collared off about mid-island in 1840, but the Empire State wouldn't be, nor would the rest of America. The city absorbs people, enriches them, affords them the confidence and security to have smaller families, and generates the capital and knowledge that move the production of food and energy off the land and into the third dimension.

Suburbs may indeed consume more material resources than cities; they certainly consume more land. But rural living consumes even more land: land is the one thing rural life tends to consume in profligate excess, because the country is the one place where land is really cheap. Viewing the suburb as mere spillover from the city is just plain wrong, demographically speaking. On their own cities don't spill out; they collapse in, because on their own cities have negative population growth. Cities grow not because they sprawl out from the center, but because they draw people in from the periphery—the distant periphery, far beyond the suburbs.

If bad policies do somehow manage to collar the city with an impregnable ring of green, the city will stop drawing people in from the country and begin sending them back out instead. As cyber-visionaries keep telling us, one doesn't have to stay in the city anymore to stay at the center of the new economy; the virtual city is where it's at, and given the choice, quite a few people may happily bid the concrete city good-bye. Chips and communica-

35

tions networks are centrifugal technologies; they make it easier to spread apart. They are very powerful already and grow more so month by month. In these circumstances, the most likely effect of collaring the city will be to spin people out farther still, well beyond the suburbs. "[T]he digital world [will] redistribute jobs and wealth, so that the concentration of opportunity need not parallel the concentration of people," declares cyber-pundit Nicholas Negroponte in *Wired*. "[T]he flow of people will be out of, not into, cities. . . . Being rural could become synonymous with being rich." Bad news for the city, if he's right. And even worse news for the wilderness.

Happily for the environment, Negroponte's digital diaspora hasn't shown up in any hard demographic data yet. And it won't, not so long as there remains the option of the healthy suburb— something most people find even more attractive than rural solitude. So long as city and suburb continue to prosper and grow, the centripetal attractions of the city will overcome the centrifugal power of bits. Indeed, as one of us has argued in these pages previously ["New York, Capital of the Information Age," Winter 1995], gigabit links to the rest of the planet could well make Citicorp, Saks, and the Met more dominant than ever, by letting them project their top-of-the-heap talent even further outward than they do today.

The right perspective is to view suburbs and city as a single economic entity, growing organically together. The suburbs wouldn't exist but for the city and its jobs and money. The city can't survive without its suburbs, which is where the human capital finds refuge from the city's worst excesses and pathologies. Without capacious suburbs, the city will simply lose altogether the people who provide the capital and knowledge that make cities so efficient: no green collar will ever persuade such people to live in places with lousy schools and high crime.

The real threat to the environment isn't that the city will continue to grow, but that it won't. The suburbs are the best defense against the rural alternative, an alternative made newly attractive today by the decentralizing technologies of the information revolution. The suburb is the buffer that lets the married with children stay near the city when they tire of living right in it, leaving room for new young immigrants in the heart of the city itself. Collar the city, halt its natural slope into suburbs, and the young, well-wired digirati may choose the country instead, as soon as their kids arrive. The city will lose, and the wilderness will lose too.

There was abroad, at one time, the notion that cities grew parasitically off the countryside, that all economic wealth derived from the land, and that the city grew rich only by expropriating the bounty of honest folk who tilled the soil. If this were ever true, it's no longer true today. The industrial revolution severed half the links between wealth and land; the information revolution has severed most of the rest. Wealth now springs from the third dimension, beneath the surface, and from the fourth, the boundless caverns of the mind. The city, its capital, and its knowledge are the fonts of those kinds of wealth. Their ultimate effect is to make land far from the city uneconomic. Which returns it to wilderness, 100 percent green.

2000

Discussion

1. Discuss the premise of the author that urban growth is beneficial to environmental preservation.
2. What is Huber's argument for rejecting the notion that urban sprawl is a debilitating factor on the environment?
3. What is Huber suggesting when he says that the "city is a population sink" and "the view from Wall Street is the greenest on earth"?
4. Why does Huber claim that environmentalists are a "great green fraud"?
5. Discuss Huber's claim that "the real threat to the environment isn't that the city will continue to grow, but that it won't."

The Regulars
MARIE WINN

Marie Winn was born in Prague, Czechoslovakia, but later became a U.S. citizen and graduated from Columbia University. Her books include The Plug in Drug, Television, Computers & Family Life *(1985) and* Children Without Childhood *(1983). Winn has translated the plays of Václav Havel, the former president of Czechoslovakia, into English. Her reportage and news stories have appeared in* The Wall Street Journal, The New York Times, The New York Times Book Review, *and* Smithsonian Magazine. *In "The Regulars" (1998), Wynn discusses the Register, a book of bird sightings, that is a compendium of observations of the rich variety of wildlife, especially birds, in New York City's Central Park. But of*

*equal interest are the people who observe the flora and fauna of
Central Park. Winn is impressed with their knowledge, compassion,
and helpfulness, traits that she believes are ample evidence of the
need for human interrelatedness with nature in the heart of an urban metropolis.*

———————— ✦ ————————

Just as the physical realities of Central Park—its plants, trees,
lakes, streams, and the wildlife within—stand in sharp contrast
to the man-made world around it, so the park's little band of
Regulars stand in relief to the culture of urban life.

The passage of time is different for the Regulars. The changing length of days, the arrivals and departures of birds, the flowering of plants, and the changing colors of leaves organize their
time far more than the calendars and clocks and schedules of
contemporary life.

The seasons do not begin for them on dates given in al-
manacs. Spring begins with the arrival of the woodcock in
February, or at the moment the first phoebe begins hawking for
insects at the Upper Lobe, or when the juncos start trilling and
the fox sparrows whistling, well before the equinox. Winter begins when the witch hazel blooms, when rafts of ruddy ducks appear on the Reservoir, when flocks of white-throated sparrows arrive and the saw-whet and long-eared owls appear in the
Shakespeare Garden hemlocks and the blue spruce at Cedar Hill.
Butterflies and dragonflies, crickets, and katydids define summer.

The Regulars notice what others have long learned to ignore:
the sights and sounds, smells, textures, and tastes of the world
around them. Forget the self and its hungry needs. Pay attention
to tiny details. One wing bar or two? Six petals or eight? Listen to
that squirrel whining. It probably means there's a hawk or an owl
nearby. Notice the wind. In May if it's from the southwest, a wave
of songbirds may be arriving. Pay attention to tree cavities. There
may be a bunch of raccoon babies poking their heads out, or a
family of young downy woodpeckers clamoring to be fed.

5   In their human relations, too, the Regulars' ways differ from
the ways of the modern world. Neither job nor income nor family
background confer a place in their hierarchy—nobody asks about
these things. They don't matter. Among the Regulars, each person's skills and abilities count to secure the others' respect and
approval. Among these are skills in observing, identifying, asking
the right kinds of questions, skills, even, in encouraging others
who might possess any of these skills to practice them. Is faithful-

ness a skill, an ability, a tendency, a trait? Whatever it is, it is admired, perhaps above all. The *regularness* of the Regulars is the feature that binds them together most powerfully. It allows them to count on each other to be there, observing, noting, keeping track. The Bird Register is their communications center.

Anyone can write in the Bird Register, and over the course of time many do. New birders, old-timers, out-of-town birdwatchers, ornithologists from the Natural History museum, tourists who want to express their delight with the park—all write occasional entries in the Bird Book.

During the spring and fall migration seasons, precisely when a greater diversity of birds shows up in the park, a diversity of contributors weighs in with entries. Names of legendary park birders appear then: Marty Sohmer, Michel Kleinbaum, Peter Post—the Big Guns, as I think of them, who write only when they spot something out of the ordinary.

The Big Guns are actively searching for esoteric birds. While many bird enthusiasts will glance at a bunch of sparrows and dismiss them as ordinary house sparrows, one of the Big Guns will spend fifteen minutes inspecting this army of drab creatures, going over them one by one, and find in their midst a single, elusive Lincoln's sparrow. This bird resembles the song sparrow, a common park bird, but the side of its face and its eye stripe are a bit grayer, its breast stripes a bit finer, its bill a tiny bit thinner. Once Kleinbaum, a bird illustrator, pointed one out to me near Willow Rock. I always see better birds when a Big Gun is in the vicinity.

The Register would be a slim volume indeed if the Big Guns were its only correspondents. In fact it is a hefty volume by the end of the year. Most entries, as I saw that first day I looked in the Register, were written by a small number of men and women whose names appeared again and again—the Regulars.

Tom Fiore and Norma Collin are the Bird Book's principal correspondents. Both in their own way keep it a complete document of the natural and human history of Central Park. 10

Sun-darkened in winter as well as in summer, Tom Fiore reminds me of Thoreau's dictum: "A tanned skin is something more than respectable, and perhaps olive is a fitter color than white for a man,—a denizen of the woods."

Tom is the Bird Register's prize reporter. Until Tom began writing in the Register, no one had ever cataloged the park's daily and year-round birdlife (and other wildlife) in such detail. No one has been so faithful a daily chronicler in the years since.

Before 1991, the first year Tom appeared in the Register, most entries in the Bird Book simply named the species seen and the location of the sighting: "Fox Sparrow, Azalea Pond" or "Pintail, N.E. Reservoir." Tom's observations involved the mind as much as the eye:

> March 6: Four or more Fox sparrows near Azalea Pond, 2 of which seemed to be showing preliminaries-to-mating behavior: one calling and singing quietly, the other following, then both facing each other almost beak to beak and generally imitating what the other would do. This went on 10 minutes or so, then they continued feeding.

"Fantastic observations! Thank you!" Christina and Marianne Girards wrote in the Register that same day. They had been regular park birdwatchers since 1960, and welcomed Tom's more informative entries. They continue to come into the park almost daily, though Chris celebrated her ninetieth birthday a few years ago. Aunt and niece, the Girards are among the Regulars who bridge the pre-Tom and post-Tom gap.

15   The Regulars have come to depend on Tom's daily entries in the Register. Once, when this quietly intense, unfailingly courteous young man took off on a bird trip to the Philippines, the birdlife of Central Park suddenly seemed *so quiet!* It's not that the other Regulars aren't fine birdwatchers; it's that Tom seems to have a seventh sense that takes him to the right place at the right time.

Almost every other spring, for instance, Tom comes upon a migrating common snipe, a hard-to-find shorebird that everyone else seems to miss. But it's hardly luck that bags him the snipe. Thanks to his knowledge of its preferred habitat, in the middle of March Tom begins searching for the long-billed bird of bogs and wet meadows in the closest place to snipe paradise the park has to offer: the swampy, reedy area between Balcony Bridge and Bank Rock Bridge.

That snipe usually arrives during the third week of March, year after year. The eastern phoebe shows up at the Upper Lobe on March 13th, give or take a day or two. Most of the other migratory birds that use the park as a stopover seem to follow a precise timetable. They'll appear on their appointed date at the same place year after year. So that must be Tom's secret: he's learned these times and places, that's all.

Actually, that's not all. In addition to knowledge, Tom *does* seem to have luck. Once he was leaning back on a bench at the south side of the Harlem Meer, listening to a jazz band playing Duke Ellington, when he saw a bird of prey come zig-zagging from the east. Something about it caught his eye, and he grabbed his binoculars to give it a closer look. It was a Mississippi kite, a bird never before seen in Central Park (or even above it).

Norma Collin may not enter the most sightings in the Register (though she writes in plenty) nor see the most elusive birds (though she is a fine birder), but she is the scribe, the town crier for the birding community. You can piece together the drama of the birdwatcher's daily life from Norma's distinctive vignettes. After reporting on fifteen species of warbler seen one morning in the middle of May, including the beautiful hooded warbler, she wrote:

> While enjoying good views of the Hooded, I looked up into the "lightning tree" and there was a raccoon having its midday nap. A tufted titmouse collecting stuff for its nest flew down to the raccoon and pulled a tuft of fur from its backside. The raccoon didn't stir, so the titmouse went back for another bill-full. This time the raccoon turned around and (if we can give it human traits) looked very surprised and slightly annoyed when the titmouse took a hunk of fur the third time. By that time around 8 birders had gathered around for the show and then went onward for a "Big" day of birding in the Ramble.

Though tufted titmice are known to gather fur or hair for their nests from live mammals, including dogs, squirrels, horses, cows, cats, and, amazingly, *Homo sapiens*, none of the texts includes the mammal that was titmouse-plundered in Central Park the following year: a red panda sleeping in an outdoor exhibit at the Central Park Zoo. The witness was Clare Flemming, a young mammalogist from the American Museum of Natural History. She subsequently reported her sighting at a meeting of the Linnaean Society, a scientific-minded club for ornithologists, birdwatchers, and nature-lovers that meets twice a month at the museum. Many Central Park birdwatchers are members and report their best park sightings at the end of the meeting when the president asks: "Are there any field notes?"

The entries in the Register resemble nature sightings in logs almost anywhere: Cape May, Point Reyes National Seashore, Muir Woods. Some of Tom's entries would not be out of place if they appeared in Henry David Thoreau's great *Journal:*

> March 11, 1854: Air full of birds,—bluebirds, song sparrows, chickadee [phoebe note] and blackbirds. Song sparrows toward

20

the water, with at least two kinds of variations of their strain hard to imitate. *Ozit, ozit, ozit, psa, te te te te te ter twe ter* is one. The other began *chip chip che we* etc. . . .

H. Thoreau

April 27, 1995—Weather: mild, s/sw wind, bringing light haze/sunny sky . . . Indigo Bunting, singing 6:20 a.m. Belvedere Castle (w. side), Red-eyed Vireo, singing, "Warbler Rock" (i.e. the trees on top of rocky outcrop, N.E. of Bow Bridge), Least Flycatcher singing: rapid Che-bek, che-bek call, Tupelo meadow area (early a.m.). . . .

T. Fiore

Yet there is the difference of a world between these observations. Thoreau described what he saw and heard in a natural surrounding unchanged for millennia. The world of Central Park is entirely man-made and its wilderness is enclosed by a city. Not even a city of well-tended gardens, with tree-shaded lanes and village greens: this is a city of skyscrapers on a bed of Manhattan schist.

"And imagine! This happened in the heart of New York City!" Nobody bothers to write these words in the Bird Register. Nevertheless, this context—the "other" world of nature within, civilization and its discontents without—informs each natural event in the park and deepens its excitement. The red-eyed vireo nest where both parents are feeding three nestlings is not hanging in a wooded glen; it is suspended over a path directly beside lamppost 7106, and as the parent birds go back and forth with large pale-green insects in their bills, legions pass directly underneath, some on foot, others on Rollerblades, bicycle, or tricycle, or in carriages or strollers pushed by parents, baby-sitters, or nannies in uniforms. And none of them have the slightest idea of the drama taking place inches above their heads.

On January 13, 1856, Thoreau found a red-eyed vireo nest at Walden Pond and wrote in his *Journal:*

> What a wonderful genius it is that leads the vireo to select the tough fibers of the inner bark, instead of the more brittle grasses, for its basket, the elastic pine needles and the twigs, curved as they dried to give it form, and, as I suppose, the silk of cocoons, etc. etc. to bind it together with!

25   His admiration for the vireo's genius would surely not have diminished at the sight of the nest at lamppost 7106, displaying bits of toilet paper, plastic wrap, and fishing line among the leaves and twigs and plant fibers.

All the regulars keep an eye on the Register. Has it been returned to its proper place? Are the pages running out? Are people writing in the locations of sightings so others can find them? Are they signing their names? The names are important. News of the sighting of a boat-tailed grackle by one of the Big Guns would immediately activate the birders' grapevine, with one person calling another until everyone was reached. For this is a bird that has never been seen in Central Park.

The name of a beginning birder at the end of an extraordinary entry will evoke a cautious and mildly skeptical reaction. How many new birdwatchers seeing the common grackle, a large iridescent blackbird that abounds in Central Park, have looked it up in Peterson's *Field Guide* and identified it as a boat-tailed grackle, a *very* large iridescent blackbird. (Size can be misleading in a field-guide illustration.) The sighting will still be checked out; impossible birds do show up every so often, which is what gives birdwatching its special excitement.

Not long ago a new birdwatcher named Ilenne Goldstein wrote in the Register that she had seen a little blue heron at Turtle Pond, the small body of water at the base of Belvedere Castle.

"Please describe in *detail* the observation of the Little Blue Heron on 5/18 and please list any additional observers. This is *extremely rare* in Central Park!!!" wrote Tom Fiore under the notation. A beginner, he knew, might look in a field guide and mistake the rare little blue for the more common great blue heron, a bird often seen wading in the mud flats at the edges of that same pond.

Ilenne responded in the Register a few days later: 30

> He was an adult, completely blue body, reddish blue neck and head, bill dark at tip and silvery looking (to me at least) at the base. It was cloudy and muggy but the light was O.K. He had long reddish plumes on his neck that blew in the breeze and a "tassel" (also red-blue) on his head similar to a Black Crowned Night Heron's. He moved to a mucky area close to the south edge of the pond to feed alongside the mallards and sandpipers there. He was about the size of the mallards only much more slender. I watched for about 20 minutes. Unfortunately there were no other observers.

An impressive beginner, everyone agreed. When E. M. Forster proposed "Only connect!" as the basic creative principle, he was starting in the middle. Birdwatchers know something else must come first: Only observe. Take note of everything, *everything* (the dark tip of the silvery bill!) in its full, detailed richness.

In the Register the next day, Tom accepted Ilenne's identification of the little blue heron. Since no one else saw the bird in question, the sighting could never be finally confirmed for the record books. It was reported as a field note at the next Linnaean Society meeting, however.

Every so often, in spite of everyone's tender care, the Bird Register disappears. It has vanished twice and had to be replaced in the six years I've been following it. Who in the world would want to swipe it? A tourist looking for a souvenir? Someone with a grudge against birdwatchers? A kid needing a new loose-leaf binder? Norma usually insists that it simply "got misplaced." Norma likes to think well of her fellow man.

The Register's disappearance inevitably brings on a feeling of dislocation, even desolation, among the Regulars. Like a family starting over after their house with all their old books and papers and *stuff* has burned to the ground, without the Register the Regulars have lost the history that tied them together. Now they seem no more than a collection of odd, disconnected people.

35   As the regulars study the natural world around them day after day, year after year, they confirm entomologist Vincent Dethier's astute observation: "Lack of knowledge is a vacuum that must be filled. Human beings are animals that must know." The Regulars share in equal measure a generous impulse to pass along what they have learned to others. One September morning when a weekly bird-study group, the Earlybirds, was walking by the Swampy Pin Oak, Dorothy Poole, a Regular and a superb birdwatcher, stopped and strained her ears. "Listen!" she said. "Do you hear that?" At first nobody did. There was just a big jumble of undifferentiated bird sound. "There it is again. That little 'whit, whit, whit.' " One by one we heard it, a tiny, repeated chip coming from the underbrush. "That's the Swainson's thrush," said Dorothy. After a few moments we could hardly imagine we had *not* heard it before. We walked farther and again Dorothy stopped to focus our attention. " 'Vi-ew, vi-ew.' Hear how different that little chip is? That's the veery." The lesson was rounded out before long by yet another thrush chip, the quicker "pip-pip-pip" of the wood thrush. How had we come to ignore these sounds before, everyone asked. Had we been deaf?

Norma Collin's knowledge of birds, plants and flowers, trees, fungi, butterflies, dragonflies, and other insects is extensive, though less encyclopedic than Nick Wagerik's. Nick, a superb birder and the park's preeminent butterfly and dragonfly expert, knows the various scientific names in the plant and animal kingdoms. Nick can draw you a perfect diagram of all the parts of a flower. The poetry of taxonomy is always at the tip of his tongue, as it was one day in the autumn when in the course of a walk in the Ramble he named and defined the various kinds of fruit in the plant kingdom: berry, pepo, hesperidium, drupe, pome, legume, follicle, capsule, silique, akene, caryopsis, samara, schizocarp, nut.

Norma may not know the textbook names of every flower, but she knows which ones are good to eat. In January Norma can show you where the field garlic is coming up; in April, the emerging young shoots of Japanese knotweed, the park's ubiquitous weed—they're quite tasty. In June Norma knows which mulberries are sweet and which taste like cardboard. (Their place in the sun matters.) Best of all, she knows where the secret wineberry bushes are and when they're due to ripen. Wineberries are more delicious than the finest raspberries, and the price in the park is right.

Norma knows where to find blackberries in August and persimmons in October. She once generously showed me the only fruit-bearing nectarine tree in Central Park, and gave me one of the "curious peaches" to sample. The tree's no longer there, by the way—done in by the drought of 1995. By September she'll have figured out which of the crabapples will produce the best fruit that year—it's not always the same ones.

And then there are mushrooms. A total of eighteen people shared in a mycological bonanza Norma discovered in Central Park one day in October—a decaying log covered with sulphur shelf mushrooms. Nick would have called them *Laetiporus sulphureus*, but Norma used one of their vernacular names—chicken mushrooms—because they taste somewhat like chicken when properly cooked. Everyone took some home and ate heartily. A sign of the special esteem in which Norma is held by her fellow Central Park nature lovers is this: it is common knowledge that some mushrooms can be deadly, but eighteen people put their lives on the line that day with perfect confidence. I'm still here to tell you that fresh *Laetiporus sulphureus* does taste like chicken, only a little better. (Her recipe: slice, sauté in a little oil, add a little water, cover, and continue cooking for about ten more minutes.)

Nick Wagerik introduced me to the butterflies of Central Park   40
on a sunny day in early June a few years ago.

Nick is a young man of medium height, solid, somewhat teddy-bearish in appearance. He lumbers when he walks, slightly hunched over. But the ursine appearance vanishes as he talks. The man is a bundle of nervous energy: His eyes dart about, taking in everything; words tumble out, a flood of information bursts forth. Nick is fiercely devoted to facts.

We were walking through a sun-dotted glade at the northwest corner of the Ramble that day when Nick pointed out a small butterfly fluttering by a rocky outcropping. "This one is an eastern comma," Nick told me, "*Polygonia comma*. It belongs to the family Nymphalidae. Commonly known as brush-footed butterflies. It's a woodland butterfly that loves glades with some sun breaking through. Like this one."

The butterfly settled on the rock, basking in the sun, and Nick took out his magnifying glass to show me a tiny silvery mark on its lower side (the ventral surface, as he called it). It did indeed look like a little comma, though I might never have noticed it if he hadn't pointed it out. Immediately afterwards I thought I saw another comma butterfly, but I was mistaken. "Look at its comma," Nick instructed. "Does it look the same?" As I peered at the insect through my binoculars, I saw that there was an almost imperceptible difference: just below the comma was a tiny dot. That dot made it a different species: a question mark butterfly, *Polygonia interrogationis*.

Nick possesses the indispensable characteristic of a great teacher: an infectious passion for his subject. As we were leaving the park after that first lesson in lepidoptera, he stopped and pointed out a pair of butterflies circling and swirling in the air just ahead. "That's the butterfly dance!" he said with emotion. "It's the most beautiful thing in nature. I could watch it forever."

45   One great common interest—birds, or butterflies, or trees, or even natural history in general—might not be enough to transform a motley collection of individuals into a cohesive entity. The birdwatching community of Central Park is also a product of those events and occasions that periodically bring them together—gatherings of the tribe, you might call them. For just as weddings or funerals provide an opportunity for members of a far-flung family to meet and reaffirm membership in the group, so these occasions serve to define the birdwatching community and to cement its rather amorphous bonds.

There are organized events: the Christmas Count, the fall migration Hawkwatch at Belvedere Castle, the occasional celebrations to mark special birthdays—usually avian ones. These are the national holidays, so to speak, of the birdwatching community, marked on all calendars well in advance.

Then there are the serendipitous gatherings of the clan whenever a rare or special bird is sighted in the park. Engraved invitations will not do for these get-togethers—time is of the essence. Hence the birders' grapevine. Who will forget the January morning when a four-star bird for Central Park, a great horned owl, was discovered on the outskirts of Muggers Woods. (In spite of its name, the little thicket just behind the Humming Tombstone attracts no more muggers than any other part of the Ramble.) Tom Fiore rushed for the phone at the Delacorte Theater, while Charles Kennedy, one of the most faithful of the Regulars, biked to the outdoor booth at the Boathouse. Each made three or four calls whose recipients made still others. On their way back to the owl, Tom and Charles passed the word to Regulars already in the park. By the end of the day a total of twenty-two people had seen the great horned owl, most of them within an hour or two of its discovery.

1998

Discussion

1. Discuss Winn's possible intentions in contrasting Henry David Thoreau's nature notes and those of the Regulars.
2. What does Winn suggest are the joys of bird-watching? What factors might motivate this kind of human behavior in the midst of a city such as New York or in any town?
3. Discuss the paradox of constructing a man-made wilderness in the heart of a city.

Dispatch from Toxic Town
TARA HULEN

Tara Hulen (1964–) is a freelance writer from Birmingham, Alabama. After graduating from Loyola University, New Orleans, she worked as a staff writer for The Birmingham News. *In 1997, she helped launch* Birmingham Weekly, *the city's first alternative newsweekly where, as senior writer and executive editor, she focused on environmental issues. She has been a freelance writer since 2000 and has published environmental op/ed pieces in news-papers throughout the southeast. Hulen's work has also been pub-lished in* Cornbread Nation 1: The Best of Southern Food Writing. *She primarily writes features for local and regional magazines, and on diverse topics, including the environment.*

――――――――― ✦ ―――――――――

Just off Interstate 20, about halfway between Birmingham and Atlanta, past a long string of malls, car dealerships, and fast-food restaurants, there is a cluster of buildings set against a back-drop of Appalachian swells. This is Anniston, population 24,000, in many respects a regular, smallish Southeastern town. The side-walks and streets are litter free, the grass in the parks is trim, and the people are friendly and talkative, the kind who might drive a stranger to where she's going, just to make sure she gets there. High school football occupies fall Friday nights, college football buzzes on radios on Saturdays and, of course, Sundays and Wednesday nights are spent in church.

It seems like the kind of place Samuel Noble and Daniel Tyler, who founded Anniston in the 1870s, would be proud of. The en-trepreneurs envisioned the city as a post-Civil War utopia, with their company, the Woodstock Iron Company, at its economic center. They paid workers $1.25 when the going rate was 75 cents. They erected churches and schools and planted thousands of trees. It was also the first city in the state to have electricity and streetcars. Impressed by this idyllic hamlet, one Atlanta newspa-per columnist nicknamed Anniston the "Model City." For years, the name stuck.

Anniston also became a military town. Fort McClellan, an Army post, came to Calhoun County in 1890, and in 1942, to house the growing supply of World War II munitions, the Anniston Army Depot opened west of the city, adding thousands of jobs to the area.

For more than a century, the people of Anniston were content with their relationships with the military and industries. That all started to change ten years ago, when a fisherman caught a de-formed largemouth bass in nearby Choccolocco Creek and went to the state for answers. The creek turned out to be full of poly-chlorinated biphenyls (PCBs), chemicals once used as insulators in electrical equipment. It also turned out that some of the com-panies and institutions that created Anniston had created Alabama's most poisonous place to live. The "Model City" now has another name: "Toxic Town."

Monsanto manufactured PCBs in west Anniston for forty 5
years, dumping a reported 10 million pounds of PCBs into land-
fills and 1.2 million pounds into streams. The company stopped
production of PCBs in 1971, and eight years later, the federal government banned them as a probable carcinogen. Today, west
Anniston is one of the worst PCB-contaminated places in the
country—and it has other problems. Lead from Woodstock Iron
Works, which shut its doors in the 1960s, migrated throughout
Anniston in loads of fill-dirt commonly given away for construction projects. And, though Congress voted to close Fort McClellan
in 1995, more than 2,000 tons of chemical weapons remain at the
depot. The Army plans to start incinerating those weapons in
early 2003, in spite of the fact that emergency-preparedness plans
won't be in place for months.

All of this has made headlines across the country. "Everybody
knows about Anniston, and that's a bad thing," says David Baker,
executive director of Community Against Pollution (CAP), an
Anniston activist group.

At a local barbecue restaurant, a group of friends replied in
perfect unison when asked how they feel about Anniston today.
"We've been dumped on," they say, as if they've been asked a hundred times before.

Sallie Bowie Franklin, sixty-six, is one of some 3,600 plaintiffs who sued Monsanto, its spin-off Solutia, and their parent
company, Pharmacia, in state court. Last February, the court
found all three liable for damage they caused by polluting
Anniston's land and waterways and poisoning its residents with
PCBs. The suit was won on the strength of Monsanto's internal
memos, which showed it suspected PCBs were dangerous to people long before it stopped manufacturing them. As far back as
1938, Monsanto knew PCBs were toxic to animals.

Today, Franklin is surrounded by nothing. Her neighbors are
gone; so are their houses. Most of the more than 1,600 people in
the area closest to the plant (now operated by Solutia) moved after the companies offered them a $45 million settlement. Solutia
then razed about a hundred homes, removed some topsoil, and
capped the area with dirt.

Until the court decides how much the damage inflicted upon 10
her and her co-plaintiffs is worth, Franklin is in limbo, stuck
waiting in a house that she can't sell and her grandkids can't play
around: "After we found out how contaminated it was, they don't
come out too often," she says. She has high levels of PCBs in her
body, and believes that's why she has lupus of the skin.

Of course, hers is just a hunch. Proving that PCBs caused a specific medical problem is difficult. The Environmental Protection Agency will soon conduct a human-health risk assessment, which will determine where the PCBs are, how much remains, and how harmful they are for people. The Centers for Disease Control is planning a comprehensive health study of the effects of Anniston's pollution on residents, but until all the lawsuits run their course and more people are free to talk, that process will be slow moving.

Shirley McCord might be a great resource for such a study. For forty-two years, she's run a west Anniston grocery store, the kind of place where locals can get credit, candy, beer, and pickled pigs' feet. A soft-spoken woman with a kind but focused manner, McCord keeps a list of people she and customers can remember dying over the years. It's more than seventeen pages long; most of the names have "cancer" written beside them.

Lots of people in west Anniston had cancer, kidney, and liver problems, but until that fish was found, no one had directly blamed Monsanto. "The people didn't want to accept it," CAP's Baker says. But they knew in their guts that the rotten-egg stench from the plant and water that turned creeks odd colors couldn't be good for them. In 1995, soil tests showed PCB contamination in Anniston to be higher than had ever been recorded.

Dr. Angela Michiko Martin, director of pediatrics at the town's Northeast Regional Medical Center, sees a lot of babies born with extremely rare brain disorders—three out of the fifteen cases worldwide of holoproscencephaly, a disease that prevents the brain from forming correctly, are in Calhoun County. "We're seeing some things we cannot explain," she says. "We lead the state in birth defects."

15   The average person's PCB load is about 2 parts per billion. CAP's Baker, fifty-one, has more than 300 parts per billion. In 1993, after a stint as a union organizer in New York City, Baker returned home, and, with self-assured bravado, became one of Anniston's loudest hell raisers. He helped organize plaintiffs for the state lawsuit and did the same for a federal trial scheduled to begin in January. That suit, which is headed by Johnny Cochran and nationally feared plaintiffs attorney Jere Beasley, involves more than 16,000 complainants. All together, some 25,000 people are involved in various cases and settlements against the companies.

Today Solutia employs just 81 people—down from 1,400 at its height—who make a heat-transfer fluid and a chemical used in acetaminophen. Plant manager David L. Cain can't comment on matters still in litigation, but he will say that he thinks it's time for the community to move forward. According to Cain, the company has spent $50 million to date collecting data on polluted land and waterways and cleaning some of those areas. This summer, it will sponsor ten of about forty homes to be built by Habitat for Humanity. It's also part of a redevelopment committee considering the construction of a walking track and a farmer's market—proposals some are skeptical of. "This is a community initiative," Cain says. "Do not look at this as a Solutia project."

2003

Discussion

1. What elements of Hulen's reportage make the story personal and likely to elicit a sympathetic response from the reader?
2. Does Hulen tend to place blame for the state of environmental affairs in Anniston? Do you think that she presents the issues fairly?
3. How does Hulen use technical information to make the environmental reportage believable on a human level?
4. Suppose that leaving town is not an option; explain what you would do if you were currently living in Anniston, Alabama.

Thinking and Writing About Chapter 2

1. How does Henry David Thoreau's "Walking" (p. 44), and his ideas about walking westward, take on the symbolism of living a better life unconta- minated by city life, public luxury, and urban excitement?
2. Discuss the clash of opposing points of view regarding the concept of town/city life and the wilderness as detailed by Thoreau in "Walking" (p. 44) and Peter Huber in "How Cities Green the Planet" (p. 53).
3. Contrast the problems facing Anniston, Alabama, as reported by Tara Hulen in "Dispatch from Toxic Town" (p. 73) with Thoreau's reasons for walking west in "Walking" (p. 44).
4. Marie Winn's view of New York City in "The Regulars" (p. 63) concen- trates on the interaction of people and wildlife. Explain how this human- istic point of view contrasts with the economic point of view developed by Huber in "How Cities Green the Planet" (p. 53).

Additional Resources

Fiction
James Fenimore Cooper. *The Pioneers* (1823)
Edward Abbey. *The Monkey-Wrench Gang* (1975)

Films
Koyaanisqati: Life Out of Balance (1983), directed by Godfrey Reggio
Erin Brokovich (2000), directed by Steven Soderberg
A Civil Action (1998), directed by Steve Zaillian

Essays
Mark Twain. *Life on the Mississippi* (1883)
Jane Jacobs. *The Death and Life of Great American Cities* (1961)
John Brinkerhoff Jackson. *Discovering the Vernacular Landscape* (1984)

Literary Criticism
Leo Marx. *The Machine and the Garden: Technology and the Pastoral Ideal in America* (1964, revised 2000)
Laurence Buell. *The Environmental Imagination: Thoreau, Nature Writing and the Formation of American Culture* (1995)

Website
Marie Winn's website at http://www.mariewinn.com

CHAPTER 3

Local
Landscapes

No environmental issues are as inflaming as those close to home, in our proverbial backyard. "Not in My Backyard," the rallying cry, is now shouted across the country as a matter of course as the health tolls of air and water pollution become better understood. Who would not complain when a shopping mall, a highway, a new factory, stream dredging, land filling—no matter the proposal—threatens? Protest over real or imagined environmental disruption inevitably follows. So vital is our sense of place, with all its implications, that the threat of change prompts a sort of territorial protectiveness.

It should not be ignored that some people find favor with the mall or the highway, both of which are viewed as necessary for improving the quality of life. A new factory may provide jobs and revive a dying community. Sarah Orne Jewett was sensitive to the debate over changing qualities of life, and her short story "A White Heron" (1886) questions the value of beauty and spiritual pleasure in a materialistic world. Jewett's hero, Sylvia, a girl of nine, is tempted both by the beauty of a wild thing, a white heron, and the ten dollars, a princely sum, she will receive from an ornithologist/hunter for disclosing its whereabouts. Sylvia's choice is intuitive and poignant, and she is a model of the kind of person Henry David Thoreau talked about in "Walking." (See p. 44.)

The debate between personal benefit/loss and universal benefit/loss can take many twists and turns, as evidenced in "Winter" from Sue Hubbell's *A Country Year: Living the Questions* (1999). The idea of damming a river and creating a lake, which will flood part of Hubbell's farm, is seen by some local people as a positive venture, a money-making scheme that will provide recreation and stimulate tourism. Hubbell suggests that good arguments can be made for the necessity of such an economic boon, but others want to preserve the land and its rural qualities. When Hubbell uncovers the fact that the U.S. Park Service had already expropriated the river and surrounding land for preservation, the argument is resolved, but not without splitting the community. A similar controversy—federal government versus private interests—is at the heart of Margaret L. Knox's "The Wilderness According to Cushman" (1993). (See p. 31.)

The control we exert over backyard nature is in many ways a testament to our attitudes toward the environment and nature. When Joy Williams elected to let nature take over her acre of land near Sarasota, Florida, her neighbors were not happy. They resented unruly nature. Williams embraced it. In her essay "One Acre: On Devaluing Real Estate to Keep Land Priceless" (2001), she asserts that to hold an acre of prime building land in a place such as Florida where real estate development is a way of life is difficult, even neurotic. The acre could have been divided into four building lots in order to garner substantial financial gain, but Williams is adamant and holds that "when land is developed, it ceases being land. It becomes covered, sealed, its own grave." Like Sylvia in Jewett's "The White Heron," Williams has to face the dilemma of establishing a balance between her love of nature, and the pressure she feels from Florida real estate developers. It is tempting to ponder this dilemma and contrast it with practicality. Williams could have taken her profit from the sale of the sole acre and undoubtedly purchased many acres elsewhere for preservation. Although that course would have been one way of solving the dilemma, the question still remains to be answered: Does this one acre in this particular location in Florida have a value to nature that warrants keeping it?

The answer to this question depends on how one looks at nature, as Rebecca Solnit reminds us in "The Orbits of Earthly Bodies" (2003). Williams looks out the window of her home to her backyard and observes what she calls nature. Solnit walks down a city street to a store and sees nature in this act, one typical of an urban dweller. We often discount human beings as part of nature. It is interesting to contemplate that city streets and city parks are the backyards of the vast majority of this country's population and, as Solnit points out, we have set up our society so that the most die-hard rural dwellers still depend on cities for their mail, cars, tax forms, and bank statements.

While most of us rejoice in nature, the danger is that we rejoice in our own vision of nature. Nature has shown itself to be very plastic. We can shove it here, bend it there, and even break it elsewhere, and it still suggests true nature. That may be good enough for most of us. But we would do well to ask ourselves as we manipulate our corner of nature whether we are acting in our own self-interest, or nature's greater interest.

A White Heron

SARAH ORNE JEWETT

Sarah Orne Jewett (1849–1909), like Sylvia, the young girl in "A White Heron" (1886), opted for nature rather than material things, independence rather than dependence. Her fiction is peopled with characters, particularly women, who live on their own and believe in themselves. Jewett was born and lived most of her life in the same house in South Berwick, Maine, a depressed inland port. Afflicted by arthritis during her childhood, Jewett was not required to attend school regularly; instead, she often accompanied her physician father on his house calls to isolated fishing communities and farm islands off the coast. Jewett began writing seriously as a teenager and published stories frequently in The Atlantic Monthly. *Her works include a collection of short stories,* Deephaven *(1877); the novels* A Country Doctor *(1884),* King of Folly *(1888), and* The Life of Nancy *(1895); and a collection of poems,* Verses *(1916). Her best writing appears in* The Country of Pointed Firs *(1896), a collection of loosely related stories that forms a kind of novel. Jewett's writing career was cut short by injuries sustained during a carriage accident, and in 1909 she died in the house where she was born.*

---------------- ✦ ----------------

1

The woods were already filled with shadows one June evening, just before eight o'clock, though a bright sunset still glimmered faintly among the trunks of the trees. A little girl was driving home her cow, a plodding, dilatory, provoking creature in her behavior, but a valued companion for all that. They were going away from the western light, and striking deep into the dark woods, but their feet were familiar with the path, and it was no matter whether their eyes could see it or not.

There was hardly a night the summer through when the old cow could be found waiting at the pasture bars; on the contrary, it was her greatest pleasure to hide herself away among the high huckleberry bushes, and though she wore a loud bell she had made the discovery that if one stood perfectly still it would not ring. So Sylvia had to hunt for her until she found her, and call Co'! Co'! with never an answering Moo, until her childish patience was quite spent. If the creature had not given good milk and plenty of it, the case would have seemed very different to her owners. Besides, Sylvia had all the time there was, and very little use to make of it. Sometimes in pleasant weather it was a consolation to look upon the cow's pranks as an intelligent attempt to play hide and seek, and as the child had no playmates she lent herself to this amusement with a good deal of zest. Though this chase had been so long that the wary animal herself had given an unusual signal of her whereabouts, Sylvia had only laughed when she came upon Mistress Moolly at the swamp-side, and urged her affectionately homeward with a twig of birch leaves. The old cow was not inclined to wander farther, she even turned in the right direction for once as they left the pasture, and stepped along the road at a good pace. She was quite ready to be milked now, and seldom stopped to browse. Sylvia wondered what her grandmother would say because they were so late. It was a great while since she had left home at half past five o'clock, but everybody knew the difficulty of making this errand a short one. Mrs. Tilley had chased the hornèd torment too many summer evenings herself to blame any one else for lingering, and was only thankful as she waited that she had Sylvia, nowadays, to give such valuable assistance. The good woman suspected that Sylvia loitered occasionally on her own account; there never was such a child for straying about out-of-doors since the world was made! Everybody said that it was a good change for a little maid who had tried to grow for eight years in a crowded manufacturing town, but, as for Sylvia herself, it seemed as if she never had been alive at all before she came to live at the farm. She thought often with wistful compassion of a wretched dry geranium that belonged to a town neighbor.

"'Afraid of folks,'" old Mrs. Tilley said to herself, with a smile, after she had made the unlikely choice of Sylvia from her daughter's houseful of children, and was returning to the farm. "'Afraid of folks,' they said! I guess she won't be troubled no great with 'em up to the old place!" When they reached the door of the lonely house and stopped to unlock it, and the cat came to purr loudly, and rub against them, a deserted pussy, indeed, but fat with young robins, Sylvia whispered that this was a beautiful placc to live in, and she never should wish to go home.

The companions followed the shady wood-road, the cow taking slow steps, and the child very fast ones. The cow stopped long at the brook to drink, as if the pasture were not half a swamp, and Sylvia stood still and waited, letting her bare feet cool themselves in the shoal water, while the great twilight moths struck softly against her. She waded on through the brook as the cow moved away, and listening to the thrushes with a heart that beat fast with pleasure. There was a stirring in the great boughs overhead. They were full of little birds and beasts that scemed to be wide-awake, and going about their world, or else saying goodnight to each other in sleepy twitters. Sylvia herself felt sleepy as she walked along. However, it was not much farther to the house, and the air was soft and sweet. She was not often in the woods so late as this, and it made her feel as if she were a part of the gray shadows and the moving leaves. She was just thinking how long it seemed since she first came to the farm a year ago, and wondering if everything went on in the noisy town just the same as when she was there; the thought of the great red-faced boy who used to chase and frighten her made her hurry along the path to escape from the shadow of the trees.

Suddenly this little woods-girl is horror-stricken to hear a   5 clear whistle not very far away. Not a bird's whistle, which would have a sort of friendliness, but a boy's whistle, determined, and somewhat aggressive. Sylvia left the cow to whatever sad fate might await her, and stepped discreetly aside into the bushes, but she was just too late. The enemy had discovered her, and called out in a very cheerful and persuasive tone, "Halloa, little girl, how far is it to the road?" and trembling Sylvia answered almost inaudibly, "A good ways."

She did not dare to look boldly at the tall young man, who carried a gun over his shoulder, but she came out of her bush and again followed the cow, while he walked alongside.

"I have been hunting for some birds," the stranger said kindly, "and I have lost my way, and need a friend very much. Don't be afraid," he added gallantly. "Speak up and tell me what your name is, and whether you think I can spend the night at your house, and go out gunning early in the morning."

Sylvia was more alarmed than before. Would not her grandmother consider her much to blame? But who could have foreseen such an accident as this? It did not appear to be her fault, and she hung her head as if the stem of it were broken, but managed to answer, "Sylvy," with much effort when her companion again asked her name.

Mrs. Tilley was standing in the doorway when the trio came into view. The cow gave a loud moo by way of explanation.

10 "Yes, you'd better speak up for yourself, you old trial! Where'd she tucked herself away this time, Sylvy?" Sylvia kept an awed silence; she knew by instinct that her grandmother did not comprehend the gravity of the situation. She must be mistaking the stranger for one of the farmer-lads of the region.

The young man stood his gun beside the door, and dropped a heavy game-bag beside it; then he bade Mrs. Tilley good-evening, and repeated his wayfarer's story, and asked if he could have a night's lodging.

"Put me anywhere you like," he said. "I must be off early in the morning, before day; but I am very hungry, indeed. You can give me some milk at any rate, that's plain."

"Dear sakes, yes," responded the hostess, whose long slumbering hospitality seemed to be easily awakened. "You might fare better if you went out on the main road a mile or so, but you're welcome to what we've got. I'll milk right off, and you make yourself at home. You can sleep on husks or feathers," she proffered graciously. "I raised them all myself. There's good pasturing for geese just below here towards the ma'sh. Now step round and set a plate for the gentleman, Sylvy!" And Sylvia promptly stepped. She was glad to have something to do, and she was hungry herself.

It was a surprise to find so clean and comfortable a little dwelling in this New England wilderness. The young man had known the horrors of its most primitive housekeeping, and the dreary squalor of that level of society which does not rebel at the companionship of hens. This was the best thrift of an old-fashioned farmstead, though on such a small scale that it seemed like a hermitage. He listened eagerly to the old woman's quaint talk, he watched Sylvia's pale face and shining gray eyes with ever growing enthusiasm, and insisted that this was the best supper he had eaten for a month; then, afterward, the new-made friends sat down in the doorway together while the moon came up.

15 Soon it would be berry-time, and Sylvia was a great help at picking. The cow was a good milker, though a plaguy thing to keep track of, the hostess gossiped frankly, adding presently that she had buried four children, so that Sylvia's mother, and a son (who might be dead) in California were all the children she had left. "Dan, my boy, was a great hand to go gunning," she explained

sadly. "I never wanted for pa'tridges or gray squer'ls while he was to home. He's been a great wand'rer, I expect, and he's no hand to write letters. There, I don't blame him, I'd ha' seen the world myself if it had been so I could.

"Sylvia takes after him," the grandmother continued affectionately, after a minute's pause. "There ain't a foot o' ground she don't know her way over, and the wild creatur's counts her one o' themselves. Squer'ls she'll tame to come an' feed right out o' her hands, and all sorts o' birds. Last winter she got the jay-birds to bangeing here, and I believe she'd 'a' scanted herself of her own meals to have plenty to throw out amongst 'em, if I had n't kep' watch. Anything but crows, I tell her, I'm willin' to help support,— though Dan he went an' tamed one o' them that did seem to have reason same as folks. It was round here a good spell after he went away. Dan an' his father they did n't hitch,—but he never held up his head ag'in after Dan had dared him an' gone off."

The guest did not notice this hint of family sorrows in his eager interest in something else.

"So Sylvy knows all about birds, does she?" he exclaimed, as he looked round at the little girl who sat, very demure but increasingly sleepy, in the moonlight. "I am making a collection of birds myself. I have been at it ever since I was a boy." (Mrs. Tilley smiled.) "There are two or three very rare ones I have been hunting for these five years. I mean to get them on my own ground if they can be found."

"Do you cage 'em up?" asked Mrs. Tilley doubtfully, in response to this enthusiastic announcement.

"Oh, no, they're stuffed and preserved, dozens and dozens of   20 them," said the ornithologist, "and I have shot or snared every one myself. I caught a glimpse of a white heron three miles from here on Saturday, and I have followed it in this direction. They have never been found in this district at all. The little white heron, it is," and he turned again to look at Sylvia with the hope of discovering that the rare bird was one of her acquaintances.

But Sylvia was watching a hop-toad in the narrow footpath.

"You would know the heron if you saw it," the stranger continued eagerly. "A queer tall white bird with soft feathers and long thin legs. And it would have a nest perhaps in the top of a high tree, made of sticks, something like a hawk's nest."

Sylvia's heart gave a wild beat; she knew that strange white bird, and had once stolen softly near where it stood in some bright green swamp grass, away over at the other side of the woods. There was an open place where the sunshine always seemed strangely yellow and hot, where tall, nodding rushes grew, and her grandmother had warned her that she might sink in the soft black mud underneath and never be heard of more. Not far beyond were the salt marshes and beyond those was the sea, the sea which Sylvia wondered and dreamed about, but never had looked upon, though its great voice could often be heard above the noise of the woods on stormy nights.

"I can't think of anything I should like so much as to find that heron's nest," the handsome stranger was saying. "I would give ten dollars to anybody who could show it to me," he added desperately, "and I mean to spend my whole vacation hunting for it if need be. Perhaps it was only migrating, or had been chased of out its own region by some bird of prey."

25   Mrs. Tilley gave amazed attention to all this, but Sylvia still watched the toad, not divining, as she might have done at some calmer time, that the creature wished to get to its hole under the doorstep, and was much hindered by the unusual spectators at that hour of the evening. No amount of thought, that night, could decide how many wished-for treasures the ten dollars, so lightly spoken of, would buy.

The next day the young sportsman hovered about the woods, and Sylvia kept him company, having lost her first fear of the friendly lad, who proved to be most kind and sympathetic. He told her many things about the birds and what they knew and where they lived and what they did with themselves. And he gave her a jack-knife, which she thought as great a treasure as if she were a desert-islander. All day long he did not once make her troubled or afraid except when he brought down some unsuspecting singing creature from its bough. Sylvia would have liked him vastly better without his gun; she could not understand why he killed the very birds he seemed to like so much. But as the day waned, Sylvia still watched the young man with loving admiration. She had never seen anybody so charming and delightful; the woman's heart, asleep in the child, was vaguely thrilled by a dream of love. Some premonition of that great power stirred and swayed these young foresters who traversed the solemn woodlands with soft-footed silent care. They stopped to listen to a bird's song; they pressed forward again eagerly, parting the branches,—speaking to each other rarely and in whispers; the young man going first and Sylvia following, fascinated, a few steps behind, with her gray eyes dark with excitement.

She grieved because the longed-for white heron was elusive, but she did not lead the guest, she only followed, and there was no such thing as speaking first. The sound of her own unquestioned voice would have terrified her,—it was hard enough to an-

swer yes or no when there was need of that. At last evening began
to fall, and they drove the cow home together, and Sylvia smiled
with pleasure when they came to the place where she heard the
whistle and was afraid only the night before.

2

Half a mile from home, at the farther edge of the woods, where
the land was highest, a great pine-tree stood, the last of its generation. Whether it was left for a boundary mark, or for what reason, no one could say; the woodchoppers who had felled its mates
were dead and gone long ago, and a whole forest of sturdy trees,
pines and oaks and maples, had grown again. But the stately head
of this old pine towered above them all and made a landmark for
sea and shore miles and miles away. Sylvia knew it well. She had
always believed that whoever climbed to the top of it could see
the ocean; and the little girl had often laid her hand on the great
rough trunk and looked up wistfully at those dark boughs that the
wind always stirred, no matter how hot and still the air might be
below. Now she thought of the tree with a new excitement, for
why, if one climbed it at break of day, could not one see all the
world, and easily discover whence the white heron flew, and mark
the place, and find the hidden nest?

What a spirit of adventure, what wild ambition! What fancied
triumph and delight and glory for the later morning when she
could make known the secret! It was almost too real and too great
for the childish heart to bear.

All night the door of the little house stood open, and the   30
whippoorwills came and sang upon the very step. The young
sportsman and old hostess were sound asleep, but Sylvia's great
design kept her broad awake and watching. She forgot to think of
sleep. The short summer night seemed as long as the winter darkness, and at last when the whippoorwills ceased, and she was
afraid the morning would after all come too soon, she stole out of
the house and followed the pasture path through the woods, has-
tening toward the open ground beyond, listening with a sense of
comfort and companionship to the drowsy twitter of a half-
awakened bird, whose perch she had jarred in passing. Alas, if the
great wave of human interest which flooded for the first time this
dull little life should sweep away the satisfactions of an existence
heart to heart with nature and the dumb life of the forest!

There was the huge tree asleep yet in the paling moonlight,
and small and hopeful Sylvia began with utmost bravery to
mount to the top of it, with tingling, eager blood coursing the

channels of her whole frame, with her bare feet and fingers, that pinched and held like bird's claws to the monstrous ladder reaching up, up, almost to the sky itself. First she must mount the white oak tree that grew alongside, where she was almost lost among the dark branches and the green leaves heavy and wet with dew; a bird fluttered off its nest, and a red squirrel ran to and fro and scolded pettishly at the harmless housebreaker. Sylvia felt her way easily. She had often climbed there, and knew that higher still one of the oak's upper branches chafed against the pine trunk, just where its lower boughts were set close together. There, when she made the dangerous pass from one tree to the other, the great enterprise would really begin.

She crept out along the swaying oak limb at last, and took the daring step across into the old pine-tree. The way was harder than she thought; she must reach far and hold fast, the sharp dry twigs caught and held her and scratched her like angry talons, the pitch made her thin little fingers clumsy and stiff as she went round and round the tree's great stem, higher and higher upward. The sparrows and robins in the woods below were beginning to wake and twitter to the dawn, yet it seemed much lighter there aloft in the pine-tree, and the child knew that she must hurry if her project were to be of any use.

The tree seemed to lengthen itself out as she went up, and to reach farther and farther upward. It was like a great main-mast to the voyaging earth; it must truly have been amazed that morning through all its ponderous frame as it felt this determined spark of human spirit creeping and climbing from higher branch to branch. Who knows how steadily the least twigs held themselves to advantage this light, weak creature on her way! The old pine must have loved his new dependent. More than all the hawks, and bats, and moths, and even the sweet-voiced thrushes, was the brave, beating heart of the solitary gray-eyed child. And the tree stood still and held away the winds that June morning while the dawn grew bright in the east.

Sylvia's face was like a pale star, if one had seen it from the ground, when the last thorny bough was past, and she stood trembling and tired but wholly triumphant, high in the tree-top. Yes, there was the sea with the dawning sun making a golden dazzle over it, and toward that glorious east flew two hawks with slow-moving pinions. How low they looked in the air from that height when before one had only seen them far up, and dark against the blue sky. Their gray feathers were as soft as moths; they seemed only a little way from the tree, and Sylvia felt as if she too could go flying away among the clouds. Westward, the

woodlands and farms reached miles and miles into the distance;
here and there were church steeples, and white villages; truly it
was a vast and awesome world.

The birds sang louder and louder. At last the sun came up be-   35
wilderingly bright. Sylvia could see the white sails of ships out at
sea, and the clouds that were purple and rose-colored and yellow
at first began to fade away. Where was the white heron's nest in
the sea of green branches, and was this wonderful sight and pag-
eant of the world the only reward for having climbed to such a
giddy height? Now look down again, Sylvia, where the green
marsh is set among the shining birches and dark hemlocks; there
where you saw the white heron once you will see him again; look,
look! a white spot of him like a single floating feather comes up
from the dead hemlock and grows larger, and rises, and comes
close at last, and goes by the landmark pine with steady sweep of
wing and outstretched slender neck and crested head. And wait!
wait! do not move a foot or a finger, little girl, do not send an arrow of light and consciousness from your two eager eyes, for the
heron has perched on a pine bough not far beyond yours, and
cries back to his mate on the nest, and plumes his feathers for the
new day!

The child gives a long sigh a minute later when a company of
shouting cat-birds comes also to the tree, and vexed by their fluttering and lawlessness the solemn heron goes away. She knows
his secret now, the wild, light, slender bird that floats and wavers,
and goes back like an arrow presently to his home in the green
world beneath. Then Sylvia, well satisfied, makes her perilous
way down again, not daring to look far below the branch she
stands on, ready to cry sometimes because her fingers ache and
her lamed feet slip. Wondering over and over again what the
stranger would say to her, and what he would think when she told
him how to find his way straight to the heron's nest.

"Sylvy, Sylvy!" called the busy old grandmother again and
again, but nobody answered, and the small husk bed was empty
and Sylvia had disappeared.

The guest waked from a dream, and remembering his day's
pleasure hurried to dress himself that it might sooner begin. He
was sure from the way the shy little girl looked once or twice yesterday that she had at least seen the white heron, and now she
must really be persuaded to tell. Here she comes now, paler than
ever, and her worn old frock is torn and tattered, and smeared
with pine pitch. The grandmother and the sportsman stand in the
door together and question her, and the splendid moment has
come to speak of the dead hemlock-tree by the green marsh.

But Sylvia does not speak after all, though the old grandmother fretfully rebukes her, and the young man's kind appealing
eyes are looking straight in her own. He can make them rich with
money; he has promised it, and they are poor now. He is so well
worth making happy, and he waits to hear the story she can tell.
40   No, she must keep silence! What is it that suddenly forbids
her and makes her dumb? Has she been nine years growing, and
now, when the great world for the first time puts out a hand to
her, must she thrust it aside for a bird's sake? The murmur of the
pine's green branches is in her ears, she remembers how the
white heron came flying through the golden air and how they
watched the sea and the morning together, and Sylvia cannot
speak; she cannot tell the heron's secret and give its life away.

Dear loyalty, that suffered a sharp pang as the guest went
away disappointed later in the day, that could have served and followed him and loved him as a dog loves! Many a night Sylvia
heard the echo of his whistle haunting the pasture path as she
came home with the loitering cow. She forgot even her sorrow at
the sharp report of his gun and the piteous sight of thrushes and
sparrows dropping silent to the ground, their songs hushed and
their pretty feathers stained and wet with blood. Were the birds
better friends than their hunter might have been,—who can tell?
Whatever treasures were lost to her, woodlands and summertime,
remember! Bring your gifts and graces and tell your secrets to
this lonely country child!

1886

Discussion

1. Explain Sylvia's identification with the heron.
2. Discuss the social and spiritual roles that the girl, the aunt, and the hunter
   play in understanding our relationship with nature.
3. Explain the process of thought and imagination that Sylvia undergoes as she
   climbs the great white pine.

Winter
SUE HUBBELL

*Sue Hubbell (1935–) has been a librarian, a commercial beekeeper,
and a naturalist, and she is now an author of popular books on biology. For twelve years, Hubbell lived on a farm as a solitary beekeeper*

in the Ozark Mountains of southern Missouri where she wrote A
Book of Bees: And How to Keep Them *(1998). Among her other
books are* Broadsides from Other Places: A Book of Bugs *(1993),*
Broadsides from Other Orders *(1998),* Waiting for Aphrodite:
Journey into a Time Before Bones *(1999), and* Shrinking the Cat:
Genetic Engineering Before We Knew About Genes *(2001). At
present, Hubbell lives in Maine and Washington, D.C.*

--------------------- ✦ ---------------------

Once I tried to stop a war, and once I really did help start a labor union at a library where I worked. But, on the whole, the
world has cheerfully and astutely resisted my attempts to save it.
And now that I've spent my winter saving my particular ninety
acres of it from the floodwaters of a dam, I am left to wonder, as
usual, what I have done. Upon examination, the dam proposal
turned out to be as lacking in reality as faerie gold, but the local
people were sure that it was real, and so perhaps it was.

The controversy got its start at the end of the summer. I was
harvesting the honey crop then, and immediately afterward
started on my autumn round of sales trips, so I didn't hear much
about it at first. But an item in the local newspaper explained that
a Lakes and Dams Association had been formed to promote the
damming of the river to create a recreational lake a few river
miles downstream from my farm, just inside the strip of land
along the banks of the river that the U.S. Park Service owns and
supervises. The officers of the association were two men who
work in the feed room at the general store. The news item
amused me; it seemed a piece of folly that local people would
laugh off. But then, home from a sales trip a month later, it took
me three hours to walk two blocks in town because people kept
stopping me to ask what I thought about the dam. I didn't know
anything about it, but I was given my questioner's full, colorful
and highly charged opinion. In the café, there was talk of nothing
else. A petition was being circulated asking the local conservative
congressman to initiate a feasibility study for the dam's construction, and several thousand people had already signed it. I went
back out on the road to sell honey, and when I returned again an
anti-dam group had formed: Citizens for a Free Flowin' River.
Aside from having a fine and ripply name, they caught my attention by issuing a map of the recreational lake which showed several portions of my farm under water. I promised myself that
when I got off the road for the winter I would spend some time
figuring out what was going on.

From the beginning, both dam and anti-dam were innocent of grubby reality. No one knew how dams got built or why. No trustworthy figures or facts were available from either side. But that was all right, because the argument took place over what was of value in this part of the Ozarks and expectations for the future—matters quite independent of reality, facts, figures or even a dam, for that matter. The people who wanted a dam were those who thought that it would be good to turn the town into the sort of place that had a McDonald's. Those who opposed it thought this would not be good at all. The dam was almost beside the point, and the eventual victory of the anti-dam forces was just a tiny rearguard action. People who want to exploit and change the Ozarks are still here, and will continue to suggest other plans for development.

Since 1909, proposals to dam this river have been made with varying degrees of seriousness. The two men in the feed room who had dusted off the plan came from families who had been involved in some of those earlier attempts. Once they started talking up a dam, others interested in development found reasons for it and the movement was born. The dam, it was said, could generate cheap electricity for the town. It would prevent damage from floods. Its construction would bring jobs to the area, and so would the businesses that a recreational lake would support. Land values would rise; indeed, property owners near the river immediately doubled the asking price for land they had for sale. The president of the local chamber of commerce was caught on television film, his eyes rolled heavenward, saying, "All I can see is dollar signs before my eyes."

5   But there was another compelling and contrary appeal that made people sign the petition for a dam. By inviting the U.S. Corps of Engineers to build a dam on U.S. Park Service land, the latter agency would get its comeuppance. It is hard for anyone accustomed to thinking of the popular U.S. Park Service as a benign bureaucracy to understand with what loathing the agency is regarded here. The local park was established in the mid-1960s to protect the river from attempts to dam it the decade before. Land along the river was bought up and removed from private to federal ownership; this shift in title to the river's banks has never been forgiven. As highways improved and it became easier for city people from Illinois and northern Missouri to get to the Ozarks, more people started floating the river, fishing in it and hiking along its banks, and the Park Service created new rules to regulate its use and protect the habitat. Local citizens, who remembered the old days when there were no rules and few

tourists, were outraged, believing that their rights had been taken from them. They also resented, as an unwarranted constraint on the chance to make a buck, the Park Service limitation on the number of private concessionaires who rented canoes to tourists.

The dammers knew that they couldn't make the Park Service go away, but they hoped they could punish it by withholding the river's waters behind a dam built by the U.S. Corps of Engineers, sensible folks, not like those fuzzy-minded park rangers who were always talking about the environment. The Corps certainly wouldn't issue a lot of silly rules that would keep local people from doing what they and their fathers and grandfathers before them had always done to and along the river.

The Free Flowin' Citizens, or at least the Ozarkers among them, didn't like the U.S. Park Service any better than did the dammers, but they didn't trust the U.S. Corps of Engineers either. They wanted the river to stay in private hands—namely, theirs, for many of them were landowners upriver. They did not like the idea of changing the town by bringing in even more tourists and outsiders than the federal park had already done. Many of them were concerned about the destruction a lake's waters could bring about to the wildlife habitat along the edge of the river.

For the past six weeks I have been spending my afternoons writing letters, telephoning and meeting in offices with appropriate government bureaucrats, elected officials and staffs of environmental organizations in order to find out how dams get built and what the impact of one would be on this area.

I discovered that this cave-riddled limestone is unsuitable for dam construction, that the Corps of Engineers builds flood-control dams only in urban and major agricultural areas, that costs of electricity generation have to be borne locally, that economic development in areas where dams have been built has disappointed local people and that rare and endangered plants in the state's Natural Areas System would be destroyed by the dam. I also found out that current practice requires large initial local funding, and that the federal government pays costs of a dam only when it can be justified for flood control—which this one could not. Other dams, such as those created for recreational lakes, would require local funding or at least half the cost. In a state still untouched by economic happiness, one which cannot afford to pay for its poor or its potholes, funding for a dam would be difficult.

I also found out that since the federal government had established the park in response to earlier efforts to dam the   10 river, it had spelled out in the first sentence of the charter that the river must remain a "free-flowing stream." Those responsible for attempts to dam it in or above U.S. Park Service land would be taken to court by the Department of the Interior. Attempts to change the charter would not meet with favor in Congress at this time. In addition, the district Corps of Engineers, in response to local talk, had reviewed the earlier proposals to dam the river, and in light of current political and economic realities had concluded that a dam on the river was "unthinkable."

However, some people I talked to reminded me that the politics of the pork barrel is a queer business, and that economic policies change. I also learned that the Corps of Engineers had been forced by budget pressures to lay off personnel it could not justify, and might have an interest in keeping staffers busy with a dam proposal if there was enough public support for one.

So I met with the Free Flowin' Citizens and told them what I had learned. The information cheered them. They wrote letters to their state and federal representatives. They began holding forth at the café and on street corners. They printed up their own petition opposing the dam and began gathering signatures.

I asked a man I knew, a forceful public speaker who did not live on the river but who owned property on it that would have been flooded by a dam, if he would be the featured speaker at a public meeting the Free Flowin' Citizens wanted to hold. He agreed, and the meeting was held. Public opinion had already begun to shift away from support of a dam, and the meeting saw it disappear. The Dammers brought several advocates to speak at the meeting, but they were no match for the Anti-Dam speaker, a man who has made a career both public and private of his persuasive personality. He carried the day, explaining the Free Flowin' arguments in a winning manner; I had staged a bit of guerrilla theater, nostalgia for an old activist.

Ever since that meeting, the dam as a topic of conversation is greeted with embarrassed silence. The issue has disappeared as though it never was. In the café now they are talking about how hard the present cold snap is on the new calves being born in the pastures, and when I went in to buy feed today, the most fiery of the dam's advocates wanted to show me pictures of his new baby.

1999

Discussion

1. Describe Hubbell's general attitude toward those who favored the dam.
2. Discuss a piece of land that you are familiar with that has either been developed or preserved. Do you think that whatever action was taken was the right one and how did it affect local people?
3. Discuss the dam versus free-flowing river from the ethical points of view espoused by Aldo Leopold in "The Land Ethic" (p. 18). When an area might be economically boosted by development, do you think Leopold's ideas are appropriate?

One Acre: On Devaluing Real Estate to Keep Land Priceless

JOY WILLIAMS

Joy Williams (1944–) was born in Maine, but she has traveled widely since. She was educated at Marietta College, Ohio, and the University of Iowa. She is best known for her short stories and novels that most often present a dark vision of life in the United States. Her stories have appeared in Esquire, The New Yorker, *and* Grand Street. *Her works include the short story collections* Taking Care: Short Stories *(1982) and* Escapes: Stories *(1990), and the novels* State of Grace *(1973),* The Changeling *(1978),* Breaking and Entering *(1988), and* The Quick and the Dead *(2000). Williams's non-fiction includes* Florida Keys: A History and Guide *(1986),* Florida *(1999), and* Ill Nature *(2001).*

———————— ✦ ————————

I had an acre in Florida, on a lagoon close by the Gulf of Mexico.

I am admittedly putting this first line up against Isak Dinesen's famous oneiric one: I had a farm in Africa, at the foot of the Ngong Hills. When Dinesen first came to Africa she confessed that she could not "live without getting a fine specimen of each single kind of African game." For her the hunt was an eroticized image of desire, "a love affair," wherein the "shot. . . . was in reality a declaration of love." She must have blushed to read this drivel later, for after ten years she found hunting "an unreasonable thing, indeed in itself ugly and vulgar, for the sake of a few hours enjoyment to put out a life that belonged in the great land-scape and had grown up on it." One could say her thinking had evolved, that she had become more conscientious. Still, when she was about to leave her beloved farm (her house, empty of furniture, was admirably "clean like a skull"), she planned to shoot her dogs and horses, dissuaded from doing so only by the pleas of her friends. The animals belonged to her, as had the land, which she ceased to own only when it became owned by another, and subject to that person's whims and policies. Of course it became hers again through writing about it, preserving it in *Out of Africa*. Once again, Art, reflective poesy, saves landscape.

I had an acre in Florida. . . . This bodes no drama. For what wonders could a single acre hold, what meaning or relevance? Although the word "Florida" is oneiric, too, and thus its own metaphor. It is an occasional place, a palmed and pleasant stage for transients. To hold fast to an acre in that vast state is almost neurotic. An acre is both too much and not enough. Its value lies in its divisibility, in how many building lots are permitted by law. Four, certainly.

I once saw a white heron in a tumbled landscape on the sprawling outskirts of Naples, a city that crowds against the Big Cypress National Preserve and Everglades National Park. The heron seemed to be beating its head against a tree knocked down by bulldozers to widen a road. Water still lay along the palmetto-dotted earth, but pipes would soon carry it away and dry the land for town houses and golf courses. Cars sped past. The heron, white as a robed angel must surely be, was beating his head against the tree. He was lost to himself, deranged, in his ruined and lost landscape.

5   I have seen all manner of beautiful waterbirds struck down by cars. I used to take them home and bury them between the mangroves and the live oaks on my lagoon. But of course it was not my lagoon, this body of water only a mile and a half long. To the north it cedes to a private road that gives access to the Sanderling Club, where the exceptionally wealthy enjoy their Gulf views. To the south it vanishes beneath the parking lot for a public beach. This is on Siesta Key, a crowded eight-mile-long island off Sarasota that is joined to the mainland by two bridges, one four lanes, the other two. The lagoon is named Heron; the beach, Turtle. Yes, the turtles still come to nest, and the volunteers who stake and guard the nests are grateful—they practically weep with gratitude—when the condo dwellers keep their lights out during the hatching weeks so as not to confuse the infant turtles in their night search for the softly luminous sea. But usually the condo

dwellers don't keep their lights out. They might accommodate the request were they there, but they are seldom there. The lights are controlled by timers and burn bright and long. The condos are investments, mostly, not homes. Like the lands they've consumed, they're cold commodities. When land is developed, it ceases being land. It becomes covered, sealed, its own grave.

Ecosystems are something large to be saved, if at all, by the government at great expense and set aside to be enjoyed by all of us in some recreational or contemplative fashion. An individual doesn't think of himself as owning an ecosystem. The responsibility! Too much. Besides, there's something about the word that denotes the impossibility of ownership. Land, on the other hand, is like a car or a house; it has economic currency. Aldo Leopold defined land as a fountain of energy flowing through a circuit of soils, plants, and animals; it was synonymous with ecosystem, and he argued that we all have an obligation to protect and preserve it. It was over fifty years ago that Leopold wrote his elegantly reasoned essay "The Land Ethic," but it has had about as much effect on the American conscience as a snowflake. Seven thousand acres are lost to development each day in this country. Ecosystem becomes land becomes parcel.

On Siesta Key, "open space" (of which there is now none), when bought by the county years ago, is being utilized as beach parking or tennis courts. "Raw" land no longer exists, though a few lots are still available, some with very nice trees, most of which will have to go (unfortunately) in order to accommodate the house that will be built on what is now considered a "site." We hardly can get all ecosystem emotional over a site. A banyan tree will most assuredly have to go because it is in its nature to grow extravagantly and demand a great deal of space. Trees, of course, cannot demand anything. As with the wild animals who have certain requirements or preferences—a clutter and cover, long natural hours of friendly concealing dark—anything they need can be ignored or removed right along with them.

In 1969, I bought Lots 27, 28, and 29 on Midnight Pass Road, a two-lane road that ended when the key did. There was a small cypress house, no beauty, and an even smaller cypress cottage. They were single-story affairs with fiat roofs, built on poured slabs. The lots together cost $24,000. In 1972, I bought Lots 30 and 31 for $12,000. Lagoon land wasn't all that desirable. There was no access to open water. Bay land was more valuable, and even then Gulf front was only for the wealthy. Beachfront is invaluable because no one can build on the sea; the view is "protected." I could hear the Gulf on my small acre; it was, in fact, only several hundred feet away, concealed by a scrim of mangroves. The houses that were to be built over there were grand but still never quite exceeded the height of the mangroves. I did not see my lagoon neighbors for my trees, my tangled careless land, though as the years passed I put up sections of wooden fence, for my neighbors changed, then changed again, and their little cypress houses were torn down in a twinkling, the "extra" lots sold. I put a wooden fence up along the road eventually. It weathered prettily but would shudder on its posts from a flung beer bottle. Sections of it were periodically demolished by errant cars. I don't believe I ever rushed sympathetically to the befuddled driver's aid. No one actually died, but they did go on, those crashes. Streetlights went up at fifty-foot intervals on the dark and curvy road. The bay side got the lights, the lagoon side got the bicycle path. Homeowners were responsible for keeping the "path" tidy, and I appeared out there dutifully with broom and rake, pushing away the small oak leaves from the trees that towered overhead, disclosing all that efficient concrete for the benefit of increasing streams of walkers and joggers. Bicyclists preferred to use the road. Any stubborn palmetto that fanned outward or seeded palm that once graced the strip of land outside my rickety wall would be snipped back by a supernumerary, doing his/her part for the public way. The bottles, cans, and wee chip bags were left for me to reap. As owner of Lots 27, 28, 29, 30, and 31, I had 370 feet of path to maintain. I became aware, outside my fence, of the well-known Florida light, a sort of blandly insistent urban light—feathery and bemused and resigned. Cars sped past. Large houses were being constructed on the bay, estates on half an acre with elaborate wrought-iron fences and electric gates. Palmetto scrub had given way to lawns. Trees existed as dramatically trimmed accents, all dead wood removed. Trees not deemed perfectly sound by landscape professionals were felled; the palms favored were "specimen" ones. Dead animals and birds appeared more and more frequently on the road. Cars sped past.

Behind my wobbly fence, I pottered about. The houses were built in the forties, and the land had the typical homesteaded accoutrements of that time—a few citrus trees, some oleander and hibiscus for color, a plot cleared for a few vegetables and Shasta daisies, a fig left to flourish for shade, and live oaks left to grow around the edges. The ghastly malleucas were available in nurseries then and were often planted in rows as a hedge. The man I bought the land from was a retired botanist, and he had planted avocado and lychee nut trees too, as well as a grove of giant bamboo from which he liked to make vases and bowls and various trinkets. There was bougainvillea, azalea, gardenia, powder puff and firecracker plant, crotons, wild lilies, sea grape, and several orchid trees. Of the palms there was a royal, sabal, many cabbage, pineapple, sago—queen and king—reclinata, fishtail, sentry, traveler's, and queen. There were cypresses, jacaranda, and two banyan trees. There was even a tiny lawn with small cement squares to place the lawn chairs on. The mangroves in this spot had been cut back for a view of the idly flowing tea-colored lagoon. Elsewhere they grew—the red and the black—in the manner each found lovely, in hoops and stands, creating bowers and thickets and mazes of rocking water and dappling light.

This was my acre in Florida. Visitors ventured that it looked 10
as though it would require an awful lot of maintenance, though they admired my prescience in buying the extra lots, which would surely be worth something someday. The house had a certain "rustic charm," but most people didn't find the un-air-conditioned, un-dehumidified air all that wholesome and wondered why I kept the place so damn dark, for there were colored floods widely available that would dramatize the "plantings." I could bounce more lights off the water, you could hardly even tell there was water out there, and what was the sense of hiding that? And despite the extraordinary variety, my land seemed unkempt. There were vines and Brazilian pepper and carrotwood, there were fire-ant mounds, rats surely lived in the fronds of the untrimmed palms. My acre looked a little hesitant, small and vulnerable, young. Even the banyan tree was relatively young. It had put down a few aerials but then stopped for a good decade as if it were thinking. . . . What's the use. I'm straddling Lots 29 & 30 and I'm not known as an accommodating tree. When the land gets sold, I'll be sold, too and will fall in screaming suttee. . . . Or sentiments of that sort.

As for the birds and animals, well, people didn't want raccoons and opossums and armadillos, and their cats would eat the baby rabbits. Too disgusting, but that's just the way nature was. And although I had cardinals and towhees and thrashers and mockingbirds and doves and woodpeckers, they did, too; as a matter of fact their cardinals were nesting in a place where they could actually see them, right near the front door, and that was getting to be quite the nuisance. As for the herons, you found them everywhere, even atop the dumpsters behind the 7-Eleven. Such beggars. You had to chase them away from your bait bucket when you were fishing from the beach. Did I fish in the lagoon? There were snapper in there, redfish, maybe even snook. I could get the mullet with nets. Why didn't I fish?

The years flowed past. Some of the properties on the lagoon fell to pure speculation. Mangroves were pruned like any hedging material; in some cases, decks were built over them, causing them to die, though they remained ghostily rooted. Landowners on the Gulf did not molest their mangrove. The lagoon to them was the equivalent of a back alley. Why would they want to regard the increasing myriad of houses huddled there? I traveled, I rented the place out, I returned. There were freezes, we were grazed by hurricanes. An immense mahoe hibiscus died back in a cold snap, and two years later a tall, slender, smooth-barked tree it had been concealing began producing hundreds of the pinkest, sweetest, juiciest grapefruit I have ever tasted. The water oaks that had reached their twenty-year limit rotted and fell. There were lovely woodpeckers. All through the winter in the nights the chuck-will's-widows would call.

That would drive me nuts, several of my acquaintances remarked.

The sound of construction was almost constant, but no one appeared to be actually living in the remodeled, enlarged, upgraded properties around me. I had cut out sections of my side fences to allow oak limbs to grow in their tortured specific manner, but my neighbor's yardmen would eventually be instructed to lop them off at the property line. This was, of course, the owner's right. There was the sound of trimmers, leaf blowers, pool pumps, pressure cleaners; the smell of chemicals from pest and lawn services. Maintenance maintenance maintenance. Then the county began cutting back the live oak limbs that extended over the bicycle path, even though one would have to be an idiot on a pogo stick to bump into one. Sliced sure as bread, the limbs, one at least five feet in diameter and green with resurrection fern and air plants, were cut back to the fence line.

15   It was then I decided to build the wall.

The year was 1990. The wall was of cement block with deep footers, and it ran the entire length of the property except for a twelve-foot opening, which was gated in cedar. It cost about $10,000, and two men did it in two months. The wall was ten feet high. It was not stuccoed. I thought it was splendid. I didn't know many people in the neighborhood by then, but word got back to me that some did not find it attractive. What did I have back there, a prison? To me, it was the people speeding past the baby Tajs on the animal-corpse-littered road who had become imprisoned. Inside was land—a mysterious, messy fountain of energy; outside was something else—not land in any meaningful sense but a diced bright salad of colorful real estate, pods of investment, its value now shrilly, sterilely economic.

Behind the wall was an Edenic acre, still known to the tax collector as Lots 27, 28, 29, 30, and 31. Untransformed by me, who was neither gardener nor crafty ecological restorer, the land had found its own rich dynamic. Behind the wall were neither grounds nor yard nor garden, nor park, nor even false jungle, but a functioning wild landscape that became more remarkable each year. Of course there was the humble house and even humbler cottage, which appeared less and less important to me in the larger order of things. They were shelters, pleasant enough but primarily places from which to look out at the beauty of a world to which I was irrelevant except for my role of preserving it, a world I could be integrated with only to the extent of my not harming it. The wildlife could hardly know that their world in that place existed only because I, rather than another, owned it. I knew, though, and the irrationality of the arrangement, the premise, angered me and made me feel powerless, for I did not feel that the land was mine at all but rather belonged to something larger that was being threatened by something absurdly small, the ill works and delusions of—as William Burroughs liked to say—homo sap.

Although the wall did not receive social approbation, its approval from an ecological point of view was resounding. The banyan, as though reassured by the audacious wall, flung down dozens of aerial roots. The understory flourished; the oaks soared, creating a great grave canopy. Plantings that had seemed tentative when I had bought them from botanical gardens years before took hold. The leaves and bark crumble built up, the ferns spread. It was odd. I fancied that I had made an inside for the outside to be safe in. From within, the wall vanished; green growth pressed against it, staining it naturally brown and green and black. It muffled the sound and heat of the road. Inside was cool and dappled, hymned with birdsong. There were owls and wood ducks. An osprey roosted each night in a casuarina that leaned out over the lagoon, a tree of no good reputation and half-dead, but the osprey deeply favored it, folding himself into it invisibly in a few seconds, each nightfall. A pair of yellow-crowned night herons nested in a slash pine in the center of Lot 30. Large birds with a large hidden nest, their young—each year three!— not hasty in their departure. A single acre was able to nurture so many lives, including mine. Its existence gave me great happiness.

And yet it was all an illusion too, a shadow box, for when I opened the gates or canoed the lagoon, I saw an utterly different world. This was a world that had fallen only in part to consortiums of developers; it had fallen mostly plat by plat to individuals, who, paradoxically, were quite conformist in their attitude toward land, or rather the scraped scaffolding upon which their real property was built. They lived in penury of a very special sort, but that was only my opinion. In their opinion they were living in perfect accord with the values of the time, successfully and cleverly, taking advantage of their advantages. Their attitudes were perfectly acceptable; they were not behaving unwisely or without foresight. They had maximized profits, and if little of nature had been preserved in the arrangement, well, nature was an adornment not to everyone's taste, a matter really of personal tolerance and sympathy. Besides, Nature was not far away, supported by everyone's tax dollars and preserved in state and federal parks. And one could show one's appreciation for these places by visiting them at any time. Public lands can be projected as having as many recreational, aesthetic, or environmental benefits as can be devised for them, but private land, on this skinny Florida key and almost everywhere in this country, is considered too economically valuable to be conserved. Despoliation of land in its many, many guises is the custom of the country. Privately, one by one, the landowner makes decisions that render land, in any other than financial terms, moot. Land is something to be "built out."

20   In contrast to its surrounds, my acre appeared an evasion of reality, a construct, a moment poised before an inevitable after. How lovely it was, how fortunate I was. Each day my heart recognized its great worth. It was invaluable to me. The moment came when I had to sell it.

Leopold speaks of the necessity of developing an ecological conscience, of having an awareness of land in a philosophical rather than an economic sense. His articulation of our ethical obligations to the land is considered by many to be quite admirable. We celebrated the fiftieth anniversary of this articulation (if not its implementation) in 1999. A pretty thought, high-minded. And yet when one has to move on (if not exactly in the final sense) one is expected to be sensible, realistic, even canny, about property. I was not in the comfortable kind of financial situation where I could deed my land to a conservation group or land trust. Even if I could have, it would probably have been sold to protect more considerable sanctuary acreage elsewhere, for it was a mere acre in a pricey neighborhood, not contiguous with additional habitat land, though the lagoon did provide a natural larger dimension. I had been developing an ecological conscience for thirty years, and I could continue to develop it still certainly, become a good steward somewhere else, because once I had decided to sell, this particular piece of land and all the creatures that found it to be a perfect earthly home would be subject to erasure in any meaningful ecological sense, and this would not be considered by society to be selfish, cruel, or irresponsible.

"Wow, it's great back here," the realtor said. "I often wondered what the heck was going on back here. I'm looking forward to showing this place."

I told him I wanted to sell the land as a single piece, with deed restrictions, these being that the land could never be subdivided; that the buildings be restricted to one house and cottage taking up no more land than the originals; and that the southern half of the property be left in its natural state as wildlife habitat.

"Nobody wants to be told what they can do with their land," he told me, frowning. "I'll mention your wishes, but you'll have to accept a significant reduction in price with those kinds of restrictions. When we get an offer you and the buyer can negotiate the wording of the agreement. I'm sure the type of person who would be attracted to this property wouldn't want to tear it all apart."

"Really," I said, "you don't think?"   25

I went through a number of realtors.

With a lawyer I drew up a simple and enforceable document that the realtors found so unnerving that they wouldn't show it right away to interested parties, preferring word wobble and expressions of goodwill. There were many people who loved the land, who loved nature, but would never buy anything that was in essence not free and clear. Or they had no problem with the restrictions personally, but when they had to sell (and Heaven forbid that they would right away of course) they could not impose such coercive restraints on others. The speculators and builders had been dismissed from the beginning. These were people of a more maverick bent, caring people who loved Florida, loved the key—wasn't it a shame there was so much development, so much change. When they saw the humble document they said 1) who does she think she is? 2) she's crazy, 3) she'll never sell it. Over the months the realtors took on a counseling manner with me as though I needed guidance through this dark stubborn wood of my own making, as though I needed to be talked down from my irrational fanciful resolve. They could sell the land for $200,000 more if I dropped the restrictions. My acre could be destroyed naturally; a hurricane could level everything, and the creatures, the birds, would have to go somewhere else anyway. With the money I'd make marketing it smartly, I could buy a hundred acres, maybe more, east of the interstate. There was a lot of pretty ranchland over there. I could conserve that. A lot of pressure would be on that land in a few years; I could do more by saving that. Sell and don't look back! That's what people did. You can't look back.

I'm not looking back, I said.

And I wasn't.

30   I was looking ahead, seeing the land behind the wall still existent, still supporting its nests and burrows—a living whole. I was leaving it—soon I would no longer be personally experiencing its loveliness—but I would not abandon it, I would despise myself if I did. If I were to be party to a normal real estate transaction, I would be dooming it, I would be—and this is not at all exaggerated—signing a warrant for its death. (Perhaps the owners of the four new houses that could—and would, most likely—be built would have the kindness to put out some birdseed.) I wanted more than money for my land, more than the mere memory of it, the luxury of conserving it falsely and sentimentally through lyrical recall. I wanted it to be.

It took eight months to find the right buyer. Leopold's "philosophers" were in short supply in the world of Florida real estate. But the ideal new owners eventually appeared, and they had no problem with the contract between themselves and the land. I had changed no hearts or minds by my attitude or actions; I had simply found—or my baffled but determined realtors had—people of my persuasion, people who had a land ethic, too. Their duties as stewards were not onerous to them. They did not consider the additional legal documents they were obliged to sign an insult to their personal freedom. They were aware that the principle was hardly radical. An aunt had done a similar thing in New England, preserving forty acres of meadow and woodland by conservation easement. They had friends in California who had similarly sold and conserved by deed four hundred acres of high desert. And here was this enchanted acre.

It had been accomplished. I had persisted. I was well pleased with myself. Selfishly I had affected the land beyond my tenure. I had gotten my way.

And with all of this, I am still allowed to miss it so.

2001

Discussion

1. What is the irony that Williams is striving to convey when she calls her backyard garden a Garden of Eden? Is it a garden at all?
2. What seems to be the point of Williams's antisocial, un-neighborly attitude? What does she gain? What does she lose?
3. Explain the symbolism of the white heron beating its head against a tree and compare Williams's use of the bird with Sarah Orne Jewett's "A White Heron" (p. 81).
4. Why do you think it took Williams so long to find a purchaser, or one of Aldo Leopold's so-called "philosophers"?

The Orbits of Earthly Bodies
REBECCA SOLNIT

Rebecca Solnit (1961–) is an essayist, art critic, and environmental activist. Her books include Savage Dreams: A Journey into the Landscape Wars of the American West *(1994),* A Book of Migrations: Some Passages in Ireland *(1997),* Wanderlust: A History of Walking *(2000),* Hollow City: The Siege of San Francisco and the Crisis of American Urbanism *(2000), As* Eve Said to the Serpent: On Landscape, Gender and Art *(2001), and* River of Shadows: Eadweard Muybridge and the Technological Wild West *(2003). Solnit's photography books include* Richard Misrach: The Sky Book *(2000) and* Extreme Horticulture *(with John Pfahl, 2003) She is a contributing writer for* Sierra, Orion, Art, Grand Street, *and* Creative Camera. *She lives in San Francisco.*

———————— ✦ ————————

I've spent a month or two of each of the past several summers at a friend's small house in rural New Mexico. Every year I'd come back to the city joking that I wasn't sure I was closer to nature, but I was definitely closer to my car. Really, it depends on how you define nature. In the country, there's more wildlife to be seen—though this place surrounded by cattle ranches was not so prolifically populated as many far more suburbanized places I know, where the deer come down and eat the tulips (or, even more thrillingly, the mountain lions eat the cocker spaniels).

Around the New Mexico house, coyotes sometimes howled at night, vultures, ravens, and swallows all had their appointed rites from dawn to dusk, and last summer a vivid violet bird I eventually pinned down as a male blue grosbeak arrived like a minor hallucination. Most of all, there was the changing light and sky. Without lifting my head from the pillow I could watch the summer sun rise in the northeast near where the constellation Cassiopeia made her regular nighttime appearance. I watched the transition from sunset to dusk every evening; the one time I went to a movie instead I sat there thinking, "I'm missing the show! I'm missing the show!" With views to the horizon and dark, dark nights, the sun, the moon, and the stars lived with me, or I with them, and with the lightning and wonderful cloud operas that passed by. That was glorious.

But my own life was strictly unnatural. Everything practical I did involved getting into a car, because there wasn't a newspaper, a stamp, or a bottle of milk for sale for many miles. It would have taken me a full day to walk to the nearest grocery store—and so I drove there, and to the houses of my friends, aunts, and uncles, to hikes in places less restrictive than the ranchlands, to everything. Out there in the little house on the car alarm-free prairie I had a great sense of cosmic time and a certain kind of slowing down—until it came time to hit the highway at seventy miles an hour, and that time came often.

Driving a whole hell of a lot is the unspoken foundation of most rural life in America, as well as a lot of wilderness adventuring (a backpack trip of a hundred miles begins with a single parking spot?). We talk about transportation as though the question is whether you drive a Yukon or a hybrid but the question could be whether you drive, and if so how often. I know people who really went back to the land, grew their own food, made staying home their business, ranchers whose work is really "out there," but most people who claim to be rural have just made the countryside into a suburb from which they commute to their real communities, jobs, research, and resources.

5   Ed Marston, publisher emeritus of the great environmental newspaper *High Country News*, once remarked that the West won't be destroyed by ranching, mining, or logging, but by ten-

acre ranchettes. And those ranchettes seem to preserve the frontier individualism of every-nuclear-unit-for-itself; they're generally antithetical to the ways community and density can consolidate resources. The urbanist Mike Davis talks of "public luxury"—of the shared libraries, pools, parks, transit of urban life—as the way to sustain a decent quality of life that's not predicated on global inequality.

The "new urbanism" could be a solution if it was really about public luxury and pedestrian space, not about dressing up suburbs like Disney's Main Street USA. The old urbanism was a solution before we really had a problem. Today, most of the United States is designed to make driving a necessity, turning those who don't or can't into shut-ins, dependents, and second-class citizens. As my own neighborhood went from working-class African American to middle-class white, it too has become much more car-dependent. A lot of people seem only to exit their houses to get into their cars, depriving themselves of the expansive sense of home pedestrian urbanism offers, or the democratic social space that's created by coexisting with strangers from, as they say, all *walks* of life. Watching this transformation taught me that urbanism and suburbia are as much the way you perceive and engage your time and space as where you live. And it made me wonder if New York City isn't, in a few key respects, the most natural and democratic space in America, one where stockbrokers and janitors daily coexist in the same space and much of the travel doesn't involve any machines whatsoever.

I've had the rare luxury of living, with rustic intermissions, in the heart of a genuine pedestrian-scale city since I was a teenager, and though the house by the creek might have been natural habitat for a blue grosbeak, the city might be mine. Scratch pedestrian-scale; call it human-scale, since humans are pedestrians when not fitted with vehicular prosthetics. In this cityscape, my body is not, as it is in the country, a housepet to be exercised with scenic walks to nowhere in particular, but a workhorse that carries books back to the library and produce home from the farmers' market.

And in this city with wild edges I can and do walk to the beach and the hilltops (from which I can see the peaks of five counties, and where blackberries, miner's lettuce, and a few other wild comestibles grow). Sometimes I think that the intermittent stroll of shopping, people-watching, and errand-running is a pleasantly degenerate form of hunting and gathering, that the city with its dangers and invitations and supplies is more like a primordial wilderness than a predator-free parkland where one leaves only footprints and takes only pictures.

Really, it's about how you define nature. I think we have tended to define nature as things to look at and think we're natural when we're looking at nature, however unnatural our own circumstances at the time. If you think of yourself as a species, the question of what your natural habitat is arises: it should be a place where you can forage, where your body is at home, where your scale is adequate, where your rites and sustenance are situated. And then, of course, cities host a kind of human biodiversity that delights me. San Francisco is not only one of the most multiethnic places in the world, but one of the most eclectic. The elderly Asian man in a rose-covered picture hat who strolled down my street one day rivaled the blue grosbeak when it comes to provoking amazement.

10   I love wilderness, wildlife, views straight to the horizon, dark nights, the Milky Way, and silence, though I love my large libraries and pedestrian practices too. I wish I could have it all, all the time. But we choose, and I think that if we changed the way we define nature and imagined our own bodies as part of it, we might more enthusiastically choose the places of public luxury and human scale, not as a sacrifice but as a kind of sanity. Besides which, I saw a golden eagle in Oakland the other day.

2003

Discussion

1. What is Solnit getting at when she says that every time she left the country and returned to the city, she was not sure that she was closer to nature or to her car?

2. Compare Solnit's feelings for big cities and their sources of energy with the argument that the cities are, in fact, saving the wilderness offered by Peter Huber in "How Cities Green the Planet" (p. 53).

3. Discuss the possible levels of meaning for Solnit's statement that New York City might be the most natural and democratic space in America.

Thinking and Writing About Chapter 3

1. If the forests that John Muir worships in "The American Forests" (p. 7) are symbolic of God's creation, what symbolic possibilities concerning American values do the heron and Sylvia suggest in Sarah Orne Jewett's "A White Heron" (p. 81)?
2. Discuss the difference, if any, of local people favoring the appropriation of private property, as described in Sue Hubbell's "Winter" (p. 90), and the same action by the government, as discussed in Margaret L. Knox's "The World According to Cushman" (p. 13).
3. How do Mary Austin in "My Neighbor's Field" (p. 13) and Joy Williams in "One Acre" (p. 95) view the land differently in their writing? Compare the two authors' attitudes toward land as a character in their writing.
4. The issue of human control of nature is very prevalent in Chapter 3, whether it be hunting a heron, damming a river, or attempting to maintain a piece of land as natural in an unnatural setting. If humans are part of nature, comment on the ethics of our influencing the state of nature to such an extent.
5. If you consider Rebecca Solnit's argument that urban areas are as natural as rural areas, discuss the place of suburbia in the spectrum between urban and rural. Include in your discussion the place of the shopping mall.
6. Do you think the idea of keeping parts of America natural through the system of national parks and state parks is wishful thinking? Is it possible to preserve any part of this country as really wild?
7. Describe some of the basic feelings you derive from spending time in a rural environment and an urban environment.
8. Discuss William's reliance on Aldo Leopold's "The Land Ethic" (p. 18) for support for her use of suburban lots.

Additional Resources

Film
The Lorax (1972), directed by Hawley Pratt

Fiction
Dr. Seuss. *The Lorax* (1971)
Leslie Marmon Silko. *Ceremony* (1977)
Dan O'Brien. "Eminent Domain: A Love Story." *Eminent Domain* (1987)

Essays
Mark Reisner. *Cadillac Dessert: The American West and Its Disappearing Waters* (1986)
James Galvin. *Meadow* (1992)

CHAPTER 4

The Human Price

Americans have long argued the value of government or corporate development of land and natural resources. Before the twentieth century, the argument was concerned with land issues alone, but by the late 1930s the intensification of industrial mechanization, improved science, and accumulation of wealth combined to set higher standards of living, especially in towns and cities. Environments were increasingly at risk. Industrial progress and economic expansion are all to the good for a burgeoning civilization, but in practice, rampant materialism had the unintended effect of separating Americans from the land. Henry David Thoreau had foreseen this in the 1840s, which led him to his cabin on Walden Pond. In his imagination he walked west to escape the materialism of the east. But it was through the persistent urging of conservationists and naturalists that land in the west became protected. In fact, it has only been in the years following 1872, when Yellowstone was established as our first national park, that the federal government has acted to protect land and natural resources from being transformed into fodder for progress. Concurrently, it has also supported the rise of multinational corporations and agribusinesses that disconnect people from strong attachments to land and a sense of place. Land itself, once an integral part of our agrarian social fabric, is now a commodity, from which people in cities are significantly disconnected. Economic and materialistic issues have so encroached on and so compromised human values that at present, a strong sense exists that unless something is done to reverse the current pattern, the imbalance will continue.

Rachel Carson decried a crucial aspect of this imbalance in "The Human Price" from her classic book, *Silent Spring* (1962), by

111

bringing to the surface the fear that environmental degradation had not stopped and, despite lobbying to the contrary, had advanced much further than imagined. It seemed that rivers and lakes everywhere were dying under the burden of chemical pollution. The air was becoming fouler with industrial smog. Carson raised the issue that insecticides and pesticides, destroying agricultural pests and wildlife alike, perhaps were also harming, if not killing, humans. Particularly, she sought to ban the use of DDT, which eventually occurred in 1973. In reaction to all the controversy, the U.S. Congress enacted legislation aimed at maintaining and improving the air, water, soil, and forests. From the mid-1960s through the 1970s, most of the major legislation affecting the environment, which still has profound importance, was set in place. Carson's arguments are, nevertheless, still under siege and have global implications since some agribusinesses and industries now advocate the use of DDT once again, this time in countries with emerging industrial development.

Michael Pollan discusses the loss of contact with the land in his examination of organic farming. In "Behind the Organic-Industrial Complex" (2001), he shows how a 1970s-era hippie, a believer in the idea of organic farming, has now been co-opted by agribusiness, in this case, organic agribusiness. Pollan is not putting us on when he points out the irony of an organic TV dinner. Although the original impetus behind organic farming was to provide consumers with an alternative to "plastic foods," the mechanization that now goes into processing so-called organically grown foods such as corn and broccoli defeats the concept of low-energy sustainability. Ironically, mega-food producers cling to the nostalgic image of the family farm that was long ago absorbed into its industrialism. Modern foods, Pollan explains, distort reality when agribusinesses embellish packages with illustrations of bucolic settings stocked with happy animals and smiling farmers. Pollan points out that the idealized vision and historical portrayal of our land are partly true, partly fiction, so it is a jolt to realize that the image of humanity and nature in harmony has long passed—or may not have ever existed. The pretty visuals of pastoral harmony that we encounter in advertising for food, automobiles, clothing, and cigarettes do not reflect reality.

The government is guilty of lying and deception, too. Terry Tempest Williams talks about her anger at government deception in "The Clan of One-Breasted Women" (1990). This piece describes how people living in the west were cautioned "your best action is not to be worried about fallout" from above-ground nuclear testing in Nevada. Later, they learned that the U.S. government knew of the real dangers but considered people in Utah "low-use segments of the population." It was not important to government bureaucrats that the environment had been poisoned, as well as the women in Williams's family, all of whom suffered from breast cancer and other maladies.

Because we are not yet accustomed to being deceived by those we want to, and are inclined to, trust, it is heartening to learn that not all corporations operate under the assumption that they can take without limit from the environment and give nothing back. Hoping to reverse its image as a polluter, British Petroleum (BP), the second largest oil company in the world, began an advertising campaign that showed how it is trying to change. But as Darcy Frey explains in "How Green Is BP?" (2002), this mega-conglomerate is caught in a dilemma of balancing its profits with environmental stability. BP's leadership claims that the company is ahead of the Kyoto Protocol (international convention on pollution that the United States has not agreed to sign) and is achieving reductions in pollutants that harm air and water. But Frey wonders if this change is real or partial hype. There is lingering distrust that a company, or any company with such a careless historical attitude toward the environment, would do an about-face. Just as we are engrained with nostalgia for the family farm, we hesitate to believe that a faceless corporation could care more about the land rather than the bottom line.

The Human Price

RACHEL CARSON

Rachel Carson (1907–1964) became an environmental hero when Silent Spring *(in which the following appeared) was published in 1962. As a professional biologist, Carson campaigned against the chemical control of nature and indiscriminate use of pesticides that were demonstrably degrading land, sea, sky, and life itself. She attributed her love of nature to her mother, who introduced her to the woods and streams when she was a child in rural Pennsylvania. Carson studied biology and did graduate work at Johns Hopkins University in Baltimore, Maryland, and the Woods Hole Oceanographic Institute in Massachusetts. After working as an aquatic biologist, she became a full-time writer and editor. Her book* The Sea Around Us *(1951) established her as a writer able to clearly*

explain the complexities of science. She got the idea for Silent
Spring *when friends wrote her a letter complaining that aerial
spraying was killing the wildlife around their home. After the book
was published, she said on a television show: "We still talk in terms
of conquest. We still haven't become mature enough to think of ourselves as only a tiny part of a vast and incredible universe." Carson's
other books include* Under Sea Wind *(1941) and* The Edge of the
Sea *(1955).*

━━━━━━━━━━━ ✦ ━━━━━━━━━━━

A s the tide of chemicals born of the Industrial Age has arisen to
engulf our environment, a drastic change has come about in
the nature of the most serious public health problems. Only yesterday mankind lived in fear of the scourges of smallpox, cholera,
and plague that once swept nations before them. Now our major
concern is no longer with the disease organisms that once were
omnipresent; sanitation, better living conditions, and new drugs
have given us a high degree of control over infectious disease.
Today we are concerned with a different kind of hazard that lurks
in our environment—a hazard we ourselves have introduced into
our world as our modern way of life has evolved.

The new environmental health problems are multiple—created by radiation in all its forms, born of the never-ending stream
of chemicals of which pesticides are a part, chemicals now per-
vading the world in which we live, acting upon us directly and indirectly, separately and collectively. Their presence casts a
shadow that is no less ominous because it is formless and obscure, no less frightening because it is simply impossible to pre-
dict the effects of lifetime exposure to chemical and physical
agents that are not part of the biological experience of man.

"We all live under the haunting fear that something may cor-
rupt the environment to the point where man joins the dinosaurs as
an obsolete form of life," says Dr. David Price of the United States
Public Health Service. "And what makes these thoughts all the
more disturbing is the knowledge that our fate could perhaps be
sealed twenty or more years before the development of symptoms."

Where do pesticides fit into the picture of environmental disease? We have seen that they now contaminate soil, water, and
food, that they have the power to make our streams fishless and
our gardens and woodlands silent and birdless. Man, however
much he may like to pretend the contrary, is part of nature. Can
he escape a pollution that is now so thoroughly distributed
throughout our world?

We know that even single exposures to these chemicals, if the   5
amount is large enough, can precipitate acute poisoning. But this
is not the major problem. The sudden illness or death of farmers,
spraymen, pilots, and others exposed to appreciable quantities of
pesticides are tragic and should not occur. For the population as a
whole, we must be more concerned with the delayed effects of ab-
sorbing small amounts of the pesticides that invisibly contaminate our world.

Responsible public health officials have pointed out that the
biological effects of chemicals are cumulative over long periods
of time, and that the hazard to the individual may depend on the
sum of exposures received throughout his lifetime. For these very
reasons the danger is easily ignored. It is human nature to shrug
off what may seem to us a vague threat of future disaster. "Men
are naturally most impressed by diseases which have obvious
manifestations," says a wise physician, Dr. René Dubos, "yet some
of their worst enemies creep on them unobtrusively."

For each of us, as for the robin in Michigan or the salmon in
the Miramichi, this is a problem of ecology, of interrelationships,
of interdependence. We poison the caddis flies in a stream and
the salmon runs dwindle and die. We poison the gnats in a lake
and the poison travels from link to link of the food chain and
soon the birds of the lake margins become its victims. We spray
our elms and the following springs are silent of robin song, not
because we sprayed the robins directly but because the poison
traveled, step by step, through the now familiar elm leaf–earth-
worm–robin cycle. These are matters of record, observable, part
of the visible world around us. They reflect the web of life—or
death—that scientists know as ecology.

But there is also an ecology of the world within our bodies. In
this unseen world minute causes produce mighty effects; the effect,
moreover, is often seemingly unrelated to the cause, appearing in a
part of the body remote from the area where the original injury was
sustained. "A change at one point, in one molecule even, may rever-
berate throughout the entire system to initiate changes in seemingly unrelated organs and tissues," says a recent summary of the
present status of medical research. When one is concerned with the
mysterious and wonderful functioning of the human body, cause
and effect are seldom simple and easily demonstrated relationships. They may be widely separated both in space and time. To
discover the agent of disease and death depends on a patient piec-
ing together of many seemingly distinct and unrelated facts developed through a vast amount of research in widely separated fields.

We are accustomed to look for the gross and immediate effect and to ignore all else. Unless this appears promptly and in such obvious form that it cannot be ignored, we deny the existence of hazard. Even research men suffer from the handicap of inadequate methods of detecting the beginnings of injury. The lack of sufficiently delicate methods to detect injury before symptoms appear is one of the great unsolved problems in medicine.

10   "But," someone will object, "I have used dieldrin sprays on the lawn many times but I have never had convulsions like the World Health Organization spraymen—so it hasn't harmed me." It is not that simple. Despite the absence of sudden and dramatic symptoms, one who handles such materials is unquestionably storing up toxic materials in his body. Storage of the chlorinated hydrocarbons, as we have seen, is cumulative, beginning with the smallest intake. The toxic materials become lodged in all the fatty tissues of the body. When these reserves of fat are drawn upon the poison may then strike quickly. A New Zealand medical journal recently provided an example. A man under treatment for obesity suddenly developed symptoms of poisoning. On examination his fat was found to contain stored dieldrin, which had been metabolized as he lost weight. The same thing could happen with loss of weight in illness.

The results of storage, on the other hand, could be even less obvious. Several years ago the *Journal of the American Medical Association* warned strongly of the hazards of insecticide storage in adipose tissue, pointing out that drugs or chemicals that are cumulative require greater caution than those having no tendency to be stored in the tissues. The adipose tissue, we are warned, is not merely a place for the deposition of fat (which makes up about 18 per cent of the body weight), but has many important functions with which the stored poisons may interfere. Furthermore, fats are very widely distributed in the organs and tissues of the whole body, even being constituents of cell membranes. It is important to remember, therefore, that the fat-soluble insecticides become stored in individual cells, where they are in position to interfere with the most vital and necessary functions of oxidation and energy production. . . .

One of the most significant facts about the chlorinated hydrocarbon insecticides is their effect on the liver. Of all organs in the body the liver is most extraordinary. In its versatility and in the indispensable nature of its functions it has no equal. It presides over so many vital activities that even the slightest damage to it is fraught with serious consequences. Not only does it provide bile for the digestion of fats, but because of its location and the special circulatory pathways that converge upon it the liver receives blood directly from the digestive tract and is deeply involved in the metabolism of all the principal foodstuffs. It stores sugar in the form of glycogen and releases it as glucose in carefully measured quantities to keep the blood sugar at a normal level. It builds body proteins, including some essential elements of blood plasma concerned with blood-clotting. It maintains cholesterol at its proper level in the blood plasma, and inactivates the male and female hormones when they reach excessive levels. It is a storehouse of many vitamins, some of which in turn contribute to its own proper functioning.

Without a normally functioning liver the body would be disarmed—defenseless against the great variety of poisons that continually invade it. Some of these are normal by-products of metabolism, which the liver swiftly and efficiently makes harmless by withdrawing their nitrogen. But poisons that have no normal place in the body may also be detoxified. The "harmless" insecticides malathion and methoxychlor are less poisonous than their relatives only because a liver enzyme deals with them, altering their molecules in such a way that their capacity for harm is lessened. In similar ways the liver deals with the majority of the toxic materials to which we are exposed.

Our line of defense against invading poisons or poisons from within is now weakened and crumbling. A liver damaged by pesticides is not only incapable of protecting us from poisons, the whole wide range of its activities may be interfered with. Not only are the consequences far-reaching, but because of their variety and the fact that they may not immediately appear they may not be attributed to their true cause.

In connection with the nearly universal use of insecticides 15 that are liver poisons, it is interesting to note the sharp rise in hepatitis that began during the 1950's and is continuing a fluctuating climb. Cirrhosis also is said to be increasing. While it is admittedly difficult, in dealing with human beings rather than laboratory animals, to "prove" that cause A produces effect B, plain common sense suggests that the relation between a soaring rate of liver disease and the prevalence of liver poisons in the environment is no coincidence. Whether or not the chlorinated hydrocarbons are the primary cause, it seems hardly sensible under the circumstances to expose ourselves to poisons that have a proven ability to damage the liver and so presumably to make it less resistant to disease.

Both major types of insecticides, the chlorinated hydrocarbons and the organic phosphates, directly affect the nervous system, although in somewhat different ways. This has been made clear by an infinite number of experiments on animals and by observations on human subjects as well. As for DDT, the first of the new organic insecticides to be widely used, its action is primarily on the central nervous system of man; the cerebellum and the higher motor cortex are thought to be the areas chiefly affected. Abnormal sensations as of prickling, burning, or itching, as well as tremors or even convulsions may follow exposure to appreciable amounts, according to a standard textbook of toxicology.

Our first knowledge of the symptoms of acute poisoning by DDT was furnished by several British investigators, who deliberately exposed themselves in order to learn the consequences. Two scientists at the British Royal Navy Physiological Laboratory invited absorption of DDT through the skin by direct contact with walls covered with a water-soluble paint containing 2 per cent DDT, overlaid with a thin film of oil. The direct effect on the nervous system is apparent in their eloquent description of their symptoms: "The tiredness, heaviness, and aching of limbs were very real things, and the mental state was also most distressing . . . [there was] extreme irritability . . . great distaste for work of any sort . . . a feeling of mental incompetence in tackling the simplest mental task. The joint pains were quite violent at times."

Another British experimenter who applied DDT in acetone solution to his skin reported heaviness and aching of limbs, muscular weakness, and "spasms of extreme nervous tension." He took a holiday and improved, but on return to work his condition deteriorated. He then spent three weeks in bed, made miserable by constant aching in limbs, insomnia, nervous tension, and feelings of acute anxiety. On occasion tremors shook his whole body—tremors of the sort now made all too familiar by the sight of birds poisoned by DDT. The experimenter lost 10 weeks from his work, and at the end of a year, when his case was reported in a British medical journal, recovery was not complete.

(Despite this evidence, several American investigators conducting an experiment with DDT on volunteer subjects dismissed the complaint of headache and "pain in every bone" as "obviously of psychoneurotic origin.")

20   There are now many cases on record in which both the symptoms and the whole course of the illness point to insecticides as the cause. Typically, such a victim has had a known exposure to one of the insecticides, his symptoms have subsided under treat-

ment which included the exclusion of all insecticides from his environment, and most significantly *have returned with each renewed contact* with the offending chemicals. This sort of evidence—and no more—forms the basis of a vast amount of medical therapy in many other disorders. There is no reason why it should not serve as a warning that it is no longer sensible to take the "calculated risk" of saturating our environment with pesticides.

Why does not everyone handling and using insecticides develop the same symptoms? Here the matter of individual sensitivity enters in. There is some evidence that women are more susceptible than men, the very young more than adults, those who lead sedentary, indoor lives more than those leading a rugged life of work or exercise in the open. Beyond these differences are others that are no less real because they are intangible. What makes one person allergic to dust or pollen, sensitive to a poison, or susceptible to an infection whereas another is not is a medical mystery for which there is at present no explanation. The problem nevertheless exists and it affects significant numbers of the population. Some physicians estimate that a third or more of their patients show signs of some form of sensitivity, and that the number is growing. And unfortunately, sensitivity may suddenly develop in a person previously insensitive. In fact, some medical men believe that intermittent exposures to chemicals may produce just such sensitivity. If this is true, it may explain why some studies on men subjected to continuous occupational exposure find little evidence of toxic effects. By their constant contact with the chemicals these men keep themselves desensitized—as an allergist keeps his patients desensitized by repeated small injections of the allergen.

The whole problem of pesticide poisoning is enormously complicated by the fact that a human being, unlike a laboratory animal living under rigidly controlled conditions, is never exposed to one chemical alone. Between the major groups of insecticides, and between them and other chemicals, there are interactions that have serious potentials. Whether released into soil or water or a man's blood, these unrelated chemicals do not remain segregated; there are mysterious and unseen changes by which one alters the power of another for harm.

There is interaction even between the two major groups of insecticides usually thought to be completely distinct in their action. The power of the organic phosphates, those poisoners of the nerve-protective enzyme cholinesterase, may become greater if the body has first been exposed to a chlorinated hydrocarbon which injures the liver. This is because, when liver function is disturbed, the cholinesterase level drops below normal. The added depressive effect of the organic phosphate may then be enough to precipitate acute symptoms. And as we have seen, pairs of the organic phosphates themselves may interact in such a way as to increase their toxicity a hundredfold. Or the organic phosphates may interact with various drugs, or with synthetic materials, food additives—who can say what else of the infinite number of man-made substances that now pervade our world?

The effect of a chemical of supposedly innocuous nature can be drastically changed by the action of another; one of the best examples is a close relative of DDT called methoxychlor. (Actually, methoxychlor may not be as free from dangerous qualities as it is generally said to be, for recent work on experimental animals shows a direct action on the uterus and a blocking effect on some of the powerful pituitary hormones—reminding us again that these are chemicals with enormous biologic effect. Other work shows that methoxychlor has a potential ability to damage the kidneys.) Because it is not stored to any great extent when given alone, we are told that methoxychlor is a safe chemical. But this is not necessarily true. If the liver has been damaged by another agent, methoxychlor is stored in the body at *100 times* its normal rate, and will then imitate the effects of DDT with long-lasting effects on the nervous system. Yet the liver damage that brings this about might be so slight as to pass unnoticed. It might have been the result of any of a number of commonplace situations—using another insecticide, using a cleaning fluid containing carbon tetrachloride, or taking one of the so-called tranquilizing drugs, a number (but not all) of which are chlorinated hydrocarbons and possess power to damage the liver.

25   Damage to the nervous system is not confined to acute poisoning; there may also be delayed effects from exposure. Long-lasting damage to brain or nerves has been reported for methoxychlor and others. Dieldrin, besides its immediate consequences, can have long delayed effects ranging from "loss of memory, insomnia, and nightmares to mania." Lindane, according to medical findings, is stored in significant amounts in the brain and functioning liver tissue and may induce "profound and long-lasting effects on the central nervous system." Yet this chemical, a form of benzene hexachloride, is much used in vaporizers, devices that pour a stream of volatilized insecticide vapor into homes, offices, restaurants.

The organic phosphates, usually considered only in relation to their more violent manifestations in acute poisoning, also have the power to produce lasting physical damage to ne and, according to recent findings, to induce mental dis— Various cases of delayed paralysis have followed use of one or another of these insecticides. A bizarre happening in the United States during the prohibition era about 1930 was an omen of things to come. It was caused not by an insecticide but by a substance belonging chemically to the same group as the organic phosphate insecticides. During that period some medicinal substances were being pressed into service as substitutes for liquor, being exempt from the prohibition law. One of these was Jamaica ginger. But the *United States Pharmacopeia* product was expensive, and boot-leggers conceived the idea of making a substitute Jamaica ginger. They succeeded so well that their spurious product responded to the appropriate chemical tests and deceived the government chemists. To give their false ginger the necessary tang they had introduced a chemical known as triorthocresyl phosphate. This chemical, like parathion and its relatives, destroys the protective enzyme cholinesterase. As a consequence of drinking the bootleggers' product some 15,000 people developed a permanently crippling type of paralysis of the leg muscles, a condition now called "ginger paralysis." The paralysis was accompanied by destruction of the nerve sheaths and by degeneration of the cells of the anterior horns of the spinal cord.

About two decades later various other organic phosphates came into use as insecticides, as we have seen, and soon cases reminiscent of the ginger paralysis episode began to occur. One was a greenhouse worker in Germany who became paralyzed several months after experiencing mild symptoms of poisoning on a few occasions after using parathion. Then a group of three chemical plant workers developed acute poisoning from exposure to other insecticides of this group. They recovered under treatment, but ten days later two of them developed muscular weakness in the legs. This persisted for 10 months in one; the other, a young woman chemist, was more severely affected, with paralysis in both legs and some involvement of the hands and arms. Two years later when her case was reported in a medical journal she was still unable to walk.

The insecticide responsible for these cases has been withdrawn from the market, but some of those now in use may be capable of like harm. Malathion (beloved of gardeners) has induced severe muscular weakness in experiments on chickens. This was attended (as in ginger paralysis) by destruction of the sheaths of the sciatic and spinal nerves.

All these consequences of organic phosphate poisoning, if survived, may be a prelude to worse. In view of the severe damage they inflict upon the nervous system, it was perhaps inevitable that these insecticides would eventually be linked with mental disease. That link has recently been supplied by investigators at the University of Melbourne and Prince Henry's Hospital in Melbourne, who reported on 16 cases of mental disease. All had a history of prolonged exposure to organic phosphorus insecticides. Three were scientists checking the efficacy of sprays; 8 worked in greenhouses; 5 were farm workers. Their symptoms ranged from impairment of memory to schizophrenic and depressive reactions. All had normal medical histories before the chemicals they were using boomeranged and struck them down.

30   Echoes of this sort of thing are to be found, as we have seen, widely scattered throughout medical literature, sometimes involving the chlorinated hydrocarbons, sometimes the organic phosphates. Confusion, delusions, loss of memory, mania—a heavy price to pay for the temporary destruction of a few insects, but a price that will continue to be exacted as long as we insist upon using chemicals that strike directly at the nervous system.

1962

Discussion

1. According to Carson, what is the human price for the indiscriminate use of insecticides?
2. What is Carson suggesting when she places human beings in the order of the natural world?
3. Why does Carson separate natural ecology from inner ecology?
4. In what ways does Carson challenge our usual thinking about how we determine the notion of cause and effect on the natural environment?

The Clan of One-Breasted Women
TERRY TEMPEST WILLIAMS

Terry Tempest Williams (1955–) is a feminist and critic of environmental pollution and its consequences. In "The Clan of One-Breasted Women" (1990), she has chronicled the women in her family who have suffered from cancer, the probable result of the ra-

diation fall-out that drifted over their homes in the Salt Lake region of Utah. Williams comes to her environmental advocacy through personal experience: The family's pipe-laying construction business has both improved and degraded the landscape of Utah; and her family has suffered from the federal government's atomic bomb testing. Despite this conflict, Williams espouses the Mormon land ethic, which believes that natural wonders are the work of God. For many years, she was the naturalist-in-residence at the Utah Museum of Natural History in Salt Lake City. Williams's works include Pieces of White Shell: A Journey to Navajoland *(1984),* Coyote's Canyon *(1989),* Earthly Messengers *(1989),* Refuge: An Unnatural History of Family and Place *(1991),* An Unspoken Hunger: Stories from the Field *(1994),* Desert Quartet: An Erotic Landscape *(1994),* The New Genesis: A Mormon Reader on Land and Community *(1998),* Leap *(2000), and* Red: Passion and Patience in the Desert *(2001). Her essays have appeared in* The New Yorker, The Nation, Outside, Audubon, Orion, The Iowa Review, *and* The New England Review.

--------------------------- ✦ ---------------------------

I belong to a Clan of One-Breasted Women. My mother, my grandmothers, and six aunts have all had mastectomies. Seven are dead. The two who survive have just completed rounds of chemotherapy and radiation.

I've had my own problems: two biopsies for breast cancer and a small tumor between my ribs diagnosed as a "borderline malignancy."

This is my family history.

Most statistics tell us breast cancer is genetic, hereditary, with rising percentages attached to fatty diets, childlessness, or becoming pregnant after thirty. What they don't say is living in Utah may be the greatest hazard of all.

We are a Mormon family with roots in Utah since 1847. The 5 "word of wisdom" in my family aligned us with good foods—no coffee, no tea, tobacco, or alcohol. For the most part, our women were finished having their babies by the time they were thirty. And only one faced breast cancer prior to 1960. Traditionally, as a group of people, Mormons have a low rate of cancer.

Is our family a cultural anomaly? The truth is, we didn't think about it. Those who did, usually the men, simply said, "bad genes." The women's attitude was stoic. Cancer was part of life. On February 16, 1971, the eve of my mother's surgery, I accidently picked up the telephone and overheard her ask my grandmother what she could expect.

"Diane, it is one of the most spiritual experiences you will ever encounter."

I quietly put down the receiver.

Two days later, my father took my brothers and me to the hospital to visit her. She met us in the lobby in a wheelchair. No bandages were visible. I'll never forget her radiance, the way she held herself in a purple velvet robe, and how she gathered us around her.

10   "Children, I am fine. I want you to know I felt the arms of God around me."

We believed her. My father cried. Our mother, his wife, was thirty-eight years old.

A little over a year after Mother's death, Dad and I were having dinner together. He had just returned from St. George, where the Tempest Company was completing the gas lines that would service southern Utah. He spoke of his love for the country, the sandstoned landscape, bare-boned and beautiful. He had just finished hiking the Kolob trail in Zion National Park. We got caught up in reminiscing, recalling with fondness our walk up Angel's Landing on his fiftieth birthday and the years our family had vacationed there.

Over dessert, I shared a recurring dream of mine. I told my father that for years, as long as I could remember, I saw this flash of light in the night in the desert—that this image had so permeated my being that I could not venture south without seeing it again, on the horizon, illuminating buttes and mesas.

"You did see it," he said.

15   "Saw what?"

"The bomb. The cloud. We were driving home from Riverside, California. You were sitting on Diane's lap. She was pregnant. In fact, I remember the day, September 7, 1957. We had just gotten out of the Service. We were driving north, past Las Vegas. It was an hour or so before dawn, when this explosion went off. We not only heard it, but felt it. I thought the oil tanker in front of us had blown up. We pulled over and suddenly, rising from the desert floor, we saw it, clearly, this golden-stemmed cloud, the mushroom. The sky seemed to vibrate with an eerie pink glow. Within a few minutes, a light ash was raining on the car."

I stared at my father.

"I thought you knew that," he said. "It was a common occurrence in the fifties."

It was at this moment that I realized the deceit I had been living under. Children growing up in the American Southwest, drinking contaminated milk from contaminated cows, even from the contaminated breasts of their mothers, my mother—members, years later, of the Clan of One-Breasted Women.

It is a well-known story in the Desert West, "The Day We   20
Bombed Utah," or more accurately, the years we bombed Utah: above ground atomic testing in Nevada took place from January 27, 1951, through July 11, 1962. Not only were the winds blowing north covering "low-use segments of the population" with fallout and leaving sheep dead in their tracks, but the climate was right. The United States of the 1950s was red, white, and blue. The Korean War was raging. McCarthyism was rampant. Ike was it, and the cold war was hot. If you were against nuclear testing, you were for a communist regime.

Much has been written about this "American nuclear tragedy." Public health was secondary to national security. The Atomic Energy Commissioner, Thomas Murray, said, "Gentlemen, we must not let anything interfere with this series of tests, nothing."

Again and again, the American public was told by its government, in spite of burns, blisters, and nausea, "It has been found that the tests may be conducted with adequate assurance of safety under conditions prevailing at the bombing reservations." Assuaging public fears was simply a matter of public relations. "Your best action," an Atomic Energy Commission booklet read, "is not to be worried about fallout." A news release typical of the times stated, "We find no basis for concluding that harm to any individual has resulted from radioactive fallout."

On August 30, 1979, during Jimmy Carter's presidency, a suit was filed, *Irene Allen v. The United States of America*. Mrs. Allen's case was the first on an alphabetical list of twenty-four test cases, representative of nearly twelve hundred plaintiffs seeking compensation from the United States government for cancers caused by nuclear testing in Nevada.

Irene Allen lived in Hurricane, Utah. She was the mother of five children and had been widowed twice. Her first husband, with their two oldest boys, had watched the tests from the roof of the local high school. He died of leukemia in 1956. Her second husband died of pancreatic cancer in 1978.

In a town meeting conducted by Utah Senator Orrin Hatch,   25
shortly before the suit was filed, Mrs. Allen said, "I am not blaming the government, I want you to know that, Senator Hatch. But

I thought if my testimony could help in any way so this wouldn't happen again to any of the generations coming up after us . . . I am happy to be here this day to bear testimony of this."

God-fearing people. This is just one story in an anthology of thousands.

On May 10, 1984, Judge Bruce S. Jenkins handed down his opinion. Ten of the plaintiffs were awarded damages. It was the first time a federal court had determined that nuclear tests had been the cause of cancers. For the remaining fourteen test cases, the proof of causation was not sufficient. In spite of the split decision, it was considered a landmark ruling. It was not to remain so for long.

In April, 1987, the Tenth Circuit Court of Appeals overturned Judge Jenkins's ruling on the ground that the United States was protected from suit by the legal doctrine of sovereign immunity, a centuries-old idea from England in the days of absolute monarchs.

In January, 1988, the Supreme Court refused to review the Appeals Court decision. To our court system it does not matter whether the United States government was irresponsible, whether it lied to its citizens, or even that citizens died from the fallout of nuclear testing. What matters is that our government is immune: "The King can do no wrong."

30   In Mormon culture, authority is respected, obedience is revered, and independent thinking is not. I was taught as a young girl not to "make waves" or "rock the boat."

"Just let it go," Mother would say. "You know how you feel, that's what counts."

For many years, I have done just that—listened, observed, and quietly formed my own opinions, in a culture that rarely asks questions because it has all the answers. But one by one, I have watched the women in my family die common, heroic deaths. We sat in waiting rooms hoping for good news, but always receiving the bad. I cared for them, bathed their scarred bodies, and kept their secrets. I watched beautiful women become bald as Cytoxan, cisplatin, and Adriamycin were injected into their veins. I held their foreheads as they vomited green-black bile, and I shot them with morphine when the pain became inhuman. In the end, I witnessed their last peaceful breaths, becoming a midwife to the rebirth of their souls.

The price of obedience has become too high.

The fear and inability to question authority that ultimately killed rural communities in Utah during atmospheric testing of atomic weapons is the same fear I saw in my mother's body. Sheep. Dead sheep. The evidence is buried.

I cannot prove that my mother, Diane Dixon Tempest, or my   35
grandmothers, Lettie Romney Dixon and Kathryn Blackett
Tempest, along with my aunts developed cancer from nuclear
fallout in Utah. But I can't prove they didn't.
My father's memory was correct. The September blast we
drove through in 1957 was part of Operation Plumbbob, one of
the most intensive series of bomb tests to be initiated. The flash
of light in the night in the desert, which I had always thought was
a dream, developed into a family nightmare. It took fourteen
years, from 1957 to 1971, for cancer to manifest in my mother—
the same time, Howard L. Andrews, an authority in radioactive
fallout at the National Institute of Health, says radiation cancer
requires to become evident. The more I learn about what it means
to be a "downwinder," the more questions I drown in.
What I do know, however, is that as a Mormon woman of the
fifth generation of Latter-day Saints, I must question everything,
even if it means losing my faith, even if it means becoming a member of a border tribe among my own people. Tolerating blind obedience in the name of patriotism or religion ultimately takes our lives.
When the Atomic Energy Commission described the country
north of the Nevada Test Site as "virtually uninhabited desert terrain," my family and the birds at Great Salt Lake were some of
the "virtual uninhabitants."

One night, I dreamed women from all over the world circled
a blazing fire in the desert. They spoke of change, how they hold
the moon in their bellies and wax and wane with its phases. They
mocked the presumption of even-tempered beings and made
promises that they would never fear the witch inside themselves.
The women danced wildly as sparks broke away from the flames
and entered the night sky as stars.
And they sang a song given to them by Shoshone grandmothers: 40

Ah ne nah, nah	Consider the rabbits
nin nah nah—	How gently they walk on the earth—
ah ne nah, nah	Consider the rabbits
nin nah nah—	How gently they walk on the earth—
Nyaga mutzi	We remember them
oh ne nay—	We can walk gently also—
Nyaga mutzi	We remember them
oh ne nay—	We can walk gently also—

The women danced and drummed and sang for weeks, preparing
themselves for what was to come. They would reclaim the desert
for the sake of their children, for the sake of the land.

A few miles downwind from the fire circle, bombs were being tested. Rabbits felt the tremors. Their soft leather pads on paws and feet recognized the shaking sands, while the roots of mesquite and sage were smoldering. Rocks were hot from the inside out and dust devils hummed unnaturally. And each time there was another nuclear test, ravens watched the desert heave. Stretch marks appeared. The land was losing its muscle.

The women couldn't bear it any longer. They were mothers. They had suffered labor pains but always under the promise of birth. The red hot pains beneath the desert promised death only, as each bomb became a stillborn. A contract had been made and broken between human beings and the land. A new contract was being drawn by the women, who understood the fate of the earth as their own.

Under the cover of darkness, ten women slipped under a barbed-wire fence and entered the contaminated country. They were trespassing. They walked toward the town of Mercury, in moonlight, taking their cues from coyote, kit fox, antelope squirrel, and quail. They moved quietly and deliberately through the maze of Joshua trees. When a hint of daylight appeared they rested, drinking tea and sharing their rations of food. The women closed their eyes. The time had come to protest with the heart, that to deny one's genealogy with the earth was to commit treason against one's soul.

At dawn, the women draped themselves in mylar, wrapping long streamers of silver plastic around their arms to blow in the breeze. They wore clear masks, that became the faces of humanity. And when they arrived at the edge of Mercury, they carried all the butterflies of a summer day in their wombs. They paused to allow their courage to settle.

45   The town that forbids pregnant women and children to enter because of radiation risks was asleep. The women moved through the streets as winged messengers, twirling around each other in slow motion, peeking inside homes and watching the easy sleep of men and women. They were astonished by such stillness and periodically would utter a shrill note or low cry just to verify life.

The residents finally awoke to these strange apparitions. Some simply stared. Others called authorities, and in time, the women were apprehended by wary soldiers dressed in desert fatigues. They were taken to a white, square building on the other edge of Mercury. When asked who they were and why they were there, the women replied, "We are mothers and we have come to reclaim the desert for our children."

The soldiers arrested them. As the ten women were blind-folded and handcuffed, they began singing:

You can't forbid us everything
You can't forbid us to think—
You can't forbid our tears to flow
And you can't stop the songs that we sing

The women continued to sing louder and louder, until they heard the voices of their sisters moving across the mesa:

Ah ne nah, nah
nin nah nah—
Ah ne nah, nah
nin nah nah—
Nyaga mutzi
oh ne nay—
Nyaga mutzi
oh ne nay—

"Call for reinforcements," one soldier said.

"We have," interrupted one woman, "we have—and you have no idea of our numbers."

I crossed the line at the Nevada Test Site and was arrested with nine other Utahns for trespassing on military lands. They are still conducting nuclear tests in the desert. Ours was an act of civil disobedience. But as I walked toward the town of Mercury, it was more than a gesture of peace. It was a gesture on behalf of the Clan of One-Breasted Women.

As one officer cinched the handcuffs around my wrists, an-   50
other frisked my body. She did not find my scars.

We were booked under an afternoon sun and bused to Tonopah, Nevada. It was a two-hour ride. This was familiar country. The Joshua trees standing their ground had been named by my ancestors, who believed they looked like prophets pointing west to the Promised Land. These were the same trees that bloomed each spring, flowers appearing like white flames in the Mojave. And I recalled a full moon in May, when Mother and I had walked among them, flushing out mourning doves and owls.

The bus stopped short of town. We were released.

The officials thought it was a cruel joke to leave us stranded in the desert with no way to get home. What they didn't realize was that we were home, soul-centered and strong, women who recognized the sweet smell of sage as fuel for our spirits.

1990

Discussion

1. How does Williams defend her criticism of federal arguments for national defense and public safety?
2. Although Williams is arguing that the federal government's atomic bomb testing has killed people, what environmental issues does she raise?
3. Explain what Williams is suggesting when she says that according to the Atomic Energy Commission, her family and the birds at Great Salt Lake had become "virtual uninhabitants."
4. What is Williams's argument against the social barriers that keep women from speaking out on environmental issues such as this one?

Behind the Organic-Industrial Complex
MICHAEL POLLAN

Michael Pollan (1955–) was raised in suburban Long Island, New York. *He was educated at Bennington College, Vermont, and at Columbia University in New York City, where he studied English literature. Pollan is recognized as a journalist who approaches complex environmental, scientific, and health issues with a personal slant to which a reader can respond. Pollan is a contributing writer to* The New York Times Magazine, *is a columnist for* House & Garden, *and was executive editor of* Harper's. *His books include* Second Nature: A Gardener's Education *(1995),* A Place of My Own: The Education of an Amateur Builder *(1998),* Tulipa: A Photographer's Botanical *(1999), and* The Botany of Desire: A Plant's-Eye View of the World *(2001).*

──────────── ✦ ────────────

I. SUPERMARKET PASTORAL

Almost overnight, the amount and variety of organic food on offer in my local supermarket has mushroomed. Fresh produce, milk, eggs, cereal, frozen food, even junk food—all of it now has its own organic doppelgänger, and more often than not these products wind up in my shopping cart. I like buying organic, for the usual salad of rational and sentimental reasons. At a time when the whole food system feels somewhat precarious, I assume that a product labeled organic is more healthful and safer, more "wholesome," though if I stop to think about it, I'm not exactly sure what that means. I also like the fact that by buying organic, I'm casting a vote for a more environmentally friendly kind of agriculture: "Better Food for a Better Planet," in the slogan of Cascadian Farm, one of the older organic brands. Compared with all the other food in the supermarket, which is happy to tell you everything about itself except how it was grown, organic food seems a lot more legible. "Organic" on the label conjures a whole story, even if it is the consumer who fills in most of the details, supplying the hero (American Family Farmer), the villain (Agribusinessman) and the literary genre, which I think of as "supermarket pastoral." Just look at the happy Vermont cow on that carton of milk, wreathed in wildflowers like a hippie at her wedding around 1973.

Look a little closer, though, and you begin to see cracks in the pastoral narrative. It took me more than a year to notice, but the label on that carton of Organic Cow has been rewritten recently. It doesn't talk about happy cows and Vermont family farmers quite so much anymore, probably because the Organic Cow has been bought out by Horizon, a Colorado company (referred to here, in proper pastoral style, as "the Horizon family of companies"). Horizon is a $127 million public corporation that has become the Microsoft of organic milk, controlling 70 percent of the retail market. Notice, too, that the milk is now "ultrapasteurized," a process the carton presents as a boon to the consumer (it pushes the freshness date into the next millennium), but which of course also allows the company to ferry its milk all over the country.

When I asked a local dairyman about this (we still have one or two in town) he said that the chief reason to ultrapasteurize—a high-heat process that "kills the milk," destroying its enzymes and many of its vitamins—is so you can sell milk over long distances. Arguably, ultrapasteurized organic milk is *less* nutritious than conventionally pasteurized conventional milk. This dairyman also bent my ear about Horizon's "factory farms" out West, where thousands of cows that never encounter a blade of grass spend their days confined to a fenced dry lot, eating (certified organic) grain and tethered to milking machines three times a day. So maybe Organic Cow milk isn't quite as legible a product as I thought.

I wasn't sure if the farmer had his facts straight (it would turn out he did), but he made me wonder whether I really knew what organic meant anymore. I understood organic to mean—in addition to being produced without synthetic chemicals—less processed, more local, easier on the animals. So I started looking more closely at some of the other organic items in the store. One of them in the frozen-food case caught my eye: an organic TV dinner (now there are three words I never expected to string together) from Cascadian Farm called Country Herb: "rice, vegetables and grilled chicken breast strips with a savory herb sauce."

5   The text-heavy box it came in told the predictable organic stories—about the chicken (raised without chemicals and allowed "to roam freely in an outdoor yard"); about the rice and vegetables (grown without synthetic chemicals); even about the carton (recycled)—but when I got to the ingredients list, I felt a small jolt of cognitive dissonance. For one thing, the list of ingredients went on forever (31 ingredients in all) and included such enigmas of modern food technology as natural chicken flavor, high-oleic safflower oil, guar and xanthan gum, soy lecithin, carrageenan and natural grill flavor, this last culinary breakthrough achieved with something called "tapioca maltodextrin." The label assured me that most of these additives are organic, which they no doubt are, and yet they seem about as jarring to my conception of organic food as, say, a cigarette boat on Walden Pond. But then, so too is the fact (mentioned nowhere on the label) that Cascadian Farm has recently become a subsidiary of General Mills, the third biggest food conglomerate in North America.

Clearly, my notion of supermarket pastoralism has fallen hopelessly out of date. The organic movement has become a $7.7 billion business: call it Industrial Organic. Although that represents but a fraction of the $400 billion business of selling Americans food, organic is now the fastest-growing category in the supermarket. Perhaps inevitably, this sort of growth—sustained at a steady 20 percent a year for more than a decade—has attracted the attention of the very agribusiness corporations to which the organic movement once presented a radical alternative and an often scalding critique. Even today, the rapid growth of organic closely tracks consumers' rising worries about the conventional food supply—about chemicals, about additives and, most recently, about genetically modified ingredients and mad cow disease; every food scare is followed by a spike in organic sales. And now that organic food has established itself as a viable alternative food chain, agribusiness has decided that the best way to deal with that alternative is simply to own it. The question now is, What will they do with it? Is the word "organic" being emptied of its meaning?

II. THE ROAD TO CASCADIAN FARM™

I don't know about you, but I never expect the bucolic scenes and slogans on my packaged food to correspond to reality (where exactly is Nature's Valley, anyway?), but it turns out the Cascadian Farm pictured on my TV dinner is a real farm that grows real food—though not quite the same food contained in my TV dinner.

Cascadian Farm occupies a narrow, breathtaking shelf of land wedged between the Skagit River and the North Cascades in the town of Rockport, Wash., 75 miles northeast of Seattle. Originally called the New Cascadian Survival and Reclamation Project, the farm was started in 1971 by Gene Kahn with the idea of growing food for the collective of environmentally minded hippies he had hooked up with in nearby Bellingham. At the time, Kahn was a 24-year-old grad-school dropout from the South Side of Chicago who, after reading "Silent Spring" and "Diet for a Small Planet," determined to go back to the land, there to change "the food system." That particular dream was not so outrageous in 1971—this was the moment, after all, when the whole counterculture was taking a rural turn—but Kahn's success in actually achieving it surely is: he went on to become a pioneer of the organic movement and did much to move organic food into the mainstream. Today, Cascadian Farm's farm is a General Mills showcase—"a P.R. farm," as its founder freely acknowledges—and Kahn, erstwhile hippie farmer, is a General Mills vice president and a millionaire. He has become one of the most successful figures in the organic community and also perhaps one of the most polarizing; for to many organic farmers and activists, he has come to symbolize the takeover of the movement by agribusiness.

"Organic is becoming what we hoped it would be an alternative to," says Roger Blobaum, who played a key role as a consumer advocate in pushing Congress to establish the U.S.D.A.'s fledgling organic program. "Gene Kahn's approach is slowly but surely taking us in that direction. He's one of the real pioneers, but there are people now who are suspicious of him." Kahn is apt to call such people "purists," "Luddites," "romantics" and "ideologues" who have failed to outgrow the "antibusiness prejudices" of the 60's. He'll tell you he's still committed to changing the food system—but now from "inside." Few in the movement doubt his sincerity or commitment, but many will tell you the food system will much sooner change Kahn, along with the whole meaning of organic.

10   On an overcast morning not long ago, Kahn drove me out to Rockport from his company's offices in Sedro-Woolley, following the twists of the Skagit River east in a new forest green Lexus with vanity plates that say "ORGANIC." Kahn is a strikingly boyish-looking 54, and after you factor in a shave and 20 pounds, it's not hard to pick his face out from the beards-beads-and-tractor photos on display in his office. Back in the farm's early days, when Kahn supervised and mentored the rotating band of itinerant hippies who would show up to work a day or a week or a year on the farm, he drove a red VW Beetle and an ancient, temperamental John Deere. Kahn lived in a modest clapboard farmhouse on Cascadian Farm until 1993. Now he lives in a McMansion high in the hills overlooking Puget Sound.

Like a lot of the early organic farmers, Kahn had no idea what he was doing at first and suffered his share of crop failures. In 1971, organic agriculture was in its infancy—a few hundred scattered amateurs learning by trial and error how to grow food without chemicals, an ad hoc grass-roots R. & D. effort for which there was precisely no institutional support. Though it did draw on various peasant-farming models, modern-day organic agriculture is a relatively novel and remarkably sophisticated system with deep roots in the counterculture. The theoretical roots of organic agriculture go back a bit further, principally to the work of a British scientist by the name of Sir Albert Howard. Based on his experiments in India and observations of peasant farms in Asia, Howard's 1940 treatise "An Agricultural Testament" demonstrated the connection between the health of the soil and the ability of plants to withstand diseases and pests. Howard's agricultural heresies were praised in the pages of "The Whole Earth Catalog" (by Wendell Berry) and popularized by J.I. Rodale in *Organic Gardening and Farming* magazine—which claimed 700,000 readers in 1971, one of whom was Gene Kahn.

But the word "organic" around 1970 connoted a great deal more than a technique for growing vegetables. The movement's pioneers set out to create not just an alternative mode of production (the farms) but of distribution (the co-ops and health-food stores) and even consumption. A "countercuisine" based on whole grains and unprocessed ingredients rose up to challenge conventional industrial "white bread" food. ("Plastic food" was an epithet you heard a lot.) For a host of reasons that seem risible in retrospect, brown food of all kinds (rice, bread, wheat, sugar) was deemed morally superior to white. Much more than just lunch, organic food was "an edible dynamic" that promised to raise consciousness about the economic order, draw critical lines of connection between the personal and the political. It was also, not incidentally, precisely what your parents didn't eat.

Such was dinner and the dinner-table conversation at Cascadian Farm and countless other counterculture tables in the early 1970's. As for an alternative mode of distributing food, Kahn recruited a hippie capitalist named Roger Weschler to help him figure out how to sell his strawberries before they rotted in the field. Weschler had helped found something called the Cooperating Community, a network of Seattle businesses committed to ecological principles and worker self-management. A new offshoot, Community Produce, began distributing the food grown at Cascadian Farm, and Weschler and Kahn set out, in the unembarrassed words of Cascadian Farm's official corporate history, "to change the world's food system." Twenty-nine years later, Weschler is still at it, operating a produce brokerage devoted to supporting family farmers. And Kahn? Weschler, who has lost neither his scraggly black beard nor his jittery intensity, told me that by going corporate, his old friend "has made a very different choice."

If Kahn were the least bit embarrassed by the compromises he has made in his organic principles since those long-ago days, he would surely have rewritten his company's official history by now— and never sent me to interview Weschler. But as we walked around the farm talking about "how everything eventually morphs into the way the world is," it seemed clear that Kahn has made his peace with that fact of life, decided that the gains outweighed the losses.

In time, Kahn became quite a good farmer and, to his surprise, an even better businessman. By the late 70's, he had discovered the virtues of adding value to his produce by processing it (freezing blueberries and strawberries, making jams), and once Cascadian Farm had begun processing, Kahn discovered he could make more money buying produce from other farmers than by growing it himself. During the 80's, Cascadian Farm became an increasingly virtual sort of farm, processing and marketing a range of packaged foods well beyond the Seattle area.

"The whole notion of a 'cooperative community' we started with gradually began to mimic the system," Kahn recalled. "We were shipping food across the country, using diesel fuel—we were industrial organic farmers. I was bit by bit becoming more of this world, and there was a lot of pressure on the business to become more privatized."

15

That pressure became irresistible in 1990, when in the aftermath of the Alar scare, Kahn nearly lost everything—and control of Cascadian Farm wound up in corporate hands. In the history of the organic movement, the Alar episode is a watershed, marking the birth pangs of the modern organic industry. After a somewhat overheated "60 Minutes" exposé on apple growers' use of Alar, a growth-regulator that the Environmental Protection Agency declared a carcinogen, middle America suddenly discovered organic. "Panic for Organic" was the cover line of one newsweekly, and, overnight, demand from the supermarket chains soared. The ragtag industry wasn't quite ready for prime time, however. Kahn borrowed heavily to finance an ambitious expansion, contracted with farmers to grow an awful lot of organic produce—and then watched in horror as the bubble of demand subsided along with the headlines about Alar. Kahn was forced to sell a majority stake in the company—to Welch's—and set out on what he calls his "corporate adventure."

"We were part of the food industry now," he told me. "But I wanted to leverage that position to redefine the way we grow food—not what people want to eat or how we distribute it. That sure as hell isn't going to change." Kahn sees himself as very much the grown-up, a sober realist in a community of unreconstructed idealists. He speaks of selling out to Welch's as "the time when I lost the company" but doesn't trouble himself with second thoughts or regrets; in fact, it was all for the best. "Welch's was my business school," he said. Kahn seems to have no doubt that his path is the right path, not only for him but for the organic movement as a whole: "You have a choice of getting sad about all that or moving on. We tried hard to build a cooperative community and a local food system, but at the end of the day it wasn't successful. This is just lunch for most people. Just lunch. We can call it sacred, we can talk about communion, but it's just lunch."

In the years after the Alar bubble burst in 1990, the organic industry recovered, embarking on a period of double-digit annual growth and rapid consolidation, as mainstream food companies began to take organic—or at least, the organic market—seriously. Gerber's, Heinz, Dole, ConAgra and A.D.M. all created or acquired organic brands. Cascadian Farm itself became a miniconglomerate, acquiring Muir Glen, the California organic tomato processors, and the combined company changed its name to Small Planet Foods. Nineteen-ninety also marked the beginning of federal recognition for organic agriculture: that year, Congress passed the Organic Food Production Act. The legislation instructed the Department of Agriculture—which historically had treated organic farming with undisguised contempt—to establish uniform national standards for organic food and farming, fixing the definition of a word that had always meant different things to different people.

Settling on that definition turned out to be a grueling decade-   20
long process, as various forces both within and outside the movement battled for control of a word that had developed a certain magic in the marketplace. Agribusiness fought to define the word as broadly as possible, in part to make it easier for mainstream companies to get into organic but also out of fear that anything deemed *not* organic would henceforth carry an official stigma. At first, the U.S.D.A., acting out of longstanding habit, obliged its agribusiness clients, issuing a watery set of standards in 1997 that, incredibly, allowed for the use of genetic modification, irradiation and sewage sludge in organic food production. But an unprecedented flood of public comment from outraged organic farmers and consumers forced the U.S.D.A. back to the drawing board, in what was widely viewed as a victory for the movement's principles.

Yet while the struggle with agribusiness over the meaning of the word "organic" was making headlines, another, equally important struggle was under way at the U.S.D.A. between Big and Little Organic, and this time the outcome was decidedly more ambiguous. Could a factory farm be organic? Was an organic cow entitled to dine on pasture? Did food additives and synthetic chemicals have a place in organic processed food? If the answers to these seem like no-brainers, then you, too, are stuck in an outdated pastoral view of organic. Big Organic won all three arguments. The final standards, which will take effect next year, are widely seen as favoring the industry's big players. The standards do an admirable job of setting the bar for a more environmentally responsible kind of farming, but as perhaps was inevitable, many of the philosophical values embedded in the word "organic" did not survive the federal rule-making process.

Gene Kahn served on the U.S.D.A.'s National Organic Standards Board from 1992 to 1997, playing a key role in making the standards safe for the organic TV dinner and a great many other processed organic foods. This was no small feat, for Kahn and his allies had to work around the 1990 legislation establishing organic standards, which prohibited synthetic food additives. Kahn argued that you couldn't have organic processed foods without synthetics. Several of the consumer representatives on the standards board contended that this was precisely the point, and if no synthetics meant no organic TV dinners, then TV dinners were something organic simply shouldn't do.

Joan Dye Gussow, a nutritionist and an outspoken standards-board member, made the case against synthetics in a 1996 article that was much debated, "Can an Organic Twinkie Be Certified?" She questioned whether organic should simply mirror the existing food supply, with its highly processed, salted and sugary junk food, or whether it should aspire to something better—a countercuisine. Kahn responded with market populism: if the consumer wants an organic Twinkie, then we should give it to him. As he put it to me on the drive back from Cascadian Farm, "Organic is not your mother." In the end, it came down to an argument between the old movement and the new industry, and the new industry won: the final standards simply ignored the 1990 law, drawing up a "national list" of permissible additives and synthetics, from ascorbic acid to xanthan gum.

"If we had lost on synthetics," Kahn told me, "we'd be out of business."

25   Kahn's victory cleared the way for the development of a parallel organic food supply: organic Heinz ketchup (already on the shelves in England), organic Hamburger Helper, organic Miracle Whip and, sooner or later, organic Twinkies. This is not a prospect everyone relishes. Even Kahn says: "I'm not looking forward to the organic Twinkie. But I will defend to the death anyone's right to create one!" Eliot Coleman, a Maine farmer and writer whose organic techniques have influenced two generations of farmers, is repulsed by the whole idea: "I don't care if the Wheaties are organic—I wouldn't use them for compost. Processed organic food is as bad as any other processed food."

III. THE SOUL OF A NEW TV DINNER

Small Planet Foods's headquarters in Sedro-Woolley occupies a downtown block of 19th-century brick storefronts in this faded and decidedly funky logging town. The storefronts have been converted into loftlike offices designed in the alternative-capitalist style: brick walls, air ducts and I-beams all in plain sight—no facades here. Since every day is dress-down day at Small Planet Foods, Friday is the day everybody takes his or her dog to work. I spent a Friday in Woolley, learning the ins and outs of formulating, manufacturing and selling an organic TV dinner.

Steve Harper, Small Planet's chief food scientist, described the challenge of keeping a frozen herb sauce from separating unappetizingly (instead of modified food starch, organic food scientists rely on things like carrageenan, a seaweed derivative, to enhance "freeze-thaw stability") and explained the algorithm governing the relative size and population of chicken chunks (fewer bigger chunks give a better "quality perception" than a larger number of dice-size cubes). He also explained how they get that salty processed-food taste right inside a chicken chunk: marinade-injecting hypodermic needles.

If Harper is responsible for the "recipe" of a Cascadian Farm TV dinner, it falls to Marv Shelby, the company's vice president for operations, to get the meal "cooked." Shelby, who came to Small Planet after a career in operations at Birds Eye, handles the considerable logistics involved in moving three dozen ingredients on time to the co-packing plant in Alberta, Canada, where they are combined in a microwaveable bowl. He described an elaborate (and energy-intensive) choreography of ingredients, packaging and processes that takes place over a half-dozen states and two countries. Fresh broccoli, for instance, travels from a farm in the Central Valley to a plant in Sanger, Calif., where it is cut into florets, blanched and frozen. From California, the broccoli is trucked to Edmonton, Alberta, there to meet up with pieces of organic chicken that have traveled from a farm in Petaluma, Calif., with a stop at a processing plant in Salem, Ore., where they were defrosted, injected with marinade, cubed, cooked and refrozen. They don't call it processed food for nothing.

Most everyone I met at Small Planet Foods expressed a fervently held belief in the value of organic farming. There was a politics to their work, and if they had had to compromise certain ideals in order to adapt their products to the mainstream food system, all this was in service to a greater good they seemed never to lose sight of: converting the greatest number of acres of American farmland to organic agriculture. The solitary exception to this outlook was a vice president for marketing, the man most responsible for developing Cascadian's new slogan, "Taste You Can Believe In." R. Brooks Gekler is a marketing star at General Mills who was installed at Small Planet Foods immediately after the acquisition. A year later, Gekler, a handsome, well-spoken New York University M.B.A., was still something of an outsider at Small Planet Foods. "There are people here who regard me as the Antichrist," he joked. I think it was around the time he explained to me, apropos of his colleagues, that "some principles can be an obstacle to success" that I understood why this might be so.

30   "I came here to help the company identify its consumer target," Gekler explained crisply, "which is different from what they believed." In marketing parlance, Small Planet (like the rest of the organic industry) had traditionally directed its products toward someone called "the true natural"—a committed, activist consumer. True naturals are the people on whom the organic food industry has been built, the outwardly directed, socially conscious consumers devoted to the proposition of "better food for a better planet." But while their numbers are growing—true naturals now represent about 10 percent of the U.S. food market, as a large proportion of Gen X'ers join their ranks—the future of organic, General Mills says, lies with a considerably larger group of even more affluent consumers called the "health seekers." It is to this group that Cascadian Farm is targeting its new TV dinners.

        Health seekers, who today represent about a quarter of the market, are less "extrinsic"—that is, more interested in their own health than that of the planet. They buy supplements, work out, drink wine, drive imported cars. They aren't interested in a countercuisine, which is why Cascadian's new line of frozen entrees eschews whole grains and embraces a decidedly middle-of-the road "flavor profile."

        The chief reason the health seeker will buy organic is for the perceived health benefits. This poses a certain marketing challenge, however, since it has always been easier to make the environmental case for organic food than the health case. Although General Mills has put its new organic division under the umbrella of its "health initiatives" group, "organic" is not, at least officially, a health, nutrition or food-safety claim, a point that Dan Glickman, then secretary of agriculture, took pains to emphasize when he unveiled the U.S.D.A.'s new label in December: organic, he stressed, is simply "a production standard."

        "At first, I thought the inability to make hard-hitting health claims"—for organic—was a hurdle," Gekler said when I asked him about this glitch. "But the reality is, all you have to say is 'organic'—you don't need to provide any more information." These particular consumers—who pay attention to the media, to food scares and to articles like this one—take their own health claims to the word.

        Suddenly the genius of Cascadian Farm's new slogan dawned on me. "Taste You Can Believe In": meaningless in and of itself, the slogan "allows the consumer to bring his or her personal beliefs to it," Gekler explained. While the true natural hears social values in the phrase "Believe In," the health seeker hears a promise of health and flavor. The slogan is an empty signifier, as the literary theorists would say, and what a good thing that is for a company like General Mills. How much better to let the consumers fill in the marketing message—*healthier, more nutritious, no pesticides, more wholesome, sustainable, safer, purer*—because these are controversial comparative claims that, as Gekler acknowledged, "make the conventional food industry very uncomfortable."

Before I left his office, I asked Gekler about his own beliefs— 35 whether or not he believed that organic food was better food. He paused for a long time, no doubt assessing the cost of either answer, and deftly punted.

"I don't know yet."

IV. DOWN ON THE INDUSTRIAL ORGANIC FARM

No farm I have ever visited before prepared me for the industrial organic farms I saw in California. When I think about organic farming, I think family farm, I think small scale, I think hedgerows and compost piles and battered pickup trucks. I don't think migrant laborers, combines, thousands of acres of broccoli reaching clear to the horizon. To the eye, these farms look exactly like any other industrial farm in California—and in fact the biggest organic operations in the state today are owned and operated by conventional mega-farms. The same farmer who is applying toxic fumigants to sterilize the soil in one field is in the next field applying compost to nurture the soil's natural fertility.

Is there something wrong with this picture? It all depends on where you stand. Gene Kahn makes the case that the scale of a farm has no bearing on its fidelity to organic principles and that unless organic "scales up" it will "never be anything more than yuppie food." To prove his point, Kahn sent me to visit large-scale farms whose organic practices were in many ways quite impressive, including the Central Valley operation that grows vegetables for his frozen dinners and tomatoes for Muir Glen.

Greenways Organic is a successful 2,000-acre organic-produce operation tucked into a 24,000-acre conventional farm outside Fresno; the crops, the machines, the crews, the rotations and the fields were indistinguishable, and yet two very different kinds of industrial agriculture are being practiced here side by side.

In place of petrochemical fertilizers, Greenways's organic 40 fields are nourished by compost made by the ton at a horse farm nearby. Insects are controlled with biological agents and beneficial insects like lacewings. Frequent and carefully timed tilling, as

well as propane torches, keeps down the weeds, perhaps the industrial organic farmer's single stiffest challenge. This approach
is at best a compromise: running tillers through the soil so frequently is destructive to its tilth, yet weeding a 160-acre block of
broccoli by hand is unrealistic.

Since Greenways grows the same crops conventionally and
organically, I was interested to hear John Diener, one of the farm's
three partners, say he knew for a fact that his organic crops were
"better," and not only because they hadn't been doused with pesticide. When Diener takes his tomatoes to the cannery, the organic
crop reliably receives higher Brix scores—a measure of the sugars
in fruits and vegetables. It seems that crops grown on nitrogen
fertilizer take up considerably more water, thereby diluting their
nutrients, sugars and flavors. The same biochemical process
could explain why many people—including the many chefs who
swear by organic ingredients—believe organic produce simply
tastes better. With less water in it, the flavor and the nutrients of a
floret of organic broccoli will be more concentrated than one
grown with chemical fertilizers.

It's too simple to say that smaller organic farms are automatically truer to the organic ideal than big ones. In fact, the organic
ideal is so exacting—a sustainable system that requires not only
no synthetic chemicals but also few purchased inputs of any kind
and that returns as much to the soil as it removes—that it is most
often honored in the breach. Yet the farmers who come closest to
achieving this ideal do tend to be smaller in scale. These are the
farmers who plant dozens of different crops in fields that resemble quilts and practice long and elaborate rotations, thereby
achieving the rich biodiversity in space and time that is the key to
making a farm sustainable.

For better or worse, these are not the kinds of farms Small
Planet Foods does business with today. It's simply more efficient
to buy from one 1,000-acre farm than ten 100-acre farms. Indeed,
Cascadian Farm the corporation can't even afford to use produce
from Cascadian Farm the farm: it's too small. So the berries
grown there are sold at a roadside stand, while the company buys
berries for freezing from as far away as Chile.

The big question is whether the logic of an industrial food
chain can be reconciled to the logic of the natural systems on
which organic agriculture has tried to model itself. Put another
way, Is "industrial organic" a contradiction in terms?

45   Kahn is convinced it is not, but others both inside and outside his company see a tension. Sarah Huntington is one of

Cascadian's oldest employees. She worked alongside Kahn on the farm and at one time or another has held just about every job in the company. "The maw of that processing plant beast eats 10 acres of cornfield an hour," she told me. "And you're locked into planting a particular variety like Jubilee that ripens all at once and holds up in processing. So you see how the system is constantly pushing you back toward monoculture, which is anathema in organic. But that's the challenge—to change the system more than it changes you."

One of the most striking ways Small Planet Foods is changing the system is by helping conventional farms convert a portion of their acreage to organic. Several thousand acres of American farmland are now organic as a result of the company's efforts, which go well beyond offering contracts to providing instruction and even management. Kahn has helped to prove to the skeptical that organic—dismissed as "hippie farming" not very long ago—can work on a large scale. The environmental benefits of this educational process shouldn't be underestimated. And yet the industrialization of organic comes at a price. The most obvious is consolidation: today five giant farms control fully one-half of the $400 million organic produce market in California. Partly as a result, the price premium for organic crops is shrinking. This is all to the good for expanding organic's market beyond yuppies, but it is crushing many of the small farmers for whom organic has represented a profitable niche, a way out of the cheap-food economics that has ravaged American farming over the last few decades. Indeed, many of the small farmers present at the creation of organic agriculture today find themselves struggling to compete against the larger players, as the familiar, dismal history of American agriculture begins to repeat itself in the organic sector.

This has opened up a gulf in the movement between Big and Little Organic and convinced many of the movement's founders that the time has come to move "beyond organic"—to raise the bar on American agriculture yet again. Some of these innovating farmers want to stress fair labor standards, others quality or growing exclusively for local markets. In Maine, Eliot Coleman has pioneered a sophisticated market garden entirely under plastic, to supply his "food shed" with local produce all winter long; even in January his solar-heated farm beats California on freshness and quality, if not price. In Virginia, Joel Salatin has developed an ingenious self-sufficient rotation of grass-fed livestock: cattle, chickens and rabbits that take turns eating, and feeding, the same small pasture. There are hundreds of these "beyond organic" farmers springing up now around the country. The fact is, however, that the word "organic"—having entered the vocabulary of both agribusiness and government—is no longer these farmers' to redefine. Coleman and Salatin, both of whom reject the U.S.D.A. organic label, are searching for new words to describe what it is they're doing. Michael Ableman, a "beyond organic" farmer near Santa Barbara, Calif., says: "We may have to give up on the word 'organic,' leave it to the Gene Kahns of the world. To be honest, I'm not sure I want the association, because what I'm doing on my farm is not just substituting materials."

Not long ago at a conference on organic agriculture, a corporate organic farmer suggested to a family farmer struggling to survive in the competitive world of industrial organic agriculture that he "should really try to develop a niche to distinguish yourself in the market." The small farmer replied: "I believe I developed that niche 20 years ago. It's called 'organic.' And now you're sitting on it."

V. GENE KAHN VISITS THE MOTHERSHIP

In March, I accompanied Gene Kahn on one of his monthly visits to the General Mills headquarters, a grassy corporate campus strewn with modern sculptures in the suburbs outside Minneapolis. In deference to Fortune 500 etiquette, I put on a suit and tie but quickly realized I was overdressed: Kahn had on his usual khakis and a denim work shirt embroidered with a bright red Muir Glen tomato. When I said something, Kahn told me he makes a point of not changing his clothes when he goes to Minneapolis. I get it: an organic farmer in an embroidered work shirt is part of what General Mills was acquiring when it acquired Small Planet Foods. Yet this particular organic farmer is presumably a far sight wealthier than most of his new corporate colleagues: when General Mills bought Small Planet Foods for an estimated $70 million, Kahn still owned 10 percent of the company.

50   Together, Kahn and I toured General Mills's Bell Technical Center, a sprawling research-and-development facility where some 900 food scientists, chemists, industrial designers and nutritionists dream up and design both the near- and long-term future of American food. This was Kahn's first visit to the facility, and as we moved from lab to lab, I could see his boyish enthusiasm mounting as he collected new ideas and business cards.

In the packaging-design lab, even before Arne Brauner could finish explaining how he engineered the boxes, bowls and cups in which General Mills sells its products, Kahn asked him, "Has there ever been a completely edible packaging for food?" Brauner rubbed his chin for a moment.

"The sausage. That was probably the first."

Kahn now told him about the bowl in which Cascadian Farm sold its frozen entrees. Plastic would have turned off the organic consumer, he explained, so they were using coated paperboard, which isn't readily recyclable. Would it be possible, Kahn wondered, to make a microwaveable bowl out of biodegradable food starch? Brauner said he had heard about a cornstarch clamshell for fast-food burgers and offered to look into it. Kahn took his card.

Kahn had another, more off-the-wall request for Perry May, the man in charge of General Mills's machine shop. This is where engineers and machinists make the machines that make the food. Kahn asked Perry if his shop could help develop a prototype for a new weeding machine he had dreamed up for organic farmers. "It would be an optical weeder with a steam generator on board," Kahn explained. "The scanner would distinguish between a weed and a corn plant, say, and then zap the weed with a jet of hot steam." May thought it might be doable; they exchanged cards.

"I feel like a kid in a candy store," Kahn told me afterward.   55
"Organic has never had these kinds of resources at its disposal."

On the drive back from Bell, Kahn grew positively effervescent about the "organic synergies" that could come from General Mills's acquisition of Pillsbury, a $10.5 billion deal now awaiting F.T.C. approval. Pillsbury owns Green Giant, and the prospect of being able to draw on that company's scientists (and patents) has planted agronomic fantasies in the fevered brain of the former farmer: broccoli specifically bred for organic production ("We've never had anything like that!"); an organic version of Niblets, Green Giant's popular proprietary corn; carrots bred for extra vitamin content. In fact, Kahn got so worked up spinning his vision of the industrial organic future that he got us lost.

So this was how Kahn proposed to change the American food system from within: by leveraging its capital and know-how on behalf of his dream. Which prompts the question, Just how does the American food system feel about all this? As Kahn and I made the rounds of General Mills's senior management, he in his work shirt, I in my suit, I tried to find out how these tribunes of agribusiness regarded their new vice president's organic dream, exactly how it fit into their vision of the future of food.

The future of food, I learned, is toward ever more health and convenience—the two most important food trends today—at no sacrifice of taste. "Our corporate philosophy," as one senior vice president, Danny Strickland, put it, "is to give consumers what they want with no trade-offs." Organic fits into this philosophy in so far as the company's market research shows that consumers increasingly want it and believe it's healthier.

The acquisition of a leading organic food company is part of a company-wide "health initiative"—along with adding calcium to various product lines and developing "functional foods" like Harmony, a soy-and-calcium-fortified cereal aimed at menopausal women. When I asked Ian Friendly, the sharp, young executive in charge of the company's health-initiative group, if this meant that General Mills believed organic was more healthful than conventional food, he deftly shifted vocabulary, suggesting that "'wellness' is perhaps a better word." Wellness is more of a whole gestalt or lifestyle, which includes things like yoga, massage and working out. It quickly became clear that in the eyes of General Mills, organic is not a revolution so much as a market niche, like menopausal women or "ethnics," and that health is really a matter of consumer perception. You did not have to buy into the organic "belief system" to sell it. When I asked Strickland if he believed that organic food was in any way better, he said: "Better? It depends. Food is subjective. Perceptions depend on circumstances."

60   I got much the same response from other General Mills executives. The words "better food," uttered so unself-consciously in Sedro-Woolley, rang in their offices like a phrase from a dead language. Steve Sanger, the company's chairman, said: "I'm certain it's better for some people. It depends on their particular beliefs." Sheri Schellhaas, vice president for research and development, said, "The question is, Do *consumers* believe organic is healthier?" Marc Belton, a senior vice president for cereals and the executive most responsible for the Small Planet acquisition, put it this way: "Is it better food? . . . You know, so much of life is what you make of it. If it's right for you, it's better—if you feel it's better, it is."

At General Mills, it would seem, the whole notion of objective truth has been replaced by a kind of value-neutral consumer constructivism, in which each sovereign shopper constructs his own reality: "Taste You Can Believe In." Kahn understands that there is no percentage in signing onto the organic belief system, not when you also have Trix and Go-Gurt and Cinnamon Toast Milk and Cereal Bars to sell, yet, as he acknowledged later, contemporary corporate relativism drives him a little nuts.

Old-fashioned objective truth did make a brief reappearance when Kahn and I visited the quality-assurance lab deep in the bowels of the Bell center. This is where technicians grind up Trix and Cheerios and run them through a mass spectrometer to make sure pesticide residues don't exceed F.D.A. "tolerances." Pesticide residues are omnipresent in the American food supply: the F.D.A. finds them in 30 to 40 percent of the food it samples. Many of them are known carcinogens, neurotoxins and endocrine disrupters—dangerous at some level of exposure. The government has established acceptable levels for these residues in crops, though whether that means they're safe to consume is debatable: in setting these tolerances the government has historically weighed the risk to our health against the benefit—to agriculture, that is. The tolerances also haven't taken into account that children's narrow diets make them especially susceptible or that the complex mixtures of chemicals to which we're exposed heighten the dangers.

Harry Leichtweis, a senior research analytical chemist at General Mills, tests for hundreds of different chemical compounds, not only the 400 pesticides currently approved by the E.P.A. but also the dozens of others that have been banned over the years as their dangers became known. Decades later, many of these toxins remain in the soil and continue to show up in our food. "We still find background levels of DDT and chlordane," he explained. Now the lab tests Small Planet Foods's products too. So I asked Leichtweis, who is a pale, rail-thin scientist with Coke-bottle specs and no discernible affect, if organic foods, as seen from the perspective of a mass spectrometer, are any different.

"Well, they don't contain pesticide."

Leichtweis had struck a blow for old-fashioned empiricism. 65
Whatever else you might say about an organic TV dinner, it almost certainly contains less pesticide than a conventional one. Gene Kahn was beaming.

VI. LOCAL FARM

My journey through the changing world of organic food has cured me of my naive supermarket pastoralism, but it hasn't put me off my organic feed. I still fill my cart with the stuff. The science might still be sketchy, but common sense tells me organic is better food—better, anyway, than the kind grown with organophosphates, with antibiotics and growth hormones, with cadmium and lead and arsenic (the E.P.A. permits the use of toxic waste in fertilizers), with sewage sludge and animal feed made from ground-up bits of other animals as well as their own manure. Very likely it's better for me and my family, and unquestionably it is better for the environment. For even if only 1 percent of

the chemical pesticides sprayed by American farmers end up as
residue in our food, the other 99 percent are going into the environment—which is to say, into our drinking water, into our rivers,
into the air that farmers and their neighbors breathe. By now it
makes little sense to distinguish the health of the individual from
that of the environment.

Still, while it surely represents real progress for agribusiness
to be selling organic food rather than fighting it, I'm not sure I
want to see industrialized organic become the only kind in the
market. Organic is nothing if not a set of values *(this* is better
than *that)*, and to the extent that the future of those values is in
the hands of companies that are finally indifferent to them, that
future will be precarious.

Also, there are values that the new corporate—and government—construction of "organic" leaves out, values that once were
part and parcel of the word but that have since been abandoned
as impractical or unprofitable. I'm thinking of things like locally
grown, like the humane treatment of animals, like the value of a
shorter and more legible food chain, the preservation of family
farms, even the promise of a countercuisine. To believe that the
U.S.D.A. label on a product ensures any of these things is, as I discovered, naive.

Yet if the word "organic" means anything, it means that all
these things are ultimately connected: that the way we grow food
is inseparable from the way we distribute food, which is inseparable from the way we eat food. The original premise, remember,
the idea that got Kahn started in 1971, was that the whole industrial food system—and not just chemical agriculture—was in
some fundamental way unsustainable. It's impossible to read the
papers these days without beginning to wonder if this insight
wasn't prophetic. I'm thinking, of course, of mad cow disease, of
the 76 million cases of food poisoning every year (a rate higher
than in 1948), of StarLink corn contamination, of the 20-year-old
farm crisis, of hoof-and-mouth disease and groundwater pollution, not to mention industrial food's dubious "solutions" to these
problems: genetic engineering and antibiotics and irradiation.
Buying food labeled organic protects me from some of these
things, but not all; industrial organic may well be necessary to fix
this system, but it won't be sufficient.

70   Many of the values that industrial organic has jettisoned in
recent years I find compelling, so I've started to shop with them
in mind. I happen to believe, for example, that farms produce
more than food; they also produce a kind of landscape, and if I
buy my organic milk from halfway across the country, the farms I

like to drive by every day will eventually grow nothing but raised ranch houses. So instead of long-haul ultrapasteurized milk from Horizon, I've started buying my milk, unpasteurized, from a dairy right here in town, Local Farm. Debra Tyler is organic, but she doesn't bother mentioning the fact on her label. Why? "My customers can see for themselves what I'm doing here," she says. What she's doing is milking nine pastured Jersey cows whose milk changes taste and hue with the seasons.

"Eat Your View!" is a save-the-farms bumper sticker you see in Europe now. I guess that's part of what I'm trying to do. But I'm also trying to get away from the transcontinental strawberry (5 calories of food energy, I've read, that it takes 435 calories of fossil-fuel energy to deliver to my door) and the organic "home meal replacement" sold in a package that will take 500 years to decompose. (Does that make me a True Natural?) So I've tracked down a local source for grass-fed beef (Chris Hopkins), eggs (Debra Tyler again) and maple syrup (Phil Hart), and on Saturday mornings I buy produce at a farmer's market in a neighboring town. I also have a line on a C.S.A. ("community supported agriculture"), or "subscription farm," a new marketing scheme from Europe that seems to be catching on here. You put up a couple of hundred dollars every spring and then receive a weekly box of produce through the summer. Not all of the farmers I'm buying from are certified organic. But I talk to them, see what they're up to, learn how they define the term. Sure, it's more trouble than buying organic food at the supermarket, but I'm resolved to do it anyway. Because organic is not the last word, and it's not just lunch.

2001

Discussion

1. What does Pollan say about the way that the word "organic" is currently used and what it means when we think about food?
2. What does Pollan suggest by the term "supermarket pastoralism"?
3. After reading Pollan's essay, do you really believe that organic food is organic?

How Green Is BP?

DARCY FREY

Darcy Frey (1961–) is a freelance writer specializing in science, medicine, technology, sports, and music. He attended Oberlin College, Ohio, and now lives in New York City. Frey is the author of The Last

Shot: City Streets, Basketball Dreams *(1994) and is working on a book about a scientist studying global warming in the Arctic. A winner of a National Magazine Award and the Livingston Award for an article that he wrote for* Harper's *Frey is also a contributing writer for* The New York Times Magazine. *His article "Does Anyone Here Think This Baby Can Live?" published in that magazine won a public-service award from the Society of Professional Journalists. His articles have also been anthologized in* Best American Essays: 1994 *and* Best American Science Writing: 2002.

——————— ✦ ———————

Last March, Lord John Browne, the group chief executive of the British oil giant BP, gave a speech at Stanford University. Had you stumbled into the auditorium partway through, you might be forgiven for assuming the man at the podium was not an oil baron, an industrialist, an extractor of fossil fuels from the tender earth but an environmentalist of the high church calling for the abolition of hydrocarbons, the very substance that had made his company and himself so fabulously rich. His subject was global climate change—in particular, the process by which humans, by burning oil and gas, have been slowly, perhaps irreversibly, warming the earth's atmosphere. And instead of hewing to the line of industry, instead of calling (as President Bush and the head of Exxon Mobil have) for caution and further research, he said, "I believe the American people expect a company like BP . . . to offer answers and not excuses." He also said, "Climate change is an issue which raises fundamental questions about the relationship between companies and society as a whole, and between one generation and the next." He even said, "Companies composed of highly skilled and trained people can't live in denial of mounting evidence gathered by hundreds of the most reputable scientists in the world."

Around the time Browne was at Stanford, sounding strikingly unlike an oil executive, BP was trying its own kind of identity shift, sounding strikingly unlike an oil company. Two years earlier, at a cost of $200 million, it began an enormous corporate rebranding exercise, shortening its name from British Petroleum to BP, coining the slogan "Beyond Petroleum" and redesigning its corporate insignia. Out went the old British Petroleum shield that had been a familiar image in Britain for more than 70 years, and in came a green, yellow and white sunburst that seemed to suggest a warm and fuzzy feeling about the earth. BP press officers were careful not to explain exactly what "Beyond Petroleum" meant, but the slogan, coupled with the cheerful sunburst, sent the message that the company was looking past oil and gas toward a benign, eco-friendly future of solar and renewable energy. New Yorkers in particular were the target of a high-saturation ad campaign that felt, at times, like an overfriendly stranger putting his arm around you in a bar. In Times Square, a huge billboard went up, reading IF ONLY WE COULD HARNESS THE ENERGY OF NEW YORK CITY. Then the stranger, perhaps feeling the need to explain his intentions, went on: SOLAR, NATURAL GAS, WIND, HYDROGEN. AND OH YES, OIL. Finally, the stranger took his arm away with a bit of a shrug: IT'S A START.

BP's print and TV ad campaign, which is winding down this month, represents one of the most dazzlingly high-profile corporate P.R. efforts in recent years. Created by Ogilvy & Mather Worldwide, it aspires to a conversational, almost confidential voice that suggests, *You know what oil companies do to the environment, and we do, too, but honestly, we're not like that at all.* "People are skeptical of oil companies—go figure!" says Jennifer Ruys, director of external affairs for BP. "And the ad campaign was designed to get at that skepticism." As the billboards announce: BP was "the first oil company to publicly recognize the risks of global climate change." BP "believes in alternative energy. Like solar and cappuccino." BP has joined forces with New York's Urban Park Rangers to, of all things, release four bald eagles into the wilds of Upper Manhattan. At the end of each ad was the same winking tag line: "It's a start."

Based in London, BP is the world's second-largest oil company (after Exxon Mobil), with gross revenues of $174 billion and 15,500 service stations in the United States. It operates in more than 100 countries and produces almost 3.5 billion barrels of oil and gas a year. Largely, this has been the handiwork of Lord Browne, who became group chief executive in 1995 (and was knighted 3 years later) and followed his own ascension by quickly expanding the once mid-size company into a huge multinational. In 1999, BP merged with Amoco in a deal worth $140 billion; a year later, it bought Atlantic Richfield for $27 billion. These megadeals have more than paid for themselves. At press time, BP shares were trading at $38, which is an 80 percent increase since Browne's rise to power seven years ago.

If Browne, 54, has made a name for himself as a high-stakes   5 deal maker, he has also shown that he is alert to the dangers of heading a colossal oil company in a world that—because of climate change, murmurings of war-for-oil and a host of other global crises—may hate oil companies, no matter how profitable they are. More than that, he has shown the ambition to redefine the very nature of Big Oil: pushing BP to confront global warming, candidly acknowledge the company's mistakes (environmental penalties against the company appear on its Web site), enter into dialogue with environmental groups, hire people with strong environmental ethics and opinions. "John Browne would be the first to say, 'Even on our best day, we're still a big dirty company,'" says one person involved in BP's rebranding effort. "But aren't there ways to do it smarter, cleaner, in a more surprising and forward-thinking way?'" He adds, "This guy's swimming upstream."

BP's multimillion-dollar campaign is the public face of Browne's convictions. At a time when anxiety over dependence on Middle Eastern oil has sent other energy companies scurrying for cover, BP is rushing to center stage, betting that, as Michael Kaye, who worked on the campaign as an associate creative director at Ogilvy, puts it, "BP can be a friend—listening to consumers, speaking in a human voice." BP is also betting that this will gain them a competitive advantage in the marketplace, that it will convince consumers that BP is, in the words of Anna Catalano, group vice president for marketing, "the company that goes beyond what you expect from an oil company—frank, open, honest and unapologetic." BP is the only oil company right now risking a huge advertising presence in this oil-wary culture. And this may turn out to be the richest deal of all.

But to persuade the public that BP is no rapacious multinational, that it is instead an organization thinking first and foremost of the public good, may not come so easily as long as BP remains an oil company, deriving the vast majority of its profits from the black stuff that—from drilling rig to oil tanker to refinery to gas station—scars the earth, pollutes the air and eventually warms the planet. And once the company tried to convey its new identity in billboard form, the contradiction only deepened. How can an oil company be "Beyond Petroleum" without actively distancing itself from its core product, and how can a company that digs big holes in the ground possibly advertise itself as a sensitive steward of the environment? BP's rebranding campaign caused fits, not only in the environmental movement, which saw it as the highest form of hypocrisy, but also within the company itself, which embraced and then disavowed its P.R. message so many times that people began to wonder if the company was beyond petroleum or merely beyond belief. The Independent of London, a vigilant BP-watcher, concluded that the company was "brimming with success, gushing with money, and very much wanting to be liked. Yet its image is confused, and its reputation is on the line as never before."

But its biggest challenge may come years, perhaps decades, from now, when the world turns to other forms of energy—in part because of dwindling oil supplies but mainly because of the mounting and unimpeachable evidence that we have a profound carbon problem on our hands; that even if we discover billions of new barrels of oil in the ground, we cannot keep burning them— and pumping vast amounts of carbon dioxide and other so-called greenhouse gases into the atmosphere—without potentially cata- strophic consequences. According to the latest findings of the United Nations Intergovernmental Panel on Climate Change, in order to stabilize greenhouse gases in the atmosphere, global emissions must be reduced to at least 60 percent below 1990 lev- els. That is a radical change in the way the world uses energy. And to accomplish that, many people feel, will require nothing less than a new industrial revolution, an overwhelming retreat from society's mass reliance on the carbon fuels—oil, gas and coal— that have powered the global economy for more than a hundred years.

Browne is uncomfortable speculating about a future com- pletely without oil. "My view is that hydrocarbons will be the bulk of the energy supply for the next 30 to 50 years," he said when I met him last spring. But clearly Browne is trying to prepare BP for the end of the fossil-fuel game—by cutting the emissions of carbon dioxide that it creates while producing oil and gas, by shifting to cleaner fuels like natural gas, which emits about half the volume of CO_2 generated from coal and ultimately by posi- tioning itself as a producer of alternative and renewable energy: hydrogen, wind, solar.

But whether the company—which made its fortunes in the oil   10 fields of Iran and later on the North Slope of Alaska—can survive the shift to a new energy economy remains an open question. "That's a huge level of wishful thinking," says one American scien- tist who has advised BP's senior management on climate change and renewable energy. "Of course they say they see themselves that way, and of course they're going to try. But whether they will have any chance of successfully outcompeting newcomers in re- newable energy is a very big question. Because historically, once those transformations have happened, the existing companies have not held the edge. These companies, some of which have ex- isted for a hundred years, are essentially about extracting petro- leum. And in a world where you don't extract petroleum anymore, the first order of expectation is that you're dead."

The Dalton Highway is a two-lane gravel road that runs some 400 miles from Fairbanks, Alaska, to the coast of the Arctic Ocean. Built by BP with a consortium of other oil companies after the huge 1968 strike at Prudhoe Bay, it has been open to the public for more than 10 years. After the highway, known as the Haul Road, descends the north slope of the Brooks Range, it begins to cross the open, boggy tundra of the Arctic coastal plain. Gradually, as the landscape grows prairie flat, natural objects lose their dominance and industrial ones take their place: pipelines, pump stations, piles of gravel. By the time you reach Prudhoe Bay, industry has completely consumed the view: wellheads, compressor stations, seawater processing plants, roads, flares, landing strips and overhead power lines stretch as far as the eye can see. Here, some 200 miles north of the Arctic Circle, in the middle of a vast boreal wilderness, is one of the largest industrial developments in the world.

Browne had overseen the company's Alaska division for many years, and when he became group chief executive in 1995, he revealed himself to be one oil man who did not believe that the oil business could—or should—go on as it had before. Soft-spoken and slightly built, with a manner more befitting a university lecture hall than an offshore oil rig, Browne consulted with dozens of scientists and took what he describes as a "deep dive" into the confusing, sometimes contradictory science of global warming. Back then, BP (along with Exxon Mobil, Royal Dutch/Shell and a few other oil companies) was still a member of the Global Climate Coalition, an international lobbying group set up specifically to cast skepticism on climate-change science and, later, to undermine support for the Kyoto Protocol, the international pact in which industrialized nations agreed to reduce their greenhouse gas emissions. But in 1997, Browne gave a speech at Stanford (a precursor to the one last spring) in which he acknowledged that there was now an "effective consensus" among the world's leading scientists regarding the human influence on the climate. "The science wasn't complete—but science is never complete," he said last spring. "But they knew enough to say that there were long-term risks and that precautionary action was necessary if we were to avoid the greater risk—of the evidence mounting to the point where draconian action was unavoidable."

In the continuing, ever-changing study of global warming, five years is an ice age, so it is hard to remember exactly how revolutionary this was, coming from the C.E.O. of a major oil company in 1997. But at the time, the American Petroleum Institute, of which BP had been a longstanding member, announced that Browne had, as he recalls, "left the church."

"BP was the first to say that climate change was a problem, the first to take responsibility and the first to have an internal target" for reducing their emissions, says Eileen Claussen, the president of the Pew Center on Global Climate Change. "They were pretty brave."

In some respects, it was an act of corporate bravery for BP and, later, Royal Dutch/Shell and a handful of other companies, to buck their own industry. Unlike the tobacco companies, which for years denied that their products were causing harm—or Exxon Mobil, which ran ads trying to discredit global warming science—BP and the others have been willing to confront the unpleasant truth that not only their business practices but also their core products are probable causes of global warming. In 1996, BP resigned from the Global Climate Coalition, then offered its support of the Kyoto Protocol and joined Claussen's Business Environmental Leadership Council, a program set up by the Pew Center to encourage private-sector involvement. In 1998, Browne publicly committed BP to cutting its carbon-dioxide emissions by 10 percent below 1990 levels by the year 2010, which was a 40 percent cut from business as usual and a target far more ambitious than the Kyoto Protocol itself.

But it is not just altruism that has convinced Browne and these other C.E.O.'s to seize the moral high ground. Despite the Bush administration's stubborn refusal to deal with the issue, Browne says that he thinks there will soon be government regulation of greenhouse gases. And companies that have anticipated regulation will not only know how to use it to their advantage; they will also, as Browne puts it, "gain a seat at the table, a chance to influence future rules."

And so, in order to meet its target for reducing its greenhouse-gas emissions, BP sought the advice of NGO's like the Pew Center and Environmental Defense and set up a system in which each of its 150 business units, spread across more than 100 countries, would be assigned a quota of emissions permits and encouraged to trade with one another. The company gave each business unit the choice of bringing itself into compliance by cutting its own emissions, buying emissions credits from other units or making enough greenhouse-gas reductions to have leftover permits that could be sold to other business units that violate their emissions ceilings. The motivation was simple enough: business units that reduced their emissions or cut their fuel consumption would have

15

those savings count toward their bottom line, which, in turn, would be reflected in pay scales and bonuses at year's end.

Many environmentalists are skeptical of such market-based solutions to global warming. For one thing, with such a vast number of different emissions sources and no single method for measuring emissions, enforcing compliance becomes hard, tempting companies to fudge the numbers. Then there's the matter of mitigation: why should polluters be allowed to trade emissions instead of being forced to solve the problem at its root? And will trading programs merely slow the growth rate of emissions when society's goal should be to engineer a fundamental shift away from fossil fuels?

But emissions trading, which is part of the compliance mechanism of the Kyoto Protocol, is supported by the vast majority of economists, who believe that market-based mechanisms may be the most cost-effective—and therefore most viable—method of cutting greenhouse gases. And though it doesn't shift the energy basis of the economy, it does cut down on carbon emissions in absolute terms. When Browne stood up at Stanford this past spring, he was there to report hard numbers: BP had not just met its target—to reduce its emissions of greenhouse gases by 10 percent below 1990 levels—it had exceeded it, done so eight years ahead of schedule and with no net economic cost. In fact, because of energy efficiency measures, the emissions reductions amounted to a net gain of $600 million. "And we are not," he told me later, "an inefficient company."

20   BP's achievement complicates matters for Bush, who has pronounced the Kyoto Protocol "fatally flawed" because regulating carbon-dioxide emissions "does not make economic sense for America."

That line of argument does not persuade Browne. "If you say to people, 'Do you want to develop the world and have a good living standard, or do you want a safer environment?' people are terrified by the choice," Browne said to me last spring. "That is a failure of leadership." Speaking of leadership, I asked, what did he think about Bush's position on the issue—that caps on emissions would be too costly for American businesses? Browne paused, then answered, careful not to mention any names in particular: "Well, it's unfair to the world to say that none of this is possible when it is."

Last summer, BP celebrated the 25th anniversary of the Trans-Alaska Pipeline. The company put on a big barbecue;

speeches were given. But those celebrations were overshadowed by the fact that BP's North Slope production, which peaked at two million barrels a day in the mid-1980's, has dwindled to less than a million today. As production has declined, BP—already the largest operator on the slope, with roughly 30 percent of the state's oil-extraction industry—has lobbied to open the Arctic National Wildlife Refuge to the east and built the first offshore oil projects in the Arctic Ocean to the north. BP's mantra is to make "zero environmental impact" and to leave only a "small industrial footprint." And by most accounts, it does wield its ground-eviscerating equipment with great care. But the bottom line is that BP's stock price—and its obligations to shareholders—hinges on locating more oil fields. And any new field, subjected to the drill bit, is a potential insult to the earth.

In the fall of 2000, Browne made it clear that if the Arctic refuge—an iconic 19-million-acre tract of land in northeast Alaska that is home to polar bears and grizzlies, wolves, musk oxen and a 125,000-strong herd of caribou—was opened up under a Republican administration, BP would be interested in exploring there. After all, the United States Geological Survey estimates that the refuge contains anywhere from 3 billion to 16 billion barrels of recoverable oil. Again on Feb. 13, 2001, three weeks after Bush took office, Browne acknowledged that BP openly supported efforts to drill.

BP's stated intentions for the refuge happened to coincide with its "Beyond Petroleum" campaign, and environmentalists had a field day pointing out the inconsistencies. Greenpeace announced that until BP started seriously investing in renewables, a more fitting corporate logo would be, in the words of one spokeswoman, "a miserable polar bear on an icecap shrinking because of global warming." John Browne himself was honored by Greenpeace for giving the "Best Impression of an Environmentalist." And referring to the company's interest in the Arctic refuge, The Independent wrote that it was "strange that a company boss with prominent green pretensions should advocate—openly—what many people would see as the industrial rape of an unspoiled wilderness."

The protests over BP's position on the Arctic refuge could not   25 have come at a worse time. Just a few months earlier, the company's new advertising campaign was met in some corners with howls of derision and even demonstrations outside its London offices. Stung by the controversy, the company tried to pull several TV spots, and where that time was locked in by contract, BP lost "several million dollars," according to two people involved in the ad campaign. In cases where ads could not be pulled, the company removed the words "Beyond Petroleum." "It's funny," says one of them, "I never doubted that they were the most progressive oil company around, but they didn't think through what it would require from a P.R. point of view. By pulling the ads, they showed weakness rather than having the courage of their convictions, which is what the whole rebranding effort was all about."

Later, when the time came to prepare for the campaign's second phase, BP once again waffled over whether to use the phrase "Beyond Petroleum." "I was in so many meetings when the answer was no, yes, no, yes," says one member of the ad team. And the company's concern over how its P.R. message was being perceived delayed the campaign for more than a year.

Eventually, the company once again embraced the phrase "Beyond Petroleum." But according to one member of the ad team, BP, fearful of exaggerating its claims and opening itself to further criticism, worried the ad copy to death. "All the definitive points they were making in the ads got slightly watered down," the ad-team member says. Finally, the company decided to use the tag line "It's a start"—which can sound frank and refreshing or, depending on your point of view, hedging and defensive.

Meanwhile, the issue of whether or not to drill in the Arctic refuge, at a time when BP's Alaska oil reserves are dwindling, still has the company tied up in knots. On the one hand, Browne no longer openly advocates drilling in the refuge, as he did in 2000 and 2001. On the other hand, when asked after his Stanford speech last spring what the company's position was, he disappointed environmentalists by refusing to rule out drilling altogether, saying, "I believe we should have no part in that debate."

A BP consultant on environmental policy says of Browne, "The impression he wants to leave is that it's all a process—first Congress has to vote for drilling, then the company needs to assess its value, etc., but that even if it's opened, the company probably won't drill." But others who work with the company have privately heard just the opposite. "One of their vice presidents told me flat out," another consultant says, " 'If it's opened, we'll drill.' "

30   BP's position on the refuge is "evolving," according to Ronald Chappell, who was head of press relations for BP Alaska and who now works in its London headquarters. In the early to mid-90's, BP was engaged in lobbying to open the refuge. "But," Chappell says, "I think that the company has sort of decided that the role of corporations in public life is one of standing back and letting gov-

ernments make decisions, trying to inform public policy but not making political contributions."

But, in fact, the company did make political contributions—$560,000 through its employee political action committee in 2000, according to a BP spokeswoman. Moreover, at the time that Chappell and I spoke, the company was a member and contributor to Arctic Power, a prodevelopment lobbying group whose Internet site highlights "top 10 reasons to support development in A.N.W.R.," and had a representative on the Arctic Power board. When I pointed this out to Chappell, he demurred, then sought me out a few minutes later, when I happened to be standing with Eileen Claussen of the Pew Center, one of John Browne's closest environmental advisers. "I misspoke," Chappell said to us. "It's true, we give to Arctic Power. We gave $50,000 last year but none so far this year. We also give to the American Petroleum Institute."

Claussen, looking at him, said what others—including many within the company—think but will not say out loud: "Shame on you." (Last month, BP withdrew from the group.)

The Arctic National Wildlife Refuge, which will once again be vulnerable to industry assault under the new Republican Congressional majority, is just one place BP may be interested in doing business. In recent years, it has also built Northstar, an artificial drilling island in the waters off Prudhoe Bay and the first offshore oil-exploration site in the Arctic Ocean, the oil flowing to the mainland through a six-mile undersea pipeline. And the company owns a 2.2 percent stake in PetroChina, the state-owned firm that is building a controversial pipeline across Tibet. These projects, as well as its interest in the refuge, have all been the subject of shareholder resolutions seeking to force BP to divest, to bring its actions in line with its rhetoric. And the resolutions (and BP's sometimes strong-arm legal tactics to quell them) all point out how difficult it is for an oil company to grow its business without also harming the environment. After violating federal clean-air laws at eight refineries across the country, BP, in January 2001, paid a $10 million penalty and agreed to spend $500 million modernizing its pollution-control technology. After delaying to report that its contractor had illegally dumped hazardous waste in northern Alaska, the company, in 1999, was fined $7 million in civil and criminal penalties.

It may seem unfair that BP is the target of environmental and social-responsibility movements. Shouldn't Greenpeace et al. be going after Exxon Mobil, which still tries to sow public skepticism toward global warming theories and has reportedly worked behind the scenes to remove a prominent scientist from the

United Nations climate change panel and still refuses to pay $5 billion in punitive damages ordered by an Alaska court after the 1989 Valdez oil spill? But BP has, by virtue of its slogans and its actions, tried to seize the moral high ground and so is judged by a different standard.

35   Browne seems to understand this, and at Stanford last spring he outlined his next set of goals, ambitious by any standard: to reduce global-warming gases from BP's own operations as well as from the products it makes, to maintain CO_2 emissions at current levels even as the company doubles its production of oil and gas, to make 50 percent of the company's pump sales worldwide come from clean fuels. Anticipating the future, BP bought Solarex in 1999 for $45 million, making it one of the largest solar companies in the world. It is also participating in fuel-cell technology research efforts with auto and engine manufacturers. And it is testing the viability of other energy sources like wind and hydrogen.

Few question the idea that BP is now the most conscientious oil company around, or that Browne is deeply committed to cleaning up BP's act. One of Browne's closest colleagues suggests that he may go into the climate-change field after he retires from the oil business. Meanwhile, its competitors, according to a Royal Dutch/Shell executive, feel pressed by BP into taking ever-greener positions—even Exxon Mobil has recently given a grant to Stanford University to study global warming. But while Browne and BP may show greater sensitivity to environmental concerns than any other company in its industry, it may also be impossible for any company that derives well over 90 percent of its revenue from fossil fuels to claim to be part of the solution. Despite its new sunburst logo and "Beyond Petroleum" slogan, BP still invests $12 billion, or 25 times more, on oil and gas than on its wind and solar division for the simple fact that, right now, there's a huge market for oil and almost none for solar panels. And that's not just BP's problem; that's ours. Ronald Chappell, the BP spokesman, says as much when he points out that all those environmentalists flying into the Arctic National Wildlife Refuge to save the planet are using up a lot of airplane fuel to do it. "That," he says, "is the devil's bargain we all have made."

2002

Discussion

1. What does Frey suggest is the connection between climate change and oil?
2. Discuss whether or not you think it is cynical for BP to hire an advertising agency to make its case to the American public. Do you think that this is just another instance of corporate greed?

3. What evidence is there of Frey's attitude toward BP? Do you believe that he is hostile, or skeptical about BP's attitudinal changes?
4. What does Frey suggest is the reason that BP waffled on the use of the phrase "Beyond Petroleum" in its advertising campaign?

Thinking and Writing About Chapter 4

1. Argue the proposition that we must have an ethical stand by which we regard agricultural practices. Base your argument on Michael Pollan's "Behind the Organic-Industrial Complex" (p. 130) and his concern that organic farming has been usurped by big agricultural corporations.
2. Compare Rachel Carson's concept of the human price in her scientific-based argument and Henry David Thoreau's humanistic argument in "Walking" (p. 44).
3. Based on your reading of Pollan's "Behind the Organic-Industrial Complex" (p. 130), discuss the irony of Gene Kahn's choice of Rachel Carson as a hero of ecology.
4. Discuss how the pretty visuals of pastoral harmony that we encounter in advertising for food, automobiles, clothing, and cigarettes are designed to entice us into believing that what we see in the media is environmental reality.

Additional Resources

Films
Soylent Green (1973), directed by Richard Fleischer
China Syndrome (1979), directed by James Bridges
Silkwood (1983), directed by Mike Nichols

Drama
Henrik Ibsen. *An Enemy of the People* (1882), adapted by Arthur Miller (1951)

Fiction
Sinclair Lewis. *The Jungle* (1906)
Willa Cather. *O Pioneers!* (1913)

Essays
Garrett Harden. "The Tragedy of the Commons," *Science* (1968)
René Dubos. *The Wooing of the Earth* (1980)
David Ehrenfeld. *The Arrogance of Humanism* (1978)

Website
www.coyoteclan.com (Terry Tempest Williams)

CHAPTER 5

Personal
Views

A personal view of the environment provides a glimpse into the soul of an author. In the context of *Listening to Earth,* we have selected personal views from a variety of starting points that remind us of our connection to nature. Although such a connection is primordial, we do not often acknowledge our close relationship to nature in all its parameters.

Edward Abbey, however, appears hell-bent on submersing himself in nature. In "The First Morning" (1968), he wants to rid himself of the stigma of human paraphernalia and values and be at one with the natural world outside the door of his trailer at Arches National Monument in Utah. The desire to be free of our trappings seems never-ending and takes many forms—extreme sports, music, drugs—to mention but a few examples. Like Thoreau, Abbey luxuriates in the observation of small things as well as large. He watches nature at work and, full of admiration, cannot help but wonder at the haste with which mankind is inclined to disregard the marvels in front of us and focus, instead, on reaching the heavens.

Although Leslie Marmon Silko possesses as deep an appreciation for the environment and nature in "Landscape, History, and the Pueblo Imagination" (1986), her view is colored by her ethnic heritage. Silko, who is part Laguna Pueblo, explains the link between character and place for some Native Americans: "The bare vastness of the Hopi Pueblo emphasizes the visual impact of every plant, every rock, every arroyo. Nothing is overlooked or taken for granted. Each ant, each lizard, each lark is imbued with great value simply because the creature is there, simply because the creature is alive in a place where any life at all is precious." Silko explains that to the Pueblo—in contrast to mainstream

163

Americans—nothing is wasted on the land. Everything we see is at some point on a journey from life to death to life, from growth to decay and back to life again. Abbey would appreciate this view. Silko's assumptions and interpretations are that the ancient Pueblos left behind a legacy of leaving the landscape as is and not tampering with it, a highly disputed opinion. She explains that survival means making the best of available resources, which includes the material and the spiritual. Unlike Western civilizations that depend on the written word, Silko points out that the Pueblo depended on an oral tradition of communal storytelling. The story of the Pueblo thus becomes the story of the land, and this makes them *of* it rather than *in* it.

Sallie Bingham's "A Woman's Land" (1990) is an ironic take on the age-old argument of property rights and wrongs. Bingham poses the question of what a woman, not a man, might do if she was the principal property owner. Turning the sexist tradition of society and property rights topsy-turvy, Bingham wonders if developing ideas and practices for land use are gender-related and open to change. With a feminist point of view, Bingham considers the fact that so few women own land. She points out that while men are apt to use land for gain or to sell it for development, women tend to regard land as a gift and as a source of spiritual pleasure. Unlike Mary Austin, in "My Neighbor's Field" (p. 13) who watched her neighbor's field lie fallow, Bingham owns her land, but she is determined that it should remain undeveloped. Like Joy Williams' in "One Acre: On Devaluing Real Estate to Keep Land Priceless" (p. 95), Bingham is content to let her weeds grow. Fortunately for Bingham, she does not need to sell her land, nor is she compelled to turn a profit on it.

Listening to Steve Chapple get off on the mosquito, in "Bugz" (1997), you would think that this was the bug which won the west. Insects, he points out from a very personal stance, do us harm; they cause disease, crop failure, destroy forests, damage furniture, and eat clothing. Chapple takes this in stride, recalling "fondly" his fishing trip in Montana where the "musquitors" made his trip Kafkaesque. Mosquitoes bigger than black flies bite him until he oozes blood and feels like drowning himself. He fears the black flies, too. In contrast to the other writers in this chapter, Chapple does not appear to appreciate the notion that the insects feeding off of him are only trying to survive; he puts distance between himself as part of nature and insects as part of nature. But he does acknowledge that without bugs, there would be no flowers or apple trees or cacti. His advice: "Strive to be strong, this bug season."

The link between a persona and place is a source of solace and pleasure. In the face of ever-increasing pressures brought on by the rapid pace of our civilization, it is refreshing to know that the land still holds us. Abbey, Silko, Bingham, and Chapple remind us how much place defines our character. Writings such as these carry the spirit of Henry David Thoreau and John Muir forward to other generations.

The First Morning
EDWARD ABBEY

Edward Abbey (1927–1989) was born in the Appalachian region of western Pennsylvania, the son of social activists. He had a troubled youth and hitchhiked to the west coast when he was seventeen, and was so deeply impressed with the southwest desert that he eventually made his life there. Abbey attended Indiana University of Pennsylvania, the University of New Mexico, and the University of Edinburgh in Scotland, where he studied philosophy, social action, and anarchism. Outwardly, he was difficult with people; inwardly, he was thoughtful and even shy. He taught at the University of Arizona and called himself a "fool professor," but that position gave him a base for his writing, some of which has become the philosophical foundation for radical environmental groups, particularly Earth First! His Desert Solitaire *(1968, in which the following work appears) made his reputation. Other works include* The Brave Cowboy *(1956),* Fire on the Mountain *(1962), and* Black Sun *(1971). His non-fiction includes* Road *(1979),* One Life at a Time, Please *(1988), and* A Voice Crying in the Wilderness *(1989). He wrote the screenplays* Lonely Are the Brave *(1962) and* Fire on the Mountain *(1981).*

✦

This is the most beautiful place on earth.

There are many such places. Every man, every woman, carries in heart and mind the image of the ideal place, the right place, the one true home, known or unknown, actual or visionary. A houseboat in Kashmir, a view down Atlantic Avenue in Brooklyn, a gray gothic farmhouse two stories high at the end of a red dog road in the Allegheny Mountains, a cabin on the shore of a blue lake in spruce and fir country, a greasy alley near the Hoboken waterfront, or even, possibly, for those of a less demanding sensibility, the world to be seen from a comfortable apartment high in the tender velvety smog of Manhattan, Chicago, Paris, Tokyo, Rio or Rome—there's no limit to the human capacity for the homing sentiment. Theologians, sky pilots, astronauts have even felt the appeal of home calling to them from up above, in the cold black outback of interstellar space.

For myself I'll take Moab, Utah. I don't mean the town itself, of course, but the country which surrounds it—the canyonlands. The slickrock desert. The red dust and the burnt cliffs and the lonely sky—all that which lies beyond the end of the roads.

The choice became apparent to me this morning when I stepped out of a Park Service housetrailer—my caravan—to watch for the first time in my life the sun come up over the hoodoo stone of Arches National Monument.

5   I wasn't able to see much of it last night. After driving all day from Albuquerque—450 miles—I reached Moab after dark in cold, windy, clouded weather. At park headquarters north of town I met the superintendent and the chief ranger, the only permanent employees, except for one maintenance man, in the particular unit of America's national park system. After coffee they gave me a key to the housetrailer and directions on how to reach it; I am required to live and work not at headquarters but at this one-man station some twenty miles back in the interior, on my own. The way I wanted it, naturally, or I'd never have asked for the job.

Leaving the headquarters area and the lights of Moab, I drove twelve miles farther north on the highway until I came to a dirt road on the right, where a small wooden sign pointed the way: Arches National Monument Eight Miles. I left the pavement, turned east into the howling wilderness. Wind roaring out of the northwest, black clouds across the stars—all I could see were clumps of brush and scattered junipers along the roadside. Then another modest signboard:

> WARNING: QUICKSAND
> DO NOT CROSS WASH
> WHEN WATER IS RUNNING

The wash looked perfectly dry in my headlights. I drove down, across, up the other side and on into the night. Glimpses of weird humps of pale rock on either side, like petrified elephants, dinosaurs, stone-age hobgoblins. Now and then something alive scurried across the road: kangaroo mice, a jackrabbit,

an animal that looked like a cross between a raccoon and a squirrel—the ringtail cat. Farther on a pair of mule deer started from
the brush and bounded obliquely through the beams of my lights,
raising puffs of dust which the wind, moving faster than my
pickup truck, caught and carried ahead of me out of sight into
the dark. The road, narrow and rocky, twisted sharply left and
right, dipped in and out of tight ravines, climbing by degrees toward a summit which I would see only in the light of the coming
day.

Snow was swirling through the air when I crossed the
unfenced line and passed the boundary marker of the park. A
quarter-mile beyond I found the ranger station—a wide place in
the road, an informational display under a lean-to shelter, and
fifty yards away the little tin government housetrailer where I
would be living for the next six months.

A cold night, a cold wind, the snow falling like confetti. In the
lights of the truck I unlocked the housetrailer, got out bedroll and
baggage and moved in. By flashlight I found the bed, unrolled my
sleeping bag, pulled off my boots and crawled in and went to
sleep at once. The last I knew was the shaking of the trailer in the
wind and the sound, from inside, of hungry mice scampering
around with the good news that their long lean lonesome winter
was over—their friend and provider had finally arrived.

This morning I awake before sunrise, stick my head out of   10
the sack, peer through a frosty window at a scene dim and vague
with flowing mists, dark fantastic shapes looming beyond. An unlikely landscape.

I get up, moving about in long underwear and socks, stooping
carefully under the low ceiling and the lower doorways of the
housetrailer, a machine for living built so efficiently and com-
pactly there's hardly room for a man to breathe. An iron lung it is,
with windows and venetian blinds.

The mice are silent, watching me from their hiding places, but
the wind is still blowing and outside the ground is covered with
snow. Cold as a tomb, a jail, a cave; I lie down on the dusty floor,
on the cold linoleum sprinkled with mouse turds, and light the pilot on the butane heater. Once this thing gets going the place
warms up fast, in a dense unhealthy way, with a layer of heat under the ceiling where my head is and nothing but frigid air from
the knees down. But we've got all the indispensable conveniences:
gas cookstove, gas refrigerator, hot water heater, sink with running
water (if the pipes aren't frozen), storage cabinets and shelves,
everything within arm's reach of everything else. The gas comes

from two steel bottles in a shed outside; the water comes by gravity flow from a tank buried in a hill close by. Quite luxurious for the wilds. There's even a shower stall and a flush toilet with a dead rat in the bowl. Pretty soft. My poor mother raised five children without any of these luxuries and might be doing without them yet if it hadn't been for Hitler, war and general prosperity.

Time to get dressed, get out and have a look at the lay of the land, fix a breakfast. I try to pull on my boots but they're stiff as iron from the cold. I light a burner on the stove and hold the boots upside down above the flame until they are malleable enough to force my feet into. I put on a coat and step outside. In the center of the world, God's navel, Abbey's country, the red wasteland.

The sun is not yet in sight but signs of the advent are plain to see. Lavender clouds sail like a fleet of ships across the pale green dawn; each cloud, planed flat on the wind, has a base of fiery gold. Southeast, twenty miles by line of sight, stand the peaks of the Sierra La Sal, twelve to thirteen thousand feet above sea level, all covered with snow and rosy in the morning sunlight. The air is dry and clear as well as cold; the last fogbanks left over from last night's storm are scudding away like ghosts fading into nothing before the wind and the sunrise.

15   The view is open and perfect in all directions except to the west where the ground rises and the skyline is only a few hundred yards away. Looking toward the mountains I can see the dark gorge of the Colorado River five or six miles away, carved through the sandstone mesa, though nothing of the river itself down inside the gorge. Southward, on the far side of the river, lies the Moab valley between thousand-foot walls of rock, with the town of Moab somewhere on the valley floor, too small to be seen from here. Beyond the Moab valley is more canyon and tableland stretching away to the Blue Mountains fifty miles south. On the north and northwest I see the Roan Cliffs and the Book Cliffs, the two-level face of the Uinta Plateau. Along the foot of those cliffs, maybe thirty miles off, invisible from where I stand, runs U.S. 6–50, a major east-west artery of commerce, traffic and rubbish, and the main line of the Denver–Rio Grande Railroad. To the east, under the spreading sunrise, are more mesas, more canyons, league on league of red cliff and arid tablelands, extending through purple haze over the bulging curve of the planet to the ranges of Colorado—a sea of desert.

Within this vast perimeter, in the middle ground and foreground of the picture, a rather personal demesne, are the 33,000 acres of Arches National Monument of which I am now sole inhabitant, usufructuary, observer and custodian.

What are the Arches? From my place in front of the house-trailer I can see several of the hundred or more of them which have been discovered in the park. These are natural arches, holes in the rock, windows in stone, no two alike, as varied in form as in dimension. They range in size from holes just big enough to walk through to openings large enough to contain the dome of the Capitol building in Washington, D.C. Some resemble jug handles or flying buttresses, others natural bridges but with this technical distinction: a natural bridge spans a watercourse—a natural arch does not. The arches were formed through hundreds of thousands of years by the weathering of the huge sandstone walls, or fins, in which they are found. Not the work of a cosmic hand, nor sculptured by sand-bearing winds, as many people prefer to believe, the arches came into being and continue to come into being through the modest wedging action of rainwater, melting snow, frost, and ice, aided by gravity. In color they shade from off-white through buff, pink, brown and red, tones which also change with the time of day and the moods of the light, the weather, the sky.

Standing there, gaping at this monstrous and inhuman spectacle of rock and cloud and sky and space, I feel a ridiculous greed and possessiveness come over me. I want to know it all, possess it all, embrace the entire scene intimately, deeply, totally, as a man desires a beautiful woman. An insane wish? Perhaps not—at least there's nothing else, no one human, to dispute possession with me.

The snow-covered ground glimmers with a dull blue light, reflecting the sky and the approaching sunrise. Leading away from me the narrow dirt road, an alluring and primitive track into nowhere, meanders down the slope and toward the heart of the labyrinth of naked stone. Near the first group of arches, looming over a bend in the road, is a balanced rock about fifty feet high, mounted on a pedestal of equal height; it looks like a head from Easter Island, a stone god or a petrified ogre.

Like a god, like an ogre? The personification of the natural is   20
exactly the tendency I wish to suppress in myself, to eliminate for good. I am here not only to evade for a while the clamor and filth and confusion of the cultural apparatus but also to confront, immediately and directly if it's possible, the bare bones of existence, the elemental and fundamental, the bedrock which sustains us. I want to be able to look at and into a juniper tree, a piece of quartz, a vulture, a spider, and see it as it is in itself, devoid of all

humanly ascribed qualities, anti-Kantian, even the categories of scientific description. To meet God or Medusa face to face, even if it means risking everything human in myself. I dream of a hard and brutal mysticism in which the naked self merges with a now human world and yet somehow survives still intact individual, separate. Paradox and bedrock.

Well—the sun will be up in a few minutes and I haven't even begun to make coffee. I take more baggage from my pickup, the grub box and cooking gear, go back in the trailer and start breakfast. Simply breathing, in a place like this, arouses the appetite. The orange juice is frozen, the milk slushy with ice. Still chilly enough inside the trailer to turn my breath to vapor. When the first rays of the sun strike the cliffs I fill a mug with steaming coffee and sit in the doorway facing the sunrise, hungry for the warmth.

Suddenly it comes, the flaming globe, blazing on the pinnacles and minarets and balanced rocks, on the canyon walls and through the windows in the sandstone fins. We greet each other, sun and I, across the black void of ninety-three million miles. The snow glitters between us, acres of diamonds almost painful to look at. Within an hour all the snow exposed to the sunlight will be gone and the rock will be damp and steaming. Within minutes, even as I watch, melting snow begins to drip from the branches of a juniper nearby; drops of water streak slowly down the side of the trailerhouse.

I am not alone after all. Three ravens are wheeling near the balanced rock, squawking at each other and at the dawn. I'm sure they're as delighted by the return of the sun as I am and I wish I knew the language. I'd sooner exchange ideas with the birds on earth than learn to carry on intergalactic communications with some obscure race of humanoids on a satellite planet from the world of Betelgeuse. First things first. The ravens cry out in husky voices, blue-black wings flapping against the golden sky. Over my shoulder comes the sizzle and smell of frying bacon.

That's the way it was this morning.

1968

Discussion

1. As Abbey drives through the desert to his house trailer, his imagination runs wild. Has a natural landscape ever affected your imagination similarly? Why does Abbey refer to the area around his trailer as "the red wasteland"?

2. Why does Abbey not want to compare the landscape around him to human-made artifacts?
3. Discuss both the similarities and differences in Abbey's view of his surrounding with those of Rebecca Solnit in "The Orbits of Earthly Bodies" (p. 105).

Landscape, History, and the Pueblo Imagination
LESLIE MARMON SILKO

Leslie Marmon Silko (1948–) was raised in the Laguna Pueblo fifty miles west of Albuquerque, New Mexico. Her family is of mixed heritage—white, Mexican, and Native American—a factor that she believes gives her stability as a writer with a sense of place. Silko was educated at the University of Albuquerque; later she taught at the University of Arizona. In 1981, she was awarded a MacArthur Foundation fellowship that enabled her to write without economic pressures. Laguna Woman *(1974) is a collection of Silko's poetry. Her reputation was sealed, however, with the publication of her novels* Ceremony *(1977),* Almanac of the Dead *(1991), and* Gardens in the Dunes *(1999). Silko's non-fiction works include* Storyteller *(1989),* Yellow Woman and a Beauty of the Spirit *(1996),* Sacred Water: Narratives and Pictures *(1993), and* Conversations with Leslie Marmon Silko *(2000).*

———————— ✦ ————————

FROM A HIGH ARID PLATEAU IN NEW MEXICO

You see that after a thing is dead, it dries up. It might take weeks or years, but eventually if you touch the thing, it crumbles under your fingers. It goes back to dust. The soul of the thing has long since departed. With the plants and wild game the soul may have already been borne back into bones and blood or thick green stalk and leaves. Nothing is wasted. What cannot be eaten by people or in some way used must then be left where other living creatures may benefit. What domestic animals or wild scavengers can't eat will be fed to the plants. The plants feed on the dust of these few remains.

The ancient Pueblo people buried the dead in vacant rooms or partially collapsed rooms adjacent to the main living quarters.

Sand and clay used to construct the roof make layers many inches deep once the roof has collapsed. The layers of sand and clay make for easy grave digging. The vacant room fills with cast-off objects and debris. When a vacant room has filled deep enough, a shallow but adequate grave can be scooped in a far corner. Archaeologists have remarked over formal burials complete with elaborate funerary objects excavated in trash middens of abandoned rooms. But the rocks and adobe mortar of collapsed walls were valued by the ancient people. Because each rock had been carefully selected for size and shape, then chiseled to an even face. Even the pink clay adobe melting with each rainstorm had to be prayed over, then dug and carried some distance. Corn cobs and husks, the rinds and stalks and animal bones were not regarded by the ancient people as filth or garbage. The remains were merely resting at a midpoint in their journey back to dust. Human remains are not so different. They should rest with the bones and rinds where they all may benefit living creatures— small rodents and insects—until their return is completed. The remains of things—animals and plants, the clay and the stones— were treated with respect. Because for the ancient people all these things had spirit and being.

The antelope merely consents to return home with the hunter. All phases of the hunt are conducted with love. The love the hunter and the people have for the Antelope People. And the love of the antelope who agree to give up their meat and blood so that human beings will not starve. Waste of meat or even the thoughtless handling of bones cooked bare will offend the antelope spirits. Next year the hunters will vainly search the dry plains for antelope. Thus it is necessary to return carefully the bones and hair, and the stalks and leaves to the earth who first created them. The spirits remain close by. They do not leave us.

The dead become dust, and in this becoming they are once more joined with the Mother. The ancient Pueblo people called the earth the Mother Creator of all things in this world. Her sister, the Corn Mother, occasionally merges with her because all succulent green life rises out of the depths of the earth.

5   Rocks and clay are part of the Mother. They emerge in various forms, but at some time before, they were smaller particles or great boulders. At a later time they may again become what they once were. Dust.

A rock shares this fate with us and with animals and plants as well. A rock has being or spirit, although we may not understand it. The spirit may differ from the spirit we know in animals or plants or in ourselves. In the end we all originate from the depths of the earth. Perhaps this is how all beings share in the spirit of the Creator. We do not know.

FROM THE EMERGENCE PLACE

Pueblo potters, the creators of petroglyphs and oral narratives, never conceived of removing themselves from the earth and sky. So long as the human consciousness remains *within* the hills, canyons, cliffs, and the plants, clouds, and sky, the term *landscape*, as it has entered the English language, is misleading. "A portion of territory the eye can comprehend in a single view" does not correctly describe the relationship between the human being and his or her surroundings. This assumes the viewer is somehow *outside* or *separate from* the territory he or she surveys. Viewers are as much a part of the landscape as the boulders they stand on. There is no high mesa edge or mountain peak where one can stand and not immediately be part of all that surrounds. Human identity is linked with all the elements of Creation through the clan: you might belong to the Sun Clan or the Lizard Clan or the Corn Clan or the Clay Clan.[1] Standing deep within the natural world, the ancient Pueblo understood the thing as it was—the squash blossom, grasshopper, or rabbit itself could never be created by the human hand. Ancient Pueblos took the modest view that the thing itself (the landscape) could not be improved upon. The ancients did not presume to tamper with what had already been created. Thus *realism*, as we now recognize it in painting and sculpture, did not catch the imaginations of Pueblo people until recently.

The squash blossom itself is *one thing:* itself. So the ancient Pueblo potter abstracted what she saw to be the key elements of the squash blossom—the four symmetrical petals, with four symmetrical stamens in the center. These key elements, while suggesting the squash flower, also link it with the four cardinal directions. By representing only its intrinsic form, the squash flower is released from a limited meaning or restricted identity. Even in the most sophisticated abstract form, a squash flower or a cloud or a lightning bolt became intricately connected with a complex system of relationships which the ancient Pueblo people maintained with each other, and with the populous natural world they lived within. A bolt of lightning is itself, but at the same time it may mean much more. It may be a messenger of good fortune when summer rains are needed. It may deliver death, perhaps the result of manipulations by the Gunnadeyahs, destructive necromancers. Lightning may strike down an evil-doer. Or lightning may strike a person of good will. If the person survives, lightning endows him or her with heightened power.

Pictographs and petroglyphs of constellations or elk or antelope draw their magic in part from the process wherein the focus of all prayer and concentration is upon the thing itself, which, in its turn, guides the hunter's hand. Connection with the spirit dimensions requires a figure or form which is all-inclusive. A "lifelike" rendering of an elk is too restrictive. Only the elk *is* itself. A *realistic* rendering of an elk would be only one particular elk anyway. The purpose of the hunt rituals and magic is to make contact with *all* the spirits of the Elk.

10   The land, the sky, and all that is within them—the landscape—includes human beings. Interrelationships in the Pueblo landscape are complex and fragile. The unpredictability of the weather, the aridity and harshness of much of the terrain in the high plateau country explain in large part the relentless attention the ancient Pueblo people gave the sky and the earth around them. Survival depended upon harmony and cooperation not only among human beings, but among all things—the animate and the less animate, since rocks and mountains were known to move, to travel occasionally.

The ancient Pueblos believed the Earth and the Sky were sisters (or sister and brother in the post-Christian version). As long as good family relations are maintained, then the Sky will continue to bless her sister, the Earth, with rain, and the Earth's children will continue to survive. But the old stories recall incidents in which troublesome spirits or beings threaten the earth. In one story, a malicious ka'tsina,[2] called the Gambler, seizes the Shiwana, or Rainclouds, the Sun's beloved children. The Shiwana are snared in magical power late one afternoon on a high mountain top. The Gambler takes the Rainclouds to his mountain stronghold where he locks them in the north room of his house. What was his idea? The Shiwana were beyond value. They brought life to all things on earth. The Gambler wanted a big stake to wager in his games of chance. But such greed, even on the part of only one being, had the effect of threatening the survival of all life on earth. Sun Youth, aided by old Grandmother Spider, outsmarts the Gambler and the rigged game, and the

Rainclouds are set free. The drought ends, and once more life thrives on earth.

THROUGH THE STORIES WE HEAR WHO WE ARE

All summer the people watch the west horizon, scanning the sky from south to north for rain clouds. Corn must have moisture at the time the tassels form. Otherwise pollination will be incomplete, and the ears will be stunted and shriveled. An inadequate harvest may bring disaster. Stories told at Hopi, Zuni, and at Acoma and Laguna describe drought and starvation as recently as 1900. Precipitation in west-central New Mexico averages fourteen inches annually. The western pueblos are located at altitudes over 5,600 feet above sea level, where winter temperatures at night fall below freezing. Yet evidence of their presence in the high desert plateau country goes back ten thousand years. The ancient Pueblo people not only survived in this environment, but many years they thrived. In A.D. 1100 the people at Chaco Canyon had built cities with apartment buildings of stone five stories high. Their sophistication as sky-watchers was surpassed only by Mayan and Inca astronomers. Yet this vast complex of knowledge and belief, amassed for thousands of years, was never recorded in writing.

Instead, the ancient Pueblo people depended upon collective memory through successive generations to maintain and transmit an entire culture, a world view complete with proven strategies for survival. The oral narrative, or "story," became the medium in which the complex of Pueblo knowledge and belief was maintained. Whatever the event or the subject, the ancient people perceived the world and themselves within that world as part of an ancient continuous story composed of innumerable bundles of other stories.

The ancient Pueblo vision of the world was inclusive. The impulse was to leave nothing out. Pueblo oral tradition necessarily embraced all levels of human experience. Otherwise, the collective knowledge and beliefs comprising ancient Pueblo culture would have been incomplete. Thus stories about the Creation and Emergence of human beings and animals into this World continue to be retold each year for four days and four nights during the winter solstice. The "humma-hah" stories related events from the time long ago when human beings were still able to communicate with animals and other living things. But, beyond these two preceding categories, the Pueblo oral tradition knew no boundaries. Accounts of the appearance of the first Europeans in Pueblo country or of the tragic encounters between Pueblo people and Apache raiders were no more and no less important than stories about the biggest mule deer ever taken or adulterous couples surprised in cornfields and chicken coops. Whatever happened, the ancient people instinctively sorted events and details into a loose narrative structure. Everything became a story.

15   Traditionally everyone, from the youngest child to the oldest person, was expected to listen and to be able to recall or tell a portion, if only a small detail, from a narrative account or story. Thus the remembering and retelling were a communal process. Even if a key figure, an elder who knew much more than others, were to die unexpectedly, the system would remain intact. Through the efforts of a great many people, the community was able to piece together valuable accounts and crucial information that might otherwise have died with an individual.

Communal storytelling was a self-correcting process in which listeners were encouraged to speak up if they noted an important fact or detail omitted. The people were happy to listen to two or three different versions of the same event or the same humma-hah story. Even conflicting versions of an incident were welcomed for the entertainment they provided. Defenders of each version might joke and tease one another, but seldom were there any direct confrontations. Implicit in the Pueblo oral tradition was the awareness that loyalties, grudges, and kinship must always influence the narrator's choices as she emphasizes to listeners this is the way *she* has always heard the story told. The ancient Pueblo people sought a communal truth, not an absolute. For them this truth lived somewhere within the web of differing versions, disputes over minor points, outright contradictions tangling with old feuds and village rivalries.

A dinner-table conversation, recalling a deer hunt forty years ago when the largest mule deer ever was taken, inevitably stimulates similar memories in listeners. But hunting stories were not merely after-dinner entertainment. These accounts contained information of critical importance about behavior and migration patterns of mule deer. Hunting stories carefully described key landmarks and locations of fresh water. Thus a deer-hunt story might also serve as a "map." Lost travelers, and lost piñon-nut gatherers, have been saved by sighting a rock formation they recognize only because they once heard a hunting story describing this rock formation.

The importance of cliff formations and water holes does not end with hunting stories. As offspring of the Mother Earth, the ancient Pueblo people could not conceive of themselves without a specific landscape. Location, or "place," nearly always plays a central role in the Pueblo oral narratives. Indeed, stories are most frequently recalled as people are passing by a specific geographical feature or the exact place where a story takes place. The precise date of the incident often is less important than the place or location of the happening. "Long, long ago," "a long time ago," "not too long ago," and "recently" are usually how stories are classified in terms of time. But the places where the stories occur are precisely located, and prominent geographical details recalled, even if the landscape is well-known to listeners. Often because the turning point in the narrative involved a peculiarity or special quality of a rock or tree or plant found only at that place. Thus, in the case of many of the Pueblo narratives, it is impossible to determine which came first: the incident or the geographical feature which begs to be brought alive in a story that features some unusual aspect of this location.

There is a giant sandstone boulder about a mile north of Old Laguna, on the road to Paguate. It is ten feet tall and twenty feet in circumference. When I was a child, and we would pass this boulder driving to Paguate village, someone usually made reference to the story about Kochininako, Yellow Woman, and the Estrucuyo, a monstrous giant who nearly ate her. The Twin Hero Brothers saved Kochininako, who had been out hunting rabbits to take home to feed her mother and sisters. The Hero Brothers had heard her cries just in time. The Estrucuyo had cornered her in a cave too small to fit its monstrous head. Kochininako had already thrown to the Estrucuyo all her rabbits, as well as her moccasins and most of her clothing. Still the creature had not been satisfied. After killing the Estrucuyo with their bows and arrows, the Twin Hero Brothers slit open the Estrucuyo and cut out its heart. They threw the heart as far as they could. The monster's heart landed there, beside the old trail to Paguate village, where the sandstone boulder rests now.

It may be argued that the existence of the boulder precipi- 20 tated the creation of a story to explain it. But sandstone boulders and sandstone formations of strange shapes abound in the Laguna Pueblo area. Yet most of them do not have stories. Often the crucial element in a narrative is the terrain—some specific detail of the setting.

A high dark mesa rises dramatically from a grassy plain fifteen miles southeast of Laguna, in an area known as Swanee.

On the grassy plain one hundred and forty years ago, my great-grandmother's uncle and his brother-in-law were grazing their herd of sheep. Because visibility on the plain extends for over twenty miles, it wasn't until the two sheepherders came near the high dark mesa that the Apaches were able to stalk them. Using the mesa to obscure their approach, the raiders swept around from both ends of the mesa. My great-grandmother's relatives were killed, and the herd lost. The high dark mesa played a critical role: the mesa had compromised the safety which the openness of the plains had seemed to assure. Pueblo and Apache alike relied upon the terrain, the very earth herself, to give them protection and aid. Human activities or needs were maneuvered to fit the existing surroundings and conditions. I imagine the last afternoon of my distant ancestors as warm and sunny for late September. They might have been traveling slowly, bringing the sheep closer to Laguna in preparation for the approach of colder weather. The grass was tall and only beginning to change from green to a yellow which matched the late-afternoon sun shining off it. There might have been comfort in the warmth and the sight of the sheep fattening on good pasture which lulled my ancestors into their fatal inattention. They might have had a rifle whereas the Apaches had only bows and arrows. But there would have been four or five Apache raiders, and the surprise attack would have canceled any advantage the rifles gave them.

Survival in any landscape comes down to making the best use of all available resources. On that particular September afternoon, the raiders made better use of the Swanee terrain than my poor ancestors did. Thus the high dark mesa and the story of the two lost Laguna herders became inextricably linked. The memory of them and their story resides in part with the high black mesa. For as long as the mesa stands, people within the family and clan will be reminded of the story of that afternoon long ago. Thus the continuity and accuracy of the oral narratives are reinforced by the landscape—and the Pueblo interpretation of that landscape is *maintained.*

THE MIGRATION STORY: AN INTERIOR JOURNEY

The Laguna Pueblo migration stories refer to specific places—mesas, springs, or cottonwood trees—not only locations which can be visited still, but also locations which lie directly on the state highway route linking Paguate village with Laguna village. In traveling this road as a child with older Laguna people I first heard a few of the stories from that much larger body of stories linked with the Emergence and Migration.[3] It may be coincidental that Laguna people continue to follow the same route which, according to the Migration story, the ancestors followed south from the Emergence Place. It may be that the route is merely the shortest and best route for car, horse, or foot traffic between Laguna and Paguate villages. But if the stories about boulders, springs, and hills are actually remnants from a ritual that retraces the creation and emergence of the Laguna Pueblo people as a culture, as the people they became, then continued use of that route creates a unique relationship between the ritual-mythic world and the actual, everyday world. A journey from Paguate to Laguna down the long incline of Paguate Hill retraces the original journey from the Emergence Place, which is located slightly north of the Paguate village. Thus the landscape between Paguate and Laguna takes on a deeper significance: the landscape resonates the spiritual or mythic dimension of the Pueblo world even today.

Although each Pueblo culture designates a specific Emergence Place—usually a small natural spring edged with mossy sandstone and full of cattails and wild watercress—it is clear that they do not agree on any single location or natural spring as the one and only true Emergence Place. Each Pueblo group recounts its own stories about Creation,[4] Emergence, and Migration, although they all believe that all human beings, with all the animals and plants, emerged at the same place and at the same time.

Natural springs are crucial sources of water for all life in the high desert plateau country. So the small spring near Paguate village is literally the source and continuance of life for the people in the area. The spring also functions on a spiritual level, recalling the original Emergence Place and linking the people and the spring water to all other people and to that moment when the Pueblo people became aware of themselves as they are even now. The Emergence was an emergence into a precise cultural identity. Thus the Pueblo stories about the Emergence and Migration are not to be taken as literally as the anthropologists might wish. Prominent geographical features and landmarks which are mentioned in the narratives exist for ritual purposes, not because the Laguna people actually journeyed south for hundreds of years

25

from Chaco Canyon or Mesa Verde, as the archaeologists say, or eight miles from the site of the natural springs at Paguate to the sandstone hilltop at Laguna.

The eight miles, marked with boulders, mesas, springs, and river crossings, are actually a ritual circuit or path which marks the interior journey the Laguna people made: a journey of awareness and imagination in which they emerged from being within the earth and from everything included in earth to the culture and people they became, differentiating themselves for the first time from all that had surrounded them, always aware that interior distances cannot be reckoned in physical miles or in calendar years.

The narratives linked with prominent features of the landscape between Paguate and Laguna delineate the complexities of the relationship which human beings must maintain with the surrounding natural world if they hope to survive in this place. Thus the journey was an interior process of the imagination, a growing awareness that being human is somehow different from all other life—animal, plant, and inanimate. Yet we are all from the same source: the awareness never deteriorated into Cartesian duality, cutting off the human from the natural world.

The people found the opening into the Fifth World too small to allow them or any of the animals to escape. They had sent a fly out through the small hole to tell them if it was the world which the Mother Creator had promised. It was, but there was the problem of getting out. The antelope tried to butt the opening to enlarge it, but the antelope enlarged it only a little. It was necessary for the badger with her long claws to assist the antelope, and at last the opening was enlarged enough so that all the people and animals were able to emerge up into the Fifth World. The human beings could not have emerged without the aid of antelope and badger. The human beings depended upon the aid and charity of the animals. Only through interdependence could the human beings survive. Families belonged to clans, and it was by clan that the human being joined with the animal and plant world. Life on the high arid plateau became viable when the human beings were able to imagine themselves as sisters and brothers to the badger, antelope, clay, yucca, and sun. Not until they could find a viable relationship to the terrain, the landscape they found themselves in, could they *emerge*. Only at the moment the requisite balance between human and *other* was realized could the Pueblo people become a culture, a distinct group whose population and survival remained stable despite the vicissitudes of climate and terrain.

Landscape thus has similarities with dreams. Both have the power to seize terrifying feelings and deep instincts and translate them into images—visual, aural, tactile—into the concrete where human beings may more readily confront and channel the terrifying instincts or powerful emotions into rituals and narratives which reassure the individual while reaffirming cherished values of the group. The identity of the individual as a part of the group and the greater Whole is strengthened, and the terror of facing the world alone is extinguished.

Even now, the people at Laguna Pueblo spend the greater   30
portion of social occasions recounting recent incidents or events which have occurred in the Laguna area. Nearly always, the discussion will precipitate the retelling of older stories about similar incidents or other stories connected with a specific place. The stories often contain disturbing or provocative material, but are nonetheless told in the presence of children and women. The effect of these interfamily or interclan exchanges is the reassurance for each person that she or he will never be separated or apart from the clan, no matter what might happen. Neither the worst blunders or disasters nor the greatest financial prosperity and joy will ever be permitted to isolate anyone from the rest of the group. In the ancient times, cohesiveness was all that stood between extinction and survival, and, while the individual certainly was recognized, it was always as an individual simultaneously bonded to family and clan by a complex bundle of custom and ritual. You are never the first to suffer a grave loss or profound humiliation. You are never the first, and you understand that you will probably not be the last to commit or be victimized by a repugnant act. Your family and clan are able to go on at length about others now passed on, others older or more experienced than you who suffered similar losses.

The wide deep arroyo near the Kings Bar (located across the reservation borderline) has over the years claimed many vehicles. A few years ago, when a Vietnam veteran's new red Volkswagen rolled backwards into the arroyo while he was inside buying a six-pack of beer, the story of his loss joined the lively and large collection of stories already connected with that big arroyo. I do not know whether the Vietnam veteran was consoled when he was told the stories about the other cars claimed by the ravenous arroyo. All his savings of combat pay had gone for the red Volkswagen. But this man could not have felt any worse than the man who, some years before, had left his children and mother-in-law in his station wagon with the engine running. When he came out of the liquor store his station wagon was gone. He found it and its passengers upside down in the big arroyo. Broken bones, cuts and bruises, and a total wreck of the car. The big arroyo has a wide mouth. Its existence needs no explanation. People in the area regard the arroyo much as they might regard a living being, which has a certain character and personality. I seldom drive past that wide deep arroyo without feeling a familiarity with and even a strange affection for this arroyo. Because as treacherous as it may be, the arroyo maintains a strong connection between human beings and the earth. The arroyo demands from us the caution and attention that constitute respect. It is this sort of respect the old believers have in mind when they tell us we must respect and love the earth.

Hopi Pueblo elders have said that the austere and, to some eyes, barren plains and hills surrounding their mesa-top villages actually help to nurture the spirituality of the Hopi *way*. The Hopi elders say the Hopi people might have settled in locations far more lush where daily life would not have been so grueling. But there on the high silent sandstone mesas that overlook the sandy arid expanses stretching to all horizons, the Hopi elders say the Hopi people must "live by their prayers" if they are to survive. The Hopi way cherishes the intangible: the riches realized from interaction and interrelationships with all beings above all else. Great abundances of material things, even food, the Hopi elders believe, tend to lure human attention away from what is most valuable and important. The views of the Hopi elders are not much different from those elders in all the Pueblos.

The bare vastness of the Hopi landscape emphasizes the visual impact of every plant, every rock, every arroyo. Nothing is overlooked or taken for granted. Each ant, each lizard, each lark is imbued with great value simply because the creature is there, simply because the creature is alive in a place where any life at all is precious. Stand on the mesa edge at Walpai and look west over the bare distances toward the pale blue outlines of the San Francisco peaks where the ka'tsina spirits reside. So little lies between you and the sky. So little lies between you and the earth. One look and you know that simply to survive is a great triumph, that every possible resource is needed, every possible ally—even the most humble insect or reptile. You realize you will be speaking with all of them if you intend to last out the year. Thus it is that the Hopi elders are grateful to the landscape for aiding them in their quest as spiritual people.

1986

Endnotes

1. Clan—A social unit composed of families sharing common ancestors who trace their lineage back to the Emergence where their ancestors allied themselves with certain plants or animals or elements.
2. Ka'tsina—Ka'tsinas are spirit beings who roam the earth and who inhabit kachina masks worn in Pueblo ceremonial dances.
3. The Emergence—All the human beings, animals, and life which had been created emerged from the four worlds below when the earth became habitable.

   The Migration—The Pueblo people emerged into the Fifth World, but they had already been warned they would have to travel and search before they found the place they were meant to live.
4. Creation—Tse'itsi'nako, Thought Woman, the Spider, thought about it, and everything she thought came into being. First she thought of three sisters for herself, and they helped her think of the rest of the Universe, including the Fifth World and the four worlds below. *The Fifth World* is the world we are living in today. There are four previous worlds below this world.

Discussion

1. Why does Silko make the point that to the Pueblo the term "landscape" is misleading?
2. Explain whether or not you agree with the ancient Pueblo perception that land cannot be improved upon.
3. What does Silko suggest by saying that landscapes and dreams have similarities?
4. What does Silko mean by "interdependence"?
5. How does Silko implicitly link the Pueblo way of life with the philosophy and attitudes of Henry David Thoreau in "Walking" (p. 44)?

A Woman's Land

SALLIE BINGHAM

Sallie Bingham (1937–) was born in Louisville, Kentucky, a member of one of the most influential and wealthiest families in the state. Until 1991, the Binghams owned the Louisville-Courier, *Kentucky's most important newspaper. Following a family squabble, however, the newspaper was sold, a drama that Bingham scathingly portrayed in* Passion and Prejudice: A Family Memoir *(1989). She is a graduate of Radcliffe College, in Cambridge,*

Massachusetts, taught at the University of Louisville, and founded the Kentucky Foundation for Women and the Sallie Bingham Center for Women's History and Culture at Duke University. Bingham, a feminist, writes about contemporary women and their attempts to live fulfilling lives. Her works include the novels Small Victories: A Novel *(1992),* Upstate *(1993), and* Matron of Honor *(1994), and a collection of stories entitled* Transgressions *(2002).*

────────────── ✦ ──────────────

Four years ago I bought a piece of wild land. Parts of it had been farmed in a haphazard sort of way, but most of it was woods, or fields on their way back to being woods. Since moving to this piece of land, which is often called a farm, I have begun to wonder about its appropriate uses and about my relation to it, as one of the very few women who own land.

So few women own land that the phrase, woman landowner, seems curious. At once we wonder how she came to own it, how she afforded it—and that recognition of the financial inequities women face obscures another question—can a woman *own* land?

We are in new territory here because we have no myths or legends, no sayings or parables to guide us. We few who own the half-acre our house stands on, or the several acres left from an old farm, or the piece of property that descended through the family, must weave our own theories; we have nothing to go on except the words of the land-patriarchs, and they have little to offer that does not offend.

Women do not usually exploit, even in situations where exploitation is possible or expected; we do not often sell our children, for example. Where poor women have been brought to barter their unborn babies for money, a concept vital to the community breaks down. The mother's heartbreak reflects the disease of her times.

5   Generally we are not farmers, but gardeners. We may raise a few flowers or some vegetables for the table. We take from the earth what we can use, or what we can enjoy without depleting the supply. Women are not usually hunters or real-estate developers. We do not always seek to convert gifts into power or cash.

The deer in the woods seems to me to have been placed there not for my purposes or for the purposes of the hunter, but to fulfill the law of her existence: to graze, sleep, procreate, or run away from danger, without reference even to my appreciation of her beauty.

The old fields in front of and behind my house seem to exist without reference to their potential productivity. Once they were treed; now, the trees and brush would return if the farmer who rents them for corn kept his machinery in the barn for one season. The land would be revitalized, no longer scoured and soured by chemical sprays and fertilizers. Perhaps in my lifetime those elements the soil has lost would be restored—if the machinery continued to stay in the barn. But soon the "field" would no longer be a field, but a wild place, accessible only to birds and small animals that can move through briars on their hidden paths.

Yet, this would not seem to me to be the land's intention either, but that cycle of change might, once again, bring beeches into maturity on this stretch. The land is given only to itself—it exists for me as the ground under my feet, but not as a possibility, a future, a hope of gain.

Does my attitude make the land into a luxury, affordable only by the very rich, who do not need to consider productivity? If so, women must find another way, for women are not rich, almost by definition, in a sexist society where we are always in charge of the spiritual and social work that holds the community together and pays poorly.

Perhaps I can form a theory based on the communal use of 10 my land, which recognizes several purposes for this piece of common acreage: relief for my eyes and for my soul, a place for my husband's sheep to graze, a horizon for my sons to escape from and through, a place for the barn cat and her kitten to fatten off grain-fed mice, and for my friends to house and tend their special animals—the llama, the three-legged deer. These two curious animals bear, symbolically, the weight of the whole place: they exist outside of the money exchange. Does that make them the curiosities of the rich? Not quite. Their caretakers are not wealthy, and yet their wealth or lack of it does not enter into the exchange. These animals live outside of the area of commerce, or are excluded from it. They are gifts.

The sheep are not gifts. They were bought with a certain end in view: to be converted into cash. However, the sheep's symbolic meaning has changed as they have begun to share the barn with the llama and the three-legged deer. They have names, or at least some of them do. Their purpose is no longer clear.

Is this sheer sentimentality? Again, a luxury of the rich, who do not toil, nor do they spin? Or is it a recognition of the ultimate independence of the sheep (an odd expression for such dumb and dumbly obedient beasts) from our aims or plans?

What defines the land is what escapes definition: the Canada geese who light on the pond and take off with a wild flurry of wings in the morning, always towards the south; the heron outside my studio window who stood for a short while on a stone in the river. These birds did not arrive here, and pause briefly, for our edification. They exist in their own worlds, which we can barely appreciate, which we cannot penetrate or convert into cash.

But what was the motive that brought a hunter to shoot one of our rare bald eagles, so well-marked with spray paint and electronic devices? Surely the hunter was a boy or a man. Surely he sought in the killing something he could take away with him, a talisman or a boast. The need to "make something out of" the experience perhaps defines the male. A woman might have wanted to make the sighting into a story or a painting. But she would not have figured, necessarily, in that story or painting, as the hunter must figure in the shooting of the eagle. The eagle would have lived to see another day, free of the woman—the artist—and her transitory usage; the eagle did not outlive the man's aim.

15   I am uncomfortable suggesting that a woman's use of the land might be better than a man's. Notions of women's superiority always have a sting in the tail. We carry enough weight in the world without taking on the weight of being morally superior. Yet, the fact remains that women do not destroy land, either as owners who sell off pastures for shopping centers or as employees who operate bulldozers that push down trees. Is it enough to say that we are powerless to commit this evil? I think not. A woman who is able to buy land probably learned something about its care from the way a woman without financial power tended her African violets.

But perhaps the difference in attitudes towards the land is not gender-related. Perhaps the artist, male or female, is able to see trees and open stretches as gifts, not as possibilities for conversion. Perhaps our addictive needs are satisfied by the manufacturing of words out of the landscape, rather than by the manufacturing of tract houses.

Artists who are men are often perceived as living on the fringes of their gender, stripling lads even in old age, Apollos without followers. Often they lack power and money. To the extent that their androgyny is corrupted by power and money, they become more male-like, more interested in conversion, in "making something out of." The rare successful artist who purchases land is perhaps more likely to sell off parts of it for subdivisions than the equally rare woman who can afford to buy and will preserve it.

If the gift survives the addiction, however, as it seems capable of doing, there will still be a need for a woman or an artist to appreciate it—although to all intents and purposes, that appreciation is inessential. Appreciation, if it is converted into action, can save land.

There will always be a few rich women who will endow a piece of land and will it to perpetuity, although for the land to survive, her heirs must accept that it does not belong to them. In how many cases has a woman been able to surmount her heirs' ideas of their rights and leave the land to continue "undeveloped"?

In the case of my land, the woman landowner's heirs despoiled it with their motorcycles and logged out all the old trees and would have sold it to the highest bidder for any purpose whatsoever if the lack of city water and sewage hadn't hampered their aims. It came to me almost by default.

Now, as I work on my will, I am trying to insure that the land remains open forever. This means that it will not be inherited by my sons, but will remain, as it is now, a gift. This is difficult, if not impossible, to do, first on a personal level. All children long to inherit what is of value to the parent; it is a way of receiving commitment and memories. In the case of my sons, their inevitable immersion in the patriarchy means that they will want to "make something out of" the land, should it pass to them. Leaving it to lie fallow, to grow up again with weeds, would seem an eccentric choice for a male landowner.

On another level, the patriarchy itself is dead set against my decision. The right of sons to inherit is fundamental to capitalism, and to the more secretive continuation of a ruling class. How then can heirs be taught to see the land as a gift? Only by stroking the three-legged deer and looking at the silent llama.

1990

Discussion

1. What is Bingham's vision for the future of the environment?
2. Describe the pros and cons of Bingham's idea of the communal use of land.
3. What does Bingham suggest when she says that the definition of land is what escapes definition?
4. Why does Bingham think that the person who shot the bald eagle is a man? Is she unfairly branding men as environmental criminals?

Bugz

STEVE CHAPPLE

Steve Chapple (1949–) grew up in Billings, Montana, and attended Yale University in New Haven, Connecticut. He has written eight books and two screenplays. Among his books are Rock 'n' Roll Is Here to Pay: The History and Politics of the Music Industry *(1978),* Don't Mind Dying: A Novel of Country Lust and Urban Decay *(1980),* Outlaws in Babylon: Shocking, True Adventures on the Marijuana Frontier *(1984),* Burning Desires: Sex in America *(1989),* Kayaking the Full Moon: A Journey Down the Yellowstone River *(1993), and* Let the Mountains Talk, Let the Rivers Run: A Call to Those Who Would Save the Earth *(with David Brower, 1996).*

---- ✦ ----

"Musquetoes troublesome."
MERIWETHER LEWIS, May 23, 1805

"Musquetors troublesome."
WILLIAM CLARK, May 23, 1805

"Musquetors verry troublesom."
CLARK, July 2, 1805

"Musquetos troublesome as usual."
LEWIS, July 8, 1805

"Musquitors verry troublesom."
CLARK, July 20, 1805

"Musquetoes uncommonly large and reather troublesome."
LEWIS, July 29, 1806

"Musquetoes extreemly troublesome."
LEWIS, July 12, 1806

"Musquetors excessively troublesom."
CLARK, August 2, 1806

"Musquitors excessively tormenting."
CLARK, September 7, 1806

There are 700,000 different kinds of known insects, 2700 species of mosquitoes, 90,000 flies, 30,000 ticks (actually eight-legged fellows related to spiders), 1800 fleas, 3500 cockroaches, and one really loathsome kind of bedbug. For each one of us, there are 200 million of them, which sifts out to about 300 pounds of bugs per person. The biomass of the ants alone weighs more than all humans put together. It gives pause.

Insects eat our zucchini. They poke holes in our squash. They discomfort us mightily at stream side.

And it only gets worse.

"Since the beginning of recorded history insects have caused the death by disease of more people than all the wars, earthquakes, hurricanes, floods, droughts and fires combined. To this immense toll of human life," reads a report for the American Museum of Natural History, "can be added incalculable economic losses caused by insects attacking food and textile crops, forests, buildings, furniture and much else."

I don't know about the furniture, but I think this might be too 5 strong an indictment of our tiny friends, the joint-footed Arthropoda. If it weren't for caddis flies, also mayflies and maybe black gnats, trout would starve, along with a goodly number of stream-running bass and walleyes.

Things balance out. It's important to keep your perspective, though the bloodsuckers can easily give you Lyme disease, make you crazy as a bedbug, drive you antsy, or—

Everybody has a scorpion in the ear story, a tale of wasps inside the tent. I remember a time in my youth (an extended and larvaelike period, looking back on it) when I became fresh meat for a large herd of *musquetors* along the shores of Fossil Lake, in the Beartooth Wilderness of Montana and northern Wyoming, where I happened to be whiling away a weekend prospecting for albino golden trout.

I was off the trail, above the tree line. There were billowing clouds of them, the *muskitors*, and since it was June, they had me to themselves. It was too late for elk and moose, too early for the more inviting German backpackers, who, in my experience, wear little else but sunscreen and shards of leiderhosen.

My feelings were described perfectly by Roger W. Crosskey, entomologist with the British Museum: "The experience of being continually bitten, unable to step outside without soon oozing blood from countless bites, is a demoralizer with few equals." This from Crosskey's remarkable treatise, *The Natural History of Blackflies*.

But these brutes were bigger than blackflies. "Two of them 10 could whip a dog," as Mark Twain said of some "lawless insects" down South. "Four of them could hold a man down; and except help come, they would kill him—butcher him."

I had no tent, back in Montana, no prophylaxis, save a clear plastic raincoat I'd picked up at the Army Navy Store in Billings for, in those days, about $4.95. I threw it over my T-shirt and jeans and zipped it up. It was the pants-suit kind, and it did the trick. Then I began to sweat. Then, as my core temperature slowly rose and the mozzies whined and whinnied outside my vinyl exoskeleton, I grew mad as a bedbug. Mine was becoming a Kafkaesque camping experience. I thought I might be undergoing some terrible metamorphosis—like a caribou. Already, extreme bedevilment was causing me to mix metaphors.

As you know, it is not unknown for caribou, in Canada, to sometimes charge into the nearest lake or river, even if that means drowning, should squadrons of blackflies descend. If there is an insect hell on earth, it is probably Canada, the whole country.

"The little [blackflies] force their way into any crevice," complained early Colossus-to-the-North explorers Louis Agassiz and Henry Walter Bates, near Lake Superior: "On the other hand they are easily killed, as they stick to their prey like bulldogs."

Personally, in fly season, I am afraid to venture north of the Milk River, and it has nothing to do with Margaret Atwood, Margaret Trudeau, or back-bacon.

15   They are a formidable enemy, the crinkly foot Arthropoda. At Fossil Lake, I lit a smudge stick from a moss-covered spruce branch and ceded the area to superior forces.

"Life on this planet can get along well without people," asserts one author who has dedicated his life to this sort of thing, "but it cannot in its present form do without insects. Without them we would die."

There would be no flowers without insects. The two evolved together. No apple trees or cactus, either. Can't live with them, can't live without them. Which brings us to the sex life of the mantids, at last.

When a male praying mantis jumps on a receptive female praying mantis, and they have only just begun to mate, the female turns over her shoulder and bites off the male's head, which she then proceeds to eat. Interestingly, the male, though now headless, does not draw back from his business. Once in a great while he does, out of lassitude or gravity, but if so, another male flies aboard. She bites his head off, too. That's how it's done in the mantid world, and bug scientists even believe the male's decapitation is the dramatic signal that causes him to release his sperm, or, since his head has just been chewed and swallowed, I believe it might be more accurate to say, *causes his sperm to be released.*

At any rate, it does not have to be this way, and it is not for most insects. Certainly, not for the bedbug, a true bug, of the homoptera, or True Bugs.

Since lady bedbugs have no genital opening (yes, I know this   20
is a family publication, but we are talking about creepy-crawlies) he ups and pokes a hole between her fifth and six abdominal segments. This probably hurts a lot, but the female bedbug is equipped with something called an organ of Berlese, which functions, claims entomologist May R. Berenbaum,

> to prevent the male's organ from doing permanent physical injury to her internal anatomy. The male bedbug then pumps in an enormous quantity of sperm, which swim into the bloodstream and eventually find the reproductive organs of the female. After the male withdraws his organ, the wound he created eventually closes and heals over, leaving a scar. The whole process is called, appropriately, traumatic insemination.

Clearly, it is a dull business, studying bugs for a living.

Modern chemicals have all but eliminated the grosser behaviors of the bedbug, along with the bedbugs themselves, most of them. Count yourself lucky this spring that you only have to shoo away the flies, squeeze off the sand fleas, and apply hot match heads to the tick butts sequestered in your secret places. Be thankful that bedbugs don't swarm.

Also, don't whine. The frequency of human whining only attracts certain beetles, anyway, like wasps to cologne.

It could be worse. In the late Carboniferous Period, dragonflies were 3 feet long, and primitive *musquetoes* stretched 8 inches, thoraxes thick as axe handles, with stingers like sailing needles. There was a lot more oxygen then.

And don't try to eat them. You already are. I like shrimp, lobster,   25
and crab—and these are the insects of the sea. Ask any biologist.

Strive to be strong, this bug season, even as you are pierced and sucked, bored and drilled. We are Americans, and we must act like Americans, not like Canadians or quitter French persons.

Remember, if Napoleon's brother-in-law, General Charles Leclerc, had not turned tail in his vain-glorious attempt to conquer Haiti and the fledgling United States after only 29,000 of the 33,000 men he set sail from Paris with had died of yellow fever, we might all be grilling truffles on hot plates. Lewis and Clark would never have made it up the Yellowstone, with all the sauger, sturgeon, pike, paddle-fish, and cutthroat trout this implies, since there would have been no Louisiana Purchase. The Yellow Stone would have stayed *La Roche Jahne*. You could say the *"troublesom musquetor"* was the bug that won the West.

Insects cannot be all bad.

1997

Discussion

1. What historical event, according to Chapple, caused the French to sell the Louisiana Territory to the United States?
2. What does Chapple suggest about ecological niches among "bugz" and fishermen?
3. What seems to be the source of Chapple's environmental humor?
4. Discuss your attitude toward biting and stinging insects. Does their presence keep you from enjoying the great outdoors?
5. What does Chapple suggest about ecological niches among "bugz" and fishermen?
6. What seems to be the source of Chapple's environmental humor?

Thinking and Writing About Chapter 5

1. Compare Edward Abbey's love of the desert in "The First Morning" (p. 165) with John Muir's attitude toward forests in "The American Forests" (p. 7).
2. Using yourself as an example, describe how your relationship with a natural place has changed with time.
3. Describe your experience of what you consider the most beautiful place on earth.
4. Compare Leslie Marmon Silko's emotional ties to the land in "Landscape, History, and the Pueblo Imagination" (p. 171) with Joy Williams's to her acre in "One Acre: On Devaluing Real Estate to Keep Land Priceless" (p. 95).
5. Compare the personal views of land ownership expressed by Sallie Bingham in "A Woman's Land" (p. 183) and Williams in "One Acre" (p. 95) with those of Mary Austin in "My Neighbor's Field" (p. 13) and Margaret L. Knox in "The Wilderness According to Cushman" (p. 31).
6. Imagine that you own land and a lucrative real estate deal comes your way. Would you sell your land to the highest bidder, or do you have a personal code that would guide your decision otherwise?
7. Discuss the feminist point of view regarding how women and men see nature differently in Bingham's "A Woman's Land" (p. 183) and Sarah Orne Jewett's "A White Heron" (p. 81).
8. Contrast Aldo Leopold's practical view of land in "The Land Ethic" (p. 18) with the personal viewpoints of Silko in "Landscape, History, and the Pueblo Imagination" (p. 171) and Austin in "My Neighbor's Field" (p. 13).

Additional Resources

Film
The Old Man and the Sea (1958), directed by John Sturges

Fiction
Ernest Hemingway. "Big Two-Hearted River, Parts I and II" (1925)
Jack London. "To Build a Fire" (1907)

Essay
Annie Dillard. *Pilgrim at Tinker Creek* (1974)

CHAPTER 6

Prospects for the Future

Over a century after John Muir pleaded with his readers to spare America's forests for both aesthetic and spiritual reasons, the stakes are now far more practical: threats from global warming, limited water supplies, dwindling oil and gas reserves, overfished oceans, and expanding populations—all imparting dangers to everyday living. In fact, it is difficult to pick up a newspaper these days without noting the proximity of environmental health to progress.

Environment and nature, in this contemporary context, are subjects of sharp debate. Are we on the road of irreversible destruction, refusing to acknowledge its results? Or have we exaggerated the consequences of environmental destruction? Have we asked ourselves whether the preservation of so much nature is really in our best interests? If you are atop a mountain in New York's Adirondacks, for example, all you can see from horizon to horizon is glorious forest. But someone else standing on the same spot might question whether all those trees are really necessary.

If you travel along the Skyline Drive in Virginia and look out on the Shenandoah Valley, the view is almost always obscured by haze. This was not so fifty years ago. What will the view be like fifty years hence? Global warming is hotly debated in Washington, D.C., (pun intended) where some contend that it is a figment of faulty computer simulations. And even if global warming is proven unalterably true, it is probable that some people will argue that we are better off as a result; increased carbon in the atmosphere—one of the prime causes of global warming—produces greater growth in plants from vegetables to forests. Discussion of the future is a feast for debaters. But one way to judge the environment of the future is its connection to what exists in the present.

The connection between the environment and economics is played out in Christopher Hallowell's "Coming to Terms" (2001), which focuses on the vital importance of the wetlands in South Louisiana that border the Gulf of Mexico. For decades, this huge coastal zone has been eroding due to a variety of assaults, principally the leveeing of the Mississippi River and dredging of canals by the oil and gas industry. Although over 3 million acres of wetlands remain, over 2 million acres have vanished, a loss that equals a football field of land every fifteen minutes. "The marsh," as it is locally called, is far more than a secluded vast region of waving grass and winding bayous, with an array of wildlife. It is a nursery that protects and nourishes the Gulf of Mexico's prodigious marine life, which translates into 40 percent of this country's seafood catch. It turns out to be a crucial buffer protecting New Orleans and other low-lying coastal cities from the ravages of hurricanes barreling in from the Gulf. If the wetlands continue to disappear, the economy as well as the physical appearance of South Louisiana will be in tatters. "Coming to Terms" weighs the merits of preserving an environmentally fragile area for the sake of the environment with the notion of preserving it for both the environment and the economy.

While the loss of economic benefits may be the key to environmental preservation efforts in the future, ethical considerations are just as important. Human activity has wiped out untold numbers of species, with more disappearing every year. But not all extinctions are our fault. Over geological time "ninety-nine percent of all the species that ever lived are now extinct," writes Edward O. Wilson in "The Environmental Ethic" (1992), a philosophical and scientific meditation on our place in the evolutionary scale. He argues that this knowledge must not stop us from protecting the remaining diversity of life on earth. We are on the cusp of unraveling the intricacies of all life, Wilson argues, but if species disappear before this happens, certain scientific and medical knowledge will be gone forever. Equally important, according to Wilson, is the diminishment of human spirituality as a result of the rapid changes that humans are inflicting on the global environment. Wilson wonders if our race toward development might imperil our own chances of survival since other species are disappearing at an accelerated rate because of human action. The ethic that Wilson proposes is based on self-interest. Since "humanity coevolved with the rest of life on this particular planet," Wilson writes, what will happen when the course of biodiversity is reduced to irrecoverable levels? Will we be paying a steep price for living comfortably in a biologically impoverished world?

Human awareness beyond our stereotypical intellectual attributes—such as language or music or a sense of design—is key to Linda Hogan's argument in "Walking" (1995). Hogan thinks that that we must listen to the earth to find a language that links one's soul with the universal soul, a tenet of her Native American heritage. Hogan explains that after much observation and contemplation, she was able to hear nature—the language of the sunflower, the beating pulse of the redwood tree, and the calling of the ocean. Like Henry David Thoreau, John Muir, and Mary Austin, Hogan has the sense that in the natural world things work together in an elemental way, and we have only to discover this once we step outside of the constrictions of civilization.

The challenge to business in the future, according to Paul Hawken, Amory Lovins, and L. Hunter Lovins in "Once Upon a Planet" (1999), is to understand how ecosystems work and how to operate within nature's rules—which are not society's rules. Their argument is that unless old stereotypes are broken, progress will stall. In fact, what the authors propose is an alteration of the current paradigm for environmental discourse and change. Because new plans for maintaining progress and stability must be devised, they do not blame either environmentalists or businesses. They see a positive future when competing factions "realize that solutions lie in understanding and interconnectedness of problems, not in confronting them in isolation." Hawken and the Lovins maintain that opportunities to make money *and* to care for the environment abound, but without understanding and respecting the way ecosystems work, they fear that greed will hasten approaching environmental catastrophe.

All the selections in Chapter 6 point toward a dire need to advance an environmental ethic based on the notion that social, economic, and industrial progress must be combined with a humanistic environmental ethic. Yes, the preservation of beautiful scenery, clean waters, and clear skies is important. But there must be a force other than aesthetics driving preservation. Economics ungrounded in comprehensive environmental ethics will fail. The consequences of taking tops off mountains to reveal coal seams or of overfishing are relatively easy to see. It is what we cannot see that we need the most—a unified environmental vision.

The Environmental Ethic

EDWARD O. WILSON

Edward O. Wilson (1929–), one of this country's most distinguished scientific thinkers, is a professor of science and curator in entomology at Harvard University. He was born in Birmingham, Alabama, and educated at the University of Alabama, Birmingham, and Harvard University, where he earned a Ph.D. in entomology. Wilson is known as the father of biodiversity, a field of study he originated, that explores how changing environments have influenced the genetic makeup of species. Although he is regarded as a leading expert on ants, he is better known for Sociobiology: The New Synthesis *(1975) and* On Human Nature *(1980). He wrote* The Diversity of Life *(1992, from which this essay is drawn), in which he makes recommendations on how to preserve diversity. Among Wilson's other important works are* The Insect Societies *(1971),* Biophila *(1984),* The Ants *(1990),* Consilience *(1998),* The Future of Life *(2002), and his biography,* Naturalist *(1994).*

---- ◆ ----

The sixth great extinction spasm of geological time is upon us, grace of mankind. Earth has at last acquired a force that can break the crucible of biodiversity. I sensed it with special poignancy that stormy night at Fazenda Dimona, when lightning flashes revealed the rain forest cut open like a cat's eye for laboratory investigation. An undisturbed forest rarely discloses its internal anatomy with such clarity. Its edge is shielded by thick secondary growth or else, along the river bank, the canopy spills down to ground level. The nighttime vision was a dying artifact, a last glimpse of savage beauty.

A few days later I got ready to leave Fazenda Dimona: gathered my muddied clothes in a bundle, gave my imitation Swiss army knife to the cook as a farewell gift, watched an overflight of Amazonian green parrots one more time, labeled and stored my specimen vials in reinforced boxes, and packed my field notebook next to a dog-eared copy of Ed McBain's police novel *Ice*, which, because I had neglected to bring any other reading matter, was now burned into my memory.

Grinding gears announced the approach of the truck sent to take me and two of the forest workers back to Manaus. In bright sunlight we watched it cross the pastureland, a terrain strewn with fire-blackened stumps and logs, the battlefield my forest had finally lost. On the ride back I tried not to look at the bare fields. Then, abandoning my tourist Portuguese, I turned inward and daydreamed. Four splendid lines of Virgil came to mind, the only ones I ever memorized, where the Sibyl warns

> The way downward is easy from Avernus.
> Black Dis's door stands open night and day.
> But to retrace your steps to heaven's air,
> There is the trouble, there is the toil . . .

For the green prehuman earth is the mystery we were chosen to solve, a guide to the birthplace of our spirit, but it is slipping away. The way back seems harder every year. If there is danger in the human trajectory, it is not so much in the survival of our own species as in the fulfillment of the ultimate irony of organic evolution: that in the instant of achieving self-understanding through the mind of man, life has doomed its most beautiful creations. And thus humanity closes the door to its past.

The creation of that diversity came slow and hard: 3 billion 5 years of evolution to start the profusion of animals that occupy the seas, another 350 million years to assemble the rain forests in which half or more of the species on earth now live. There was a succession of dynasties. Some species split into two or several daughter species, and their daughters split yet again to create swarms of descendants that deployed as plant feeders, carnivores, free swimmers, gliders, sprinters, and burrowers, in countless motley combinations. These ensembles then gave way by partial or total extinction to newer dynasties, and so on to form a gentle upward swell that carried biodiversity to a peak—just before the arrival of humans. Life had stalled on plateaus along the way, and on five occasions it suffered extinction spasms that took 10 million years to repair. But the thrust was upward. Today the diversity of life is greater than it was a 100 million years ago—and far greater than 500 million years before that.

Most dynasties contained a few species that expanded disproportionately to create satrapies of lesser rank. Each species and its descendants, a silver of the whole, lived an average of hundreds of thousands to millions of years. Longevity varied according to taxonomic group. Echinoderm lineages, for example, persisted longer than those of flowering plants, and both endured longer than those of mammals.

Ninety-nine percent of all the species that ever lived are now extinct. The modern fauna and flora are composed of survivors that somehow managed to dodge and weave through all the radiations and extinctions of geological history. Many contemporary world-dominant groups, such as rats, ranid frogs, nymphalid butterflies, and plants of the aster family Compositae, attained their status not long before the Age of Man. Young or old, all living species are direct descendants of the organisms that lived 3.8 billion years ago. They are living genetic libraries, composed of nucleotide sequences, the equivalent of words and sentences, which record evolutionary events all across that immense span of time. Organisms more complex than bacteria—protists, fungi, plants, animals—contain between 1 and 10 billion nucleotide letters, more than enough in pure information to compose an equivalent of the *Encyclopaedia Britannica*. Each species is the product of mutations and recombinations too complex to be grasped by unaided intuition. It was sculpted and burnished by an astronomical number of events in natural selection, which killed off or otherwise blocked from reproduction the vast majority of its member organisms before they completed their lifespans. Viewed from the perspective of evolutionary time, all other species are our distant kin because we share a remote ancestry. We still use a common vocabulary, the nucleic-acid code, even though it has been sorted into radically different hereditary languages.

Such is the ultimate and cryptic truth of every kind of organism, large and small, every bug and weed. The flower in the crannied wall—it *is* a miracle. If not in the way Tennyson, the Victorian romantic, bespoke the portent of full knowledge (by which "I should know what God and man is"), then certainly a consequence of all we understand from modern biology. Every kind of organism has reached this moment in time by threading one needle after another, throwing up brilliant artifices to survive and reproduce against nearly impossible odds.

Organisms are all the more remarkable in combination. Pull out the flower from its crannied retreat, shake the soil from the roots into the cupped hand, magnify it for close examination. The black earth is alive with a riot of algae, fungi, nematodes, mites, springtails, enchytraeid worms, thousands of species of bacteria. The handful may be only a tiny fragment of one ecosystem, but because of the genetic codes of its residents it holds more order than can be found on the surfaces of all the planets combined. It is a sample of the living force that runs the earth—and will continue to do so with or without us.

We may think that the world has been completely explored. 10
Almost all the mountains and rivers, it is true, have been named,
the coast and geodetic surveys completed, the ocean floor
mapped to the deepest trenches, the atmosphere transected and
chemically analyzed. The planet is now continuously monitored
from space by satellites; and, not least, Antarctica, the last virgin
continent, has become a research station and expensive tourist
stop. The biosphere, however, remains obscure. Even though
some 1.4 million species of organisms have been discovered (in
the minimal sense of having specimens collected and formal scientific names attached), the total number alive on earth is somewhere between 10 and 100 million. No one can say with confidence which of these figures is the closer. Of the species given
scientific names, fewer than 10 percent have been studied at a
level deeper than gross anatomy. The revolution in molecular biology and medicine was achieved with a still smaller fraction, including colon bacteria, corn, fruit flies, Norway rats, rhesus monkeys, and human beings, altogether comprising no more than a
hundred species.

Enchanted by the continuous emergence of new technologies
and supported by generous funding for medical research, biologists have probed deeply along a narrow sector of the front. Now
it is time to expand laterally, to get on with the great Linnean enterprise and finish mapping the biosphere. The most compelling
reason for the broadening of goals is that, unlike the rest of science, the study of biodiversity has a time limit. Species are disappearing at an accelerating rate through human action, primarily
habitat destruction but also pollution and the introduction of ex-
otic species into residual natural environments. I have said that a
fifth or more of the species of plants and animals could vanish or
be doomed to early extinction by the year 2020 unless better efforts are made to save them. This estimate comes from the known
quantitative relation between the area of habitats and the diversity that habitats can sustain. These area-biodiversity curves are
supported by the general but not universal principle that when
certain groups of organisms are studied closely, such as snails
and fishes and flowering plants, extinction is determined to be
widespread. And the corollary: among plant and animal remains
in archaeological deposits, we usually find extinct species and
races. As the last forests are felled in forest strongholds like the
Philippines and Ecuador, the decline of species will accelerate
even more. In the world as a whole, extinction rates are already
hundreds or thousands of times higher than before the coming of

man. They cannot be balanced by new evolution in any period of time that has meaning for the human race.

Why should we care? What difference does it make if some species are extinguished, if even half of all the species on earth disappear? Let me count the ways. New sources of scientific information will be lost. Vast potential biological wealth will be destroyed. Still undeveloped medicines, crops, pharmaceuticals, timber, fibers, pulp, soil-restoring vegetation, petroleum substitutes, and other products and amenities will never come to light. It is fashionable in some quarters to wave aside the small and obscure, the bugs and weeds, forgetting that an obscure moth from Latin America saved Australia's pastureland from overgrowth by cactus, that the rosy periwinkle provided the cure for Hodgkin's disease and childhood lymphocytic leukemia, that the bark of the Pacific yew offers hope for victims of ovarian and breast cancer, that a chemical from the saliva of leeches dissolves blood clots during surgery, and so on down a roster already grown long and illustrious despite the limited research addressed to it.

In amnesiac revery it is also easy to overlook the services that ecosystems provide humanity. They enrich the soil and create the very air we breathe. Without these amenities, the remaining tenure of the human race would be nasty and brief. The life-sustaining matrix is built of green plants with legions of microorganisms and mostly small, obscure animals—in other words, weeds and bugs. Such organisms support the world with efficiency because they are so diverse, allowing them to divide labor and swarm over every square meter of the earth's surface. They run the world precisely as we would wish it to be run, because humanity evolved within living communities and our bodily functions are finely adjusted to the idiosyncratic environment already created. Mother Earth, lately called Gaia, is no more than the commonality of organisms and the physical environment they maintain with each passing moment, an environment that will destabilize and turn lethal if the organisms are disturbed too much. A near infinity of other mother planets can be envisioned, each with its own fauna and flora, all producing physical environments uncongenial to human life. To disregard the diversity of life is to risk catapulting ourselves into an alien environment. We will have become like the pilot whales that inexplicably beach themselves on New England shores.

Humanity coevolved with the rest of life on this particular planet; other worlds are not in our genes. Because scientists have yet to put names on most kinds of organisms, and because they entertain only a vague idea of how ecosystems work, it is reckless to suppose that biodiversity can be diminished indefinitely without threatening humanity itself. Field studies show that as biodiversity is reduced, so is the quality of the services provided by ecosystems. Records of stressed ecosystems also demonstrate that the descent can be unpredictably abrupt. As extinction spreads, some of the lost forms prove to be keystone species, whose disappearance brings down other species and triggers a ripple effect through the demographies of the survivors. The loss of a keystone species is like a drill accidentally striking a powerline. It causes lights to go out all over.

These services are important to human welfare. But they cannot form the whole foundation of an enduring environmental ethic. If a price can be put on something, that something can be devalued, sold, and discarded. It is also possible for some to dream that people will go on living comfortably in a biologically impoverished world. They suppose that a prosthetic environment is within the power of technology, that human life can still flourish in a completely humanized world, where medicines would all be synthesized from chemicals off the shelf, food grown from a few dozen domestic crop species, the atmosphere and climate regulated by computer-driven fusion energy, and the earth made over until it becomes a literal spaceship rather than a metaphorical one, with people reading displays and touching buttons on the bridge. Such is the terminus of the philosophy of exemptionalism: do not weep for the past, humanity is a new order of life, let species die if they block progress, scientific and technological genius will find another way. Look up and see the stars awaiting us.

But consider: human advance is determined not by reason alone but by emotions peculiar to our species, aided and tempered by reason. What makes us people and not computers is emotion. We have little grasp of our true nature, of what it is to be human and therefore where our descendants might someday wish we had directed Spaceship Earth. Our troubles, as Vercors said in *You Shall Know Them*, arise from the fact that we do not know what we are and cannot agree on what we want to be. The primary cause of this intellectual failure is ignorance of our origins. We did not arrive on this planet as aliens. Humanity is part of nature, a species that evolved among other species. The more closely we identify ourselves with the rest of life, the more quickly we will be able to discover the sources of human sensibility and acquire the knowledge on which an enduring ethic, a sense of preferred direction, can be built.

The human heritage does not go back only for the convention-ally recognized 8,000 years or so of recorded history, but for at least 2 million years, to the appearance of the first "true" human beings, the earliest species composing the genus *Homo*. Across thousands of generations, the emergence of culture must have been profoundly influenced by simultaneous events in genetic evo-lution, especially those occurring in the anatomy and physiology of the brain. Conversely, genetic evolution must have been guided forcefully by the kinds of selection rising within culture.

Only in the last moment of human history has the delusion arisen that people can flourish apart from the rest of the living world. Preliterate societies were in intimate contact with a bewil-dering array of life forms. Their minds could only partly adapt to that challenge. But they struggled to understand the most rele-vant parts, aware that the right responses gave life and fulfill-ment, the wrong ones sickness, hunger, and death. The imprint of that effort cannot have been erased in a few generations of urban existence. I suggest that it is to be found among the particularities of human nature, among which are these:

- People acquire phobias, abrupt and intractable aversions, to the objects and circumstances that threaten humanity in natu-ral environments: heights, closed spaces, open spaces, running water, wolves, spiders, snakes. They rarely form phobias to the recently invented contrivances that are far more dangerous, such as guns, knives, automobiles, and electric sockets.
- People are both repelled and fascinated by snakes, even when they have never seen one in nature. In most cultures the serpent is the dominant wild animal of mythical and reli-gious symbolism. Manhattanites dream of them with the same frequency as Zulus. This response appears to be Darwinian in origin. Poisonous snakes have been an impor-tant cause of mortality almost everywhere, from Finland to Tasmania, Canada to Patagonia; an untutored alertness in their presence saves lives. We note a kindred response in many primates, including Old World monkeys and chim-panzees: the animals pull back, alert others, watch closely, and follow each potentially dangerous snake until it moves away. For human beings, in a larger metaphorical sense, the mythic, transformed serpent has come to possess both con-structive and destructive powers: Ashtoreth of the Canaanites, the demons Fu-Hsi and Nu Kua of the Han Chinese, Mudamma and Manasa of Hindu India, the triple-headed giant Nehebkau of the ancient Egyptians, the serpent

of Genesis conferring knowledge and death, and, among the Aztecs, Cihuacoatl, goddess of childbirth and mother of the human race, the rain god Tlaloc, and Quetzalcoatl, the plumed serpent with a human head who reigned as lord of the morning and evening star. Ophidian power spills over into modern life: two serpents entwine the caduceus, first the winged staff of Mercury as messenger of the gods, then the safe-conduct pass of ambassadors and heralds, and today the universal emblem of the medical profession.

- The favored living place of most peoples is a prominence near water from which parkland can be viewed. On such heights are found the abodes of the powerful and rich, tombs of the great, temples, parliaments, and monuments commemorating tribal glory. The location is today an aesthetic choice and, by the implied freedom to settle there, a symbol of status. In ancient, more practical times the topography provided a place to retreat and a sweeping prospect from which to spot the distant approach of storms and enemy forces. Every animal species selects a habitat in which its members gain a favorable mix of security and food. For most of deep history, human beings lived in tropical and subtropical savanna in East Africa, open country sprinkled with streams and lakes, trees and copses. In similar topography modern peoples choose their residences and design their parks and gardens, if given a free choice. They simulate neither dense jungles, toward which gibbons are drawn, nor dry grasslands, preferred by hamadryas baboons. In their gardens they plant trees that resemble the acacias, sterculias, and other native trees of the African savannas. The ideal tree crown sought is consistently wider than tall, with spreading lowermost branches close enough to the ground to touch and climb, clothed with compound or needle-shaped leaves.

- Given the means and sufficient leisure, a large portion of the populace backpacks, hunts, fishes, birdwatches, and gardens. In the United States and Canada more people visit zoos and aquariums than attend all professional athletic events combined. They crowd the national parks to view natural landscapes, looking from the tops of prominences out across rugged terrain for a glimpse of tumbling water and animals living free. They travel long distances to stroll along the seashore, for reasons they can't put into words.

These are examples of what I have called *biophilia*, the connections that human beings subconsciously seek with the rest of life. To biophilia can be added the idea of wilderness, all the land

and communities of plants and animals still unsullied by human occupation. Into wilderness people travel in search of new life and wonder, and from wilderness they return to the parts of the earth that have been humanized and made physically secure. Wilderness settles peace on the soul because it needs no help; it is beyond human contrivance. Wilderness is a metaphor of unlimited opportunity, rising from the tribal memory of a time when humanity spread across the world, valley to valley, island to island, godstruck, firm in the belief that virgin land went on forever past the horizon.

20   I cite these common preferences of mind not as proof of an innate human nature but rather to suggest that we think more carefully and turn philosophy to the central questions of human origins in the wild environment. We do not understand ourselves yet and descend farther from heaven's air if we forget how much the natural world means to us. Signals abound that the loss of life's diversity endangers not just the body but the spirit. If that much is true, the changes occurring now will visit harm on all generations to come.

The ethical imperative should therefore be, first of all, prudence. We should judge every scrap of biodiversity as priceless while we learn to use it and come to understand what it means to humanity. We should not knowingly allow any species or race to go extinct. And let us go beyond mere salvage to begin the restoration of natural environments, in order to enlarge wild populations and stanch the hemorrhaging of biological wealth. There can be no purpose more enspiriting than to begin the age of restoration, reweaving the wondrous diversity of life that still surrounds us.

The evidence of swift environmental change calls for an ethic uncoupled from other systems of belief. Those committed by religion to believe that life was put on earth in one divine stroke will recognize that we are destroying the Creation, and those who perceive biodiversity to be the product of blind evolution will agree. Across the other great philosophical divide, it does not matter whether species have independent rights or, conversely, that moral reasoning is uniquely a human concern. Defenders of both premises seem destined to gravitate toward the same position on conservation.

The stewardship of environment is a domain on the near side of metaphysics where all reflective persons can surely find common ground. For what, in the final analysis, is morality but the command of conscience seasoned by a rational examination of consequences? And what is a fundamental precept but one that serves all generations? An enduring environmental ethic will aim to preserve not only the health and freedom of our species, but access to the world in which the human spirit was born.

1992

Discussion

1. What do you think is the point of Wilson's quoting from Virgil's *Aeneid*, a poem written in praise of Rome and published in 19 B.C.E.?
2. Why does Wilson say that a handful of soil "holds more order than can be found on the surfaces of all the planets combined"? What is the significance of this realization?
3. Why is it important to map the biosphere? If we are aware of only a fraction of all life that exists on earth, why should we care about the unknown?
4. Discuss Wilson's belief that human evolution is advanced by emotions as well as intellect.
5. What does Wilson mean by "biophilia"?
6. What does Wilson suggest is the central illusion of humanity?

Walking

LINDA HOGAN

Linda Hogan (1947–) was born in Denver, raised in Colorado Springs, and spent much of her childhood on her grandparents' farm in Oklahoma. She left school at fifteen but eventually finished her studies at the University of Colorado. Hogan's family is one of mixed heritage, with a white mother and a Chickasaw father, but she identifies herself as a Native American. Hogan's ideas about nature and rural living were formed in her youth and still provide the dominant themes and subjects of her writing. Her experience of walking, like that of Henry David Thoreau, led Hogan to a profound belief in the value of observing nature while being part of it. Hogan's works include a play, A Piece of Moon *(1980), and several volumes of poetry,* Calling Myself Home *(1979),* Daughters: I Love You *(1981),* Eclipse *(1983),* Seeing Through the Sun *(1985),* Savings *(1991), and* The Book of Medicines *(1993). Her fiction includes* Mean Spirit *(1990),* Solar Storms *(1995), and* The Woman Who Watches over the World: A Native Memoir *(2002).*

---- ◆ ----

It began in dark and underground weather, a slow hunger moving toward light. It grew in a dry gulley beside the road where I live, a place where entire hillsides are sometimes yellow, wind-blown tides of sunflower plants. But this plant was different. It was alone and larger than the countless others that had established their lives farther up the hill. This one was a traveler, a settler, and like a dream beginning in conflict, it grew where the land had been disturbed.

I saw it first in early summer. It was a green and sleeping bud, raising itself toward the sun. Ants worked around the unopened bloom, gathering aphids and sap. A few days later, it was a tender young flower, soft and new, with a pale green center and a troop of silver-gray insects climbing up and down the stalk. Over the summer this sunflower grew into a plant of incredible beauty, turning its face daily toward the sun in the most subtle of ways, the black center of it dark and alive with a deep blue light, as if flint had sparked an elemental fire there, in community with rain, mineral, mountain air, and sand.

As summer changed from green to yellow there were new visitors daily, the lace-winged insects, the bees whose legs were fat with pollen, and grasshoppers with their clattering wings and desperate hunger. There were other lives I missed, those too small or hidden to see. It was as if this plant with its host of lives was a society, one in which moment by moment, depending on light and moisture, there was great and diverse change.

There were changes in the next larger world around the plant as well. One day I rounded a bend in the road to find the disturbing sight of a dead horse, black and still against a hillside, eyes rolled back. Another day I was nearly lifted by a wind and sandstorm so fierce and hot that I had to wait for it to pass before I could return home. On this day the faded dry petals of the sunflower were swept across the land. That was when the birds arrived to carry the new seeds to another future.

5   In this one plant, in one summer season, a drama of need and survival took place. Hungers were filled. Insects coupled. There was escape, exhaustion, and death. Lives touched down a moment and were gone.

I was an outsider. I only watched. I never learned the sunflower's golden language or the tongues of its citizens. I had a small understanding, nothing more than a shallow observation of the flower, insects, and birds. But they knew what to do, how to live. An old voice from somewhere, gene or cell, told the plant how to evade the pull of gravity and find its way upward, how to open. It was instinct, intuition, necessity. A certain knowing directed the seed-bearing birds on paths to ancestral homelands they had never seen. They believed it. They followed.

There are other summons and calls, some even more mysterious than those commandments to birds or those survival journeys
of insects. In bamboo plants, for instance, with their thin green
canopy of light and golden stalks that creak in the wind. Once a century, all of a certain kind of bamboo flower on the same day. Neither
the plants' location, in Malaysia or in a greenhouse in Minnesota,
nor their age or size make a difference. They flower. Some current
of an inner language passes among them, through space and separation, in ways we cannot explain in our language. They are all,
somehow, one plant, each with a share of communal knowledge.

John Hay, in *The Immortal Wilderness*, has written: "There are
occasions when you can hear the mysterious language of the
Earth, in water, or coming through the trees, emanating from the
mosses, seeping through the undercurrents of the soil, but you
have to be willing to wait and receive."

Sometimes I hear it talking. The light of the sunflower was
one language, but there are others more audible. Once, in the redwood forest, I heard a beat, something like a drum or heart coming from the ground and trees and wind. That underground current stirred a kind of knowing inside me, a kinship and longing, a
dream barely remembered that disappeared back to the body.
Another time, there was the booming voice of an ocean storm
thundering from far out at sea, telling about what lived in the distance, about the rough water that would arrive, wave after wave
revealing the disturbance at center.

Tonight I walk. I am watching the sky. I think of the people   10
who came before me and how they knew the placement of stars in
the sky, watched the moving sun long and hard enough to witness
how a certain angle of light touched a stone only once a year.
Without written records, they knew the gods of every night, the
small, fine details of the world around them and of immensity
above them.

Walking, I can almost hear the redwoods beating. And the
oceans are above me here, rolling clouds, heavy and dark, considering snow. On the dry, red road, I pass the place of the sunflower,
that dark and secret location where creation took place. I wonder
if it will return this summer, if it will multiply and move up to the
other stand of flowers in a territorial struggle.

It's winter and there is smoke from the fires. The square,
lighted windows of houses are fogging over. It is a world of elemental attention, of all things working together, listening to what
speaks in the blood. Whichever road I follow, I walk in the land of
many gods, and they love and eat one another. Walking, I am listening to a deeper way. Suddenly all my ancestors are behind me.

Be still, they say. Watch and listen. You are the result of the love of thousands.

1995

Discussion

1. What does Hogan learn about herself by walking?
2. Do you think that Hogan's direct observations of nature would take up too much time in our technological and career-driven world?
3. Why is Hogan so fascinated by the growth of the sunflower? What does she learn about life by observing it?
4. Do you believe that the separation of life from nature that Hogan discusses is lessening as a result of increased environmental awareness?
5. Compare Hogan's keen sense of observing natural change with that of Mary Austin in "My Neighbor's Field" (p. 13).

Once Upon a Planet

PAUL HAWKEN, AMORY LOVINS, AND L. HUNTER LOVINS

Paul Hawken's Growing a Business *(1987) is the basis for a public television series by the same name. He also wrote* The Ecology of Commerce *(1993). He currently serves as chairman of the Natural Step, an educational foundation dedicated to environmental sustainability. Amory Lovins, a physicist, is director of research of Rocky Mountain Institute, a not-for-profit resource policy institute in Snowmass, Colorado. L. Hunter Lovins is the Rocky Mountain Institute's president and executive director. The Lovins have written or coauthored* World Energy Strategies *(1975),* Energy Controversy: Soft Path Questions and Answers *(1979),* Brittle Power *(1982),* Energy and War: Breaking the Nuclear Link *(1980),* Green Development: Integrating Ecology & Real Estate *(1997), and the* Harvard Business Review on Business & the Environment *(2000).*

———————— ✦ ————————

The environmental debate is conducted in a predictable cycle. Science discovers another negative human impact on the environment. Trade groups and businesses counter, the media reports both sides, and the issue eventually gets consigned to a growing list of unresolved problems. The point is not that one side is right and the other wrong but that the episodic nature of the news, and the compartmentalization of each successive issue, inhibit devising solutions. Environmentalists appear like Cassandra, business looks like Pandora, apologists sound like Dr. Pangloss, and the public feels paralyzed.

The Worldwatch Institute's *1998 State of the World* report again reported that the trend in environmental indicators was downward: "Forests are shrinking, water tables are falling, soils are eroding, wetlands are disappearing, fisheries are collapsing, rangelands are deteriorating, rivers are running dry, temperatures are rising, coral reefs are dying and plant and animal species are disappearing."

Predictably, Worldwatch's critics argued that the report was unduly gloomy. "In every single report in 15 years, [Worldwatch has] said we are outgrowing the planet's capacity. For 15 years, that's proved to be absolutely in every way false [sic]," retorted Jerry Taylor of the libertarian Cato Institute. Taylor cited increased life expectancy, decreasing child mortality, and improved nutritional intake as proving that standards of living improve as population grows.

Ignored by the media is the likelihood that both sets of data are correct. It is unquestionable that humanity has made astonishing progress. Average life spans continue to increase, a middle-class person can travel the world, and people in developed countries have the highest standard of living in history. But those facts do not make the Worldwatch observations wrong. Seemingly contradictory trends in the environment and society should not be portrayed as mutually exclusive. Both sets of data are credible and can be explained by the concept of overshoot: the ability to exceed temporarily the carrying capacity of the earth can help people to live longer, but put our natural capital into decline. Stated in another way, the ability to accelerate a car that is low on gasoline does not prove the tank is full.

Although such debates make good fodder for reporters and   5 can help expose gaps in knowledge, the cacophony has unfortunate effects. One is the "expert's dilemma." If you went for your annual physical and were diagnosed by two doctors who fought and argued every step of the way as to whether you were sick or healthy, you would come away confused, numbed, and probably angry. When citizens who are not experts in climatology watch *Nightline* and hear one scientist state that automotive emissions of CO_2 could lead to killer hurricanes and massive crop loss while the other says that not using carbon-based fuels will signal the end of Western civilization, the citizens are left confused and disheartened. Mediagenic arguments allow little room for consensus or shared frameworks. Though great for ratings, such media-devised wrangling ignores the possibility that innovative, pragmatic solutions might exist that can satisfy the vast majority of Americans and make the wrangling irrelevant.

Remembering Einstein's dictum on mind-sets, cited at the beginning of this book, it might be useful to review a matrix of four worldviews on the emotional and intellectual frameworks that business, citizens, and governments use to negotiate and choose about economics and the environment. Biophysicist Donella Meadows, adjunct professor of environmental studies at Dartmouth College, outlined them in *The Economist*. She stated that she has become less interested in winning the environmental debate and more concerned with the "intransigent nature of the discussion." Each of the worldviews discussed below—which are color-coded with only a slight bias—is a systems view reflecting a perspective common among business, labor, environmentalists, and synthesists, in that order.

The *Blues* are mainstream free-marketers. Such people have a positive bias toward the future based on technological optimism and the strength of the economy. They are armed with a strong statistical case, based on the vigorous and dynamic economies of Western and (until 1998) Asian nations. Their approach is deeply rooted in conventional economics, and their number-crunching reveals a world vastly improved and rapidly ascending. Blues believe that reliance on innovation, investment, and individual freedom will ensure a shining future for humankind, and a level of material well-being that has strong appeal to virtually everyone in the world. Their optimism also extends to the environment, believing that in most cases, markets will send strong and appropriate price signals that will elicit timely responses, mitigating environmental damage or causing technological breakthroughs in efficiency and productivity.

The *Reds* represent the sundry forms of socialism. Although one might expect them to have been discredited by the downfall of the erstwhile Soviet Union, their worldview is very much alive. They find validation in the chaotic and horrific economic conditions that the rise of bandit capitalism has brought to contemporary Russia, a country whose economic machinery now benefits a minority at the expense of a materially and socially disadvantaged majority. The growing and worldwide gap between rich and poor confirms the Reds' analyses, which are as accurate about poverty and suffering as the Blues' observations are accurate about growth and change. While Blues focus on the promise of growth and technology, Reds focus on its shadow and try to discern its root causes. They view labor—one aspect of human capital—as the principal source of wealth and see its exploitation as the basis of injustice, impoverishment, and ignorance. The Reds generally have little to say about the environment, seeing it as a distraction from fundamentally important social issues.

The *Greens* see the world primarily in terms of ecosystems, and thus concentrate on depletion, damage, pollution, and population growth. They focus on carrying capacity and want to bring about better understanding of how large the economy can grow before it outstrips its host. Their policy focuses on how many and how much, the number of people, and the amount of impact each person can have upon the environment. Greens are not usually technophobes; most see technology as an important tool to reduce human impact. More recently, some have become interested in free-market mechanisms, and want externalities presently borne by society to be fully integrated into producer costs and consumer prices so that markets become, in David Korten's phrase, "mindful." The Greens, and to some extent the Reds, host bigger tents in that they hold a bolder and broader diversity of views. But this also keeps them splintered and self-canceling, as Greens tend to unite their enemies and divide their friends, a good formula for political failure. They are often portrayed as caring less for people than animals, more about halogenated compounds than waterborne diseases.

The *Whites* are the synthesists, and do not entirely oppose or   10
agree with any of the three other views. With an optimistic view of humankind, they believe that process will win the day, that people who tell others what is right lead society astray. Since Blues, Reds, and Greens all fall into that category, Whites reject them all, preferring a middle way of integration, reform, respect, and reliance. They reject ideologies whether based on markets, class, or nature, and trust that informed people can solve their own problems. On the environmental level, they argue that all issues are local. On business, they say the fabled level playing field never existed because of market imperfections, lobbying, subsidies, and capital concentration. On social problems, they argue that solutions will naturally arise from place and culture rather than from ideology. Leadership in the White world is reminiscent of the Taoist reminder that good rulers make their subjects feel as if they succeeded by themselves. Environmental and social solutions can emerge only when local people are empowered and honored.

While many individuals have traits of two or more of these typologies, the different views tend to become isolated and to define the others by their own internal logic. Blues see Reds as anachronistic, even fascistic. Reds return the compliment and neither think much of the Greens, who they say are hindering progress and speaking for a privileged minority. Blues win points (among Blues) by lumping Greens in with the Reds. All three tend to ignore the Whites but will take credit when any White-type scheme works in their sphere. Meadows asks:

> What would we see if we were willing to approach the question of human population growth and planetary limits purely scientifically? What if we could divest ourselves of hopes, fears, and ideologies long enough to entertain all arguments and judge them fairly? What we would see, I think, is that all sides are partly right and mostly incomplete. Each is focusing on one piece of a very complex system. Each is seeing its piece correctly. But because no side is seeing the whole, no side is coming to wholly supportable conclusions.
>
> The Greens are correct: Population growth that causes people to level forests and overgraze lands exacerbates poverty. The Reds are correct: The helplessness of poverty creates the motivation for parents to have many children, as their only hope of providing for themselves. The Blues are right: Economic development can bring down birthrates. The Whites are right: Development schemes work, but not when they are imposed by large bureaucratic institutions such as the World Bank. Capital can be the scarcest factor of production at some times and places, labor at other times and places, materials and energy and pollution-absorption capacity at still others. The limits the Greens point out really are there. So are the injustices that anger the Reds. So are the market and technical responses the Blues have faith in. And so is the wisdom of the people that the Whites respect.

A successful business in the new era of natural capitalism will respect and understand all four views. It will realize that solutions lie in understanding the interconnectedness of problems, not in confronting them in isolation.

Moreover, it will seek a common framework of understanding about the functions of the earth itself, and the dynamics of society. While interpretation of data is subject to culture, education, and outlook, the basic principles that govern the earth are well established and commonly agreed upon by all scientists. But you would hardly know that by reading heated op-ed columns or listening to legislative debates. Although you can go to a bookstore and find books that explain the tenets, principles, and rules for everything from golf and dominoes to taxes, judo, and war, there's no user's manual for how to live and operate on the earth, the most important and complex system known.

David Brower, the éminence grise of the environmental movement, once humorously proposed such a manual years ago. The instructions might read: (1) The planet has been delivered in perfect working condition and cannot be exchanged for a new one. (2) Please don't adjust the thermostat or the atmosphere—controls were preset at the factory. (3) The biosphere was thoroughly tested and developed during a 3-billion-year breaking-in period and is powered by a maintenance-free fusion reactor that will supply energy for another 5 billion years. (4) Air and water are in limited supply and are not replaceable; they will cycle and purify themselves automatically if there are not too many aboard. (5) There is only one life per passenger and it should be treated with dignity. Instructions covering the birth, operation and maintenance, and disposal of each living entity have been thoughtfully provided, encoded in a computer language whose operation is fully automatic. If these instructions are lost or damaged, the filling of reorders is subject to long delays. (6) If there are too many passengers and conditions get crowded, read the emergency load manual and be ever more diligent that no foreign or toxic substances are introduced into the air, food, and water.

Why would the inhabitants of earth need a manual? Ideally, it would provide everyone with a shared mental model of the system they are influencing and participating in. A generally accepted set of standards and principles in sports, finance, education, and other sectors enables society to function efficiently, harmoniously, and safely, allowing us to drive in traffic, land jumbo jets at O'Hare, and communicate globally through telephony and computers. A critical difference between a user's manual for such societal activities, however, and one for the environment is that earth's operating guidelines are inherent, not imposed. They cannot be made up, only recognized. Author Bill McKibben put it succinctly in a speech to corporate executives: "The laws of Congress and the laws of physics have grown increasingly divergent, and the laws of physics are not likely to yield."

Tens of thousands of organizations in the world have taken on the task of assembling the ingredients of a real operating manual for the planet. Some are specifically addressing the responsibilities and opportunities of business. These include:

Rocky Mountain Institute, The Natural Step, The Wuppertal Institute, World Resources Institute, SustainAbility (London), CERES, Redefining Progress, Product-Life Institute, World Business Council for Sustainable Development (Switzerland), Center for Clean Products and Clean Technologies at the University of Tennessee, United Nations Environment Programme (UNEP) and Development Program (UNDP), Institute for Sustainable Design and Commerce at the University of Virginia (Charlottesville), Forum for the Future (London), International Institute for Sustainable Development (Canada), Businesses for Social Responsibility, and the Stockholm Environmental Institute. They are joined by approximately one hundred transnational corporations and tens of thousands of smaller companies that have pledged to take an active role in reshaping the role of business in the environment and society.

In addition, tens of thousands of institutes, associations, foundations, colleges, universities, churches, outdoor clubs, land trusts, and nongovernmental organizations are addressing the complete range of environmental issues. These include such remarkable groups as Ecotrust, Ashoka, the Society for Ecological Restoration, Worldwatch Institute, Friends of the River, Environmental Research Foundation, Development Alternatives (Delhi), Land Stewardship Council, The Just Transition Consortium, Instituto de Ecología Politica (Santiago, Chile), International Society of Ecological Economics, International Institute for Industrial Environmental Economics (Lund), Earth Island Institute, Congress for the New Urbanism, American Farmland Trust, the Energy Foundation, Southwest Organizing Project, RIVM (Holland), Center for a New American Dream, One Thousand Friends of Oregon, the Cenozoic Society, Indigenous Environmental Network, World Wildlife Fund, IUCN, Friends of the Earth, and many more. Together, these thousands of organizations, however they may be collectively identified, have quietly become the world's largest and fastest-growing activist movement. Arguably they have now become the world's real capitalists. By addressing such issues as greenhouse gases, social equity, chemical contamination, and the loss of fisheries, wildlife corridors, and primary forests, they are doing more to preserve a viable business future than are all the world's chambers of commerce put together.

The largest institution addressing mental models is our schools. Colleges, universities, and public schools can change their impact on the environment in two fundamental ways. They create the citizens, MBAs, engineers, and architects that create our world. At the same time, they spend $564 billion a year to do so, including $17 billion annually in new construction on colleges and universities. Oberlin Professor David Orr, the leading spokesperson for integrating the environment and education, points out that a large segment of that money is spent to purchase energy, materials, food, and water in ways that are every bit as inefficient as this book outlines. Orr believes that changing the procurement, design, and investments made by our educational systems represents a "hidden curriculum" that can teach, as "powerfully as any overt curriculum, a more comprehensive way of seeing the world that is the foundation for a radically different curriculum than that presently offered virtually anywhere. In every respect this is a challenge of how we think which makes it a challenge for those institutions purporting to improve thinking. Much of the change in outlook and perspective called for will not happen in the time available unless schools, colleges, and education get it.

Only once in the history of this planet—now—have total flows and movement of materials by one species matched or exceeded natural planetary flows. Humans place more than three hundred times more lead into the environment than can dissipate naturally, twenty-three times more zinc, and thirty-eight times more antimony. Scientific analysis of bubbles in the Vostok ice core from Antarctica show CO_2 in the atmosphere at the highest level in 420,000 years; it took only 100 years of industrial combustion to bring this about. Global temperatures in the next century are expected to exceed a 10,000-year record.

Traditional forecasting examines prior events and present 20 trends and traces both forward to a probable tomorrow. Most of the time this method works, even with natural events, so long as projections don't extend too far into the future. Sometimes, however, traditional planning fails catastrophically, as when an unforeseen event changes all the terms of the equation. When the Soviet Empire fell, Southern California went into a near-depression as 250,000 defense jobs were lost. Real estate prices plummeted, taxes declined, alcoholism and abusive behavior increased among the unemployed, and the ripple effects were partly responsible for increased racism, anti-immigration laws, and the social uprising that occurred in South Central Los Angeles. Conventional economic forecasts of Los Angeles's future proved to be wrong simply because no one had projected an "optimistic" scenario in which the United States finally "won" the Cold War.

A big question for society is whether it is willing to place its faith in so-far-so-good forecasts that presume there will be no significant environmental problems in the future. Increasingly, it makes more sense to take into account possible downsides so that if some environmental crisis does occur, it will have the least possible effect. The rub here is that the environment never really goes "wrong" but merely changes according to the principles of nature. In that context, the most unlikely environmental scenario is that nothing unlikely happens. The biggest surprise would be no surprises. While it is unwise to believe in any one environmental projection of the future, it is important to bear in mind that nature bats last *and* owns the stadium.

Today, comprehensive planning is critical for any institution. Business faces increasing demands on all fronts, including globalization, shorter product life-cycles, the Internet, overcapacity, complex regulations, currency volatility, and changing governmental policies. In such a world, it is critical to have a long-term view that will be responsive to and complement future events. Businesses and governments often avoid the task of planning for issues related to the environment or society because the time frames for environmental and social change always seem over the horizon, whereas the challenges and modification times required in other areas are measured in years if not months. Yet any attempt to form a coherent assessment of the future that does not take into account what is happening to the natural and human capital is incomplete strategic thinking.

The lesson of this book with respect to forecasting is simple and clear: No matter what future one believes in, building the principles of natural capitalism into our planning will make the foundations of society firmer. In scenarios in which the environment begins to change rapidly (or in which its services are clearly declining), resource productivity can also buy time, buffering society against sudden changes. As futurist Peter Schwartz counsels, the best option for an uncertain future is the one that leaves the most options open.

University of North Carolina Business School Professor Stuart Hart has asked whether corporations are ready for the natural capitalism revolution. Typically, business revolutions do not arise within existing industries but from forces outside. Hart believes meeting the multitude of challenges facing business and society will bring about economic discontinuities that are unprecedented in rate and scope and will require business to adopt new approaches. It will have to leapfrog over existing technologies rather than incrementally improve them. This may mean abandoning research in core products while they are still "winners," simply because new products or systems offer vastly improved performance. Why would anyone have wanted to create incremental improvements in vacuum tubes when the transistor was coming over the horizon? Similarly, the Big Three automakers will have to determine at just what point the internal combustion engine will simply become uneconomical to re-engineer. That point may already be here.

To understand the opportunities offered by the resource productivity revolution and the other principles of natural capitalism, business will need to move across industrial sectors and solicit cooperation from competitors, critics, and perceived adversaries alike. This may seem like something no sane business would ever do, but an increasing number of leading companies are doing just that. Such organizations as World Resources Institute and Rocky Mountain Institute consult regularly for companies as well as for governments and communities. One of the largest forest products companies in the world is meeting with Rainforest Action Network and Greenpeace, its former archenemies, to formulate a strategic plan for their futures. Mitsubishi Electric worked with 160 nongovernmental environmental organizations to forge a new vision for the company.

The success of resource productivity as a societal strategy may augur an entirely new relationship between business and government. Just as traditional industrial activity may no longer be economic when natural capital becomes the limiting factor, relaxed governmental regulations that once "benefited" business may now actually harm it. Once business realizes that its existence is threatened by decreasing functions of ecosystems, it may need to take positions diametrically opposed to its prior stands and even argue for stricter regulations. For example, the oil industry, with few exceptions, has led the fight against global emissions limits for CO_2. This strategy makes as much sense as defending typewriters. Although the oil industry faces a cloudy future in the long run, energy companies and especially energy service companies do not. But regulation can exert selective pressures favoring the agile, alert, and green. By fighting the wrong battle, most oil companies delay innovation and ensure potent new competition.

In contrast, OK Petroleum, Sweden's largest refiner and retailer of gasoline, fought for higher carbon taxes because it no longer sees itself as being in the petroleum business: It is a clean

25

energy company. After formulating low-carbon gasoline, it found that it was being penalized by the per-liter fuel taxes levied in Sweden. Since the taxes were assessed on the quantity of the gasoline rather than the content of carbon that creates greenhouse gases, OK joined with twenty-four other companies to lobby the government to *increase* carbon taxes. Those businesses were thinking long-term. Having already achieved large improvements in resource productivity, they wanted a "boost" from incentives to go further. By raising resource prices, Swedish companies also thought they (like Germany and Japan before them) might gain greater advantages over their competitors in the United States, rendered somnolent by artificially cheap energy. Similarly, the U.S. firms working to create totally recyclable or compostable carpets are all fierce competitors, yet if they jointly lobbied for prohibitions on landfilling carpet, it would give them a competitive advantage, seriously putting the screws to laggards in their industry.

Just as businesses are beginning to see the loss of natural capital or ecosystem function as harmful to both their short- and long-term interests, they may also come to realize that social inequities are harmful to their interests as well. When the African writer Ken Saro-Wiwa and seven of his colleagues were hanged by the Nigerian military dictatorship after being convicted in a kangaroo court for leading the protests against the environmental degradation in Ogoniland caused by multinational petroleum companies, Shell stations in Germany were burned to the ground, boycotts in Holland slashed sales, and employees in London were chastised by family and friends. Since that time, Shell has begun to reexamine all its racial, economic, and environmental policies. Nevertheless, Shell has yet to apologize for its actions in Nigeria that helped lead to Saro-Wiwa's execution, and protests against the company continue.

While facing such challenges, it is easy to overlook the social part and go straight to the technical. Social issues are human and messy. Social includes children, women, the elderly, the next generation, and government. It is hard to grapple with what may seem unrelated issues, starting with the rights, health, education, and economic opportunities available to women. But the example of Curitiba shows that design integration of social and technical innovations is necessary and can enhance both.

30   It will not be trivial to establish sensible policies. Emphasizing resource productivity will require the reversal of two hundred years of policies in taxes, labor, industry, and trade meant to en-

courage extraction, depletion, and disposal. Trade policies will need to be recast so as to protect environmental capital, cultural heritage, indigenous rights, and social equity. At present, world-wide trade policies are going in exactly the opposite direction. The global economy that is presently envisaged and imposed upon the world can, in Wendell Berry's words, "only institution-alize a global ignorance, in which producers and consumers cannot know or care about one another and in which the histories of all products will be lost. In such a circumstance, the degradation of products and places, producers and consumers is inevitable."

In finance, central banks, lenders, investors, pension funds, and regulatory agencies will need to be engaged so that capital allocations properly account for the loss of natural and social capital. These institutions will need to create a financial system where all value is placed on the balance sheet, and where nothing is marginalized or externalized because social or biological values don't "fit" into accepted accounting procedures.

In a decade characterized by mega-mergers in the banking industry, one hopeful sign has been the vigorous emergence of the community development finance movement. From small-scale loan funds to start-up banks, and with private and federal support, a whole set of new community institutions provide credit in innovative ways at the community level, rebuilding human and social capital in hundreds of towns and cities. Not surprisingly, it is here rather than in mainstream commercial banks that banking with a natural capital focus has taken root. Shorebank Corporation, the community development pioneer, teamed up with Portland, Oregon, based Ecotrust to create ShoreBank Pacific, a commercial bank dedicated to community development and environmental restoration in the coastal and metropolitan Pacific Northwest. The bank and its nonprofit affiliate Shorebank Enterprise Pacific have together lent millions of dollars to small and medium-size businesses that enhance profitability through improved environmental management and dedication to social equity. The bank's loans are backed by "ecodeposits" from all fifty states.

In short, business has to begin to take on and engage in questions and dialogue that it has, until now, largely avoided. If natural capital is diminishing while manufactured capital is expanding, business must ultimately create production and distribution systems that reverse the loss and eventually increase the supply of natural capital. That will involve more than product design, more than marketing and competition. It will mean a fundamental reevaluation of business's roles and responsibilities.

As this book has shown, however, business will find large, unexpected benefits. While increasing labor productivity to improve competitiveness requires huge investments in capital, materials, and energy supplies to sustain its momentum, increasing resource productivity frees up large amounts of capital that can be invested in strengthening the company and in rebuilding human capital and restoring natural capital. Businesses that are moving toward advanced resource productivity are also discovering an unexpected cultural consequence to their actions. Yes, they save energy and money, create competitive advantage, and help restore the environment. But even more important, they also save people. Not only do they rebalance the roles of workers and of resource-fed machines, but they also create a renewed sense of purpose and mission. For the first time, employees' activities at work are fully and directly aligned with what is best for their children and grandchildren at home.

35   In a few decades, historians may write a history of our times that goes something like this: Now that the private sector has taken its proper place as the main implementer of sustainable practices, simply because they work better and cost less, the 1970s and 1980s approach of micromanagement by intensive government regulation is only a bad memory. Battles between industry and environmentalists are confined to backward countries, where inefficient and polluting industries cling to life beneath a shield of central planning. Today, the central issues for thoughtful and successful industries—the two being increasingly identical—relate not to how best to produce the goods and services needed for a satisfying life—that's now pretty well worked out—but rather to what is worth producing, what will make us better human beings, how we can stop trying to meet nonmaterial needs by material means, and how much is enough.

For many, the prospect of an economic system based on increasing the productivity with which we use natural capital, eliminating the concept of waste, and reinvesting in the earth's living systems and its people is so upbeat that it calls into question its economic viability. To answer that question, just reverse it and ask: How is it that we have created an economic system that tells us it is cheaper to destroy the earth and exhaust its people than to nurture them both? Is it rational to have a pricing system that discounts the future and sells off the past? How did we create an economic system that confuses capital liquidation with income?

Wasting resources to achieve profits is far from fair, wasting people to achieve higher GDP doesn't raise standards of living, and wasting the environment to achieve economic growth is neither economic nor growth.

To make people better off requires no new theories, and needs only common sense. It is based on the simple proposition that *all* capital be valued. While there may be no "right" way to value a forest, a river, or a child, the wrong way is to give it no value at all. If there are doubts about how to value a seven-hundred-year-old tree, ask how much it would cost to make a new one. Or a new atmosphere, or a new culture. What is remarkable about this period in history is the degree of agreement that is forming globally about the relationship between human and living systems. The tens of thousands of organizations that are working toward a sustainable world are, on the whole, diverse, local, underfunded, and tenuous. Scattered across the globe, from Siberia to Chile to Kenya to Bozeman, Montana, people and institutions are organizing to defend human life and the life of the planet. Although largely uncoordinated and mostly disconnected, the mandates, directives, principles, declarations, and other statements of purpose drafted by these groups are extraordinarily consonant. Now they are being joined by the deeper voices of international organizations, and companies, large and small. The Brundtland Report ("Our Common Future"), the World Conservation Strategy by the International Union for the Conservation of Nature, the CERES Principles, the Siena Declaration, the United Nations World Charter for Nature, the Convention on Biological Diversity and the Framework Convention on Climate Change from the Earth Summit, the Hannover Principles, and hundreds more documents obscure and known are being published, circulated, and acted upon. They are important for three reasons. First, the statements are not just about preferences: Often they suggest practical solutions that flow from the principles of whole-system thinking and design. Second, the statements represent a broad consensus that is emerging from the breadth of society rather than only from its ruling structures. Third, never before in history have such disparate and independent groups created common frameworks of understanding around the world. This has never happened in politics, economics, or religion, but it is happening in the growing movement—increasingly joined now by both religion and science—toward what is being called "sustainability." Businesspeople and governments should pay close attention. In these statements, the future is writ large and in the plainest of languages.

Ernst von Weizsäcker, member of the German Bundestag, has put it this way: "We are entering the century of the environment, whether we want to or not. In this century everyone who considers himself a realist will be forced to justify his behavior in light of the contribution it made toward the preservation of the environment." Away from the shrill divisiveness of media and politics, people are remarkably consistent in what kind of future they envision for their children and grandchildren. The potential outcome of natural capitalism and sustainability also aligns almost perfectly with what American voters are saying: They want better schools, a better environment, safer communities, family-wage jobs, more economic security, stronger family support, lower taxes, more effective governments, and more local control. In this, we are like all people and they are like us.

40   Natural capitalism is not about fomenting social upheaval. On the contrary, that is the consequence that will surely arise if fundamental social and environmental problems are not responsibly addressed. Natural capitalism is about choices we can make that can start to tip economic and social outcomes in positive directions. And it is already occurring—because it is necessary, possible, and practical.

1999

Discussion

1. Why do the authors disparage "mediagenic" environmental arguments? How do the authors define the idea of natural capitalism?
2. What are the positions of the Blues, Reds, and Greens? How do the authors see them interacting with the Whites?
3. Explain how the manual for planet Earth composed by Paul Brower, a past president of the Sierra Club, is taken seriously by the authors in their desire to persuade environmentalists and business that their ideas of progress are not antithetical.

Coming to Terms
CHRISTOPHER HALLOWELL

Christopher Hallowell (1945–) was raised in rural Massachusetts and educated at Harvard College and the Columbia University School of Journalism. He has a special interest in science and envi-

ronmental journalism. Hallowell is the author of five books, most recently, Holding Back the Sea *(in which the following essay appeared), which is an investigative work concerning the devastation of the Gulf of Mexico. He is a frequent speaker on wetlands and coastal issues. Hallowell's works include* The Father to the Man *(1987),* Growing Old, Staying Young *(1993), and* People of the Bayou *(1979), reissued in 2003. He has written about environmental issues and science for* Time, The New York Times Magazine, The Christian Science Monitor, Audubon, Geo, Natural History, *and* The American Scholar.

✦

It takes him a while to come to the door. He shuffles over eventually, slides it open, and shoos away the dog that has been guarding the home under the great live oaks. Frank J. Ehret, Jr., eighty-three, looks okay. He is a tiny man, barely five feet high. His eyes behind thick spectacles give the appearance of being the biggest thing about him. They sparkle like stars aflame. But he says he's not well. He says he almost called to tell me not to come to visit today, but he misplaced my telephone number. His breathing has acted up. He had such chest pain last night that he was on the verge of asking his daughter to take him to the emergency room. He decided against it. He says that after three heart operations and a pacemaker and a five-month ordeal with a staph infection following one of the procedures, he'll do anything to avoid hospitals. So, I am glad that I am here just in time, to be able to meet the man people in South Louisiana call the father and founder of the Barataria Preserve, part of the Jean Lafitte National Historical Park.

The 20,000 acre park, ten miles south of New Orleans, is the only effort by the National Park Service to preserve a piece of the state's coastal environment where the public is permitted easy access and education.[1] Its facilities and educational programs are works in progress, mere shadows of the boardwalk complexes and programs offered in the Everglades. But its fauna and flora are comparable, if not more intimate. Rather large alligators reside only a few feet from some of the trails, not readily noticeable to the million-plus visitors who pad next to their waiting jaws each year. I sought Frank out because as the sole instigator for the park, he was obviously a man with a vision for the future of South Louisiana. I wondered if enforced preservation is the best way this rare land can survive.

The name Ehret is prominent in Marrero, a town on the west bank of the Mississippi where the preserve is located, a thirty-minute drive from downtown New Orleans. There's a high school named after Frank's grandfather, part of the Jefferson Parish school system, where Frank spent his professional career as a special education teacher. Frank lives on Ehret Street. His ancestors came here from Germany in the 1720s, when the nascent French colony was in the throes of some severe growing pains. New Orleans was filling with settlers, mostly craftsmen and vagabonds. They knew little about growing crops. The Indians who had helped supply the newcomers with food could not keep up with the demand. Starvation was approaching. Germany came to the rescue, sending thousands of small farmers who settled the west bank of the Mississippi and raised New Orleans's table food. The Ehret family settled back then in just about the same spot as where Frank now dwells.

When Frank was a young man, Marrero was a river town, with a main street, neighborhood bars, dance halls, and small-town intimacies. It had changed its name from Amesville, founded around the docking facilities that the Texas Oil Company, the forerunner of Texaco, built on the river. Oil from Spindletop Field in Beaumont, Texas, was barged up the Mississippi to the docks and sold to the sugar plantations in the area. During the annual late-fall processing of cane, the unrefined oil was used as fuel to boil down the syrup.

5   Now Marrero has lost its connection to the river. Route 90 bisects it in one direction, Barataria Boulevard in the other. Enormous shopping plazas collide with each other, rendering a boxy, neon-lit landscape of Piggly-Wigglies, Home Depots, Wal-Marts, and the occasional pawnshop. And then the subdivisions begin, marching in step formation into the marsh.

Keep going down Barataria Boulevard past the subdivisions, and you will come to Frank's life achievement, *his* park, really, of swamp and marsh, bayous and great cypress trees. It took him a quarter century of lonely battle to save this land from the developers. Now part of the National Park Service, it could be seen as an answer to South Louisiana's crisis—protected and preserved forever, open to visitors but not to dwellers.

Frank is proud of his triumph, as he should be. Most people have forgotten that he is largely responsible for the park. He likes to tell the story about its founding. Besides, his wife has died; his grown children are gone, though they live nearby with their own families. The house is too quiet. So, with grace, he sweeps me into his living room where the TV is blaring to an audience of one whose mind is much too lively for its fodder.

The dark-paneled walls of his living room are covered with plaques and awards from allies-come-lately honoring him for his long fight. The most recent commendation is dated 1989, the year he received the National Conservation Achievement Award from the National Wildlife Federation. The plaque recognizes him as a hero, a man who grabbed a chunk of nature and set it in stone like a diamond, away from the grasp of greedy neighbors who wished to reap financial rewards from it, as have the oil and gas companies and land grabbers like Edward Wisner for generations.

The walls also hold evidence of another side of Frank's life— his life in the swamps where he, ironically, appears to have held little sacred. Photographs of Frank and his friends holding up strings of fish, of shot deer lying at their feet, of piles of ducks, testaments to a life of abundance that the marsh has always provided are lined up like trophies. On a mantel, exquisitely detailed and painted decoys collect dust, carved by Frank out of cypress or tupelo gum, some used in the hunt. A couple of half-finished ones clutter the threshold. They will never be completed, Frank tells me. His eyes have given out on him for detail work.

The photographs and decoys say more to me than all the   10
framed accolades. They speak of a place in nature that is recklessly pillaged rather than treated with the respect due a nurturer and provider over the centuries. The absurd bounty of bleeding wildlife complicates for me the picture that I am trying to bring to focus of Frank, the preservationist as well as the hunter. Is he any different from those many people in South Louisiana who tolerate the dredging of canals haphazardly through the wetlands and the dumping of pollutants on their fragility, and then profess such love for this land, all in a bewildering mix of adoration and abuse?

He begins to talk, fumbling through a battered folder. I have to help him, and what comes out is a large-format scrapbook he has pasted together of the volumes of newspaper articles over the years about his victories and defeats and, at last, his ultimate triumph. Finally, he turns the TV off and offers me a seat. He is out of breath and I urge him to slow down. He shrugs off my concern, insists on standing, and talks terribly fast.

He tells me that what has happened to his beloved South Louisiana—its disintegration and disappearance—is an affront against nature. As he tells me how he has seen and felt the land die, I begin to equate him with a sort of prodigal son. A young man now become an old man, he once may not have understood that these wetlands had any end to them, but then realized that they, like the deer and ducks he hunted, can be killed. He came back to the land to embrace and protect it.

As a boy, he hunted and fished Barataria Bay with his daddy. His daddy loved the land, too; he ran a charter boat service between Lafitte and Grand Isle, for weekenders going to the Oleana Hotel, still in business near the beach behind the levee that holds back the rising Gulf. A photograph of the boat on the living room wall reveals her to be a beauty, a forty-five-foot converted oyster lugger named the *Snappy Stepper*. She had a sleek cabin running her length and a full deck overhead where the Kid Thomas Jazz Band played as the boat plied Barataria Bayou. When it neared Manila Village, all the Chinese shrimp fishermen and dryers would come out on their skiffs and start dancing on the aft decks. Oh, it was a sight, says Frank, his eyes burning.

In the 1950s, the developers came. They weren't strangers from the Midwest. Frank had gone to school with them, fished and hunted with some of them. These men had looked across the river to New Orleans which was beginning to sprawl. They saw the marsh in their backyards not as a continuation of their lives but as the beginning of new lives. They saw money and began to talk about the beautiful homes that would soon line the bayous and drainage canals. Frank saw a disaster in the making. There was Huey Long on a stump, saying that this was the best thing that had ever happened to Louisiana. He said he was going to sell all the land around Barataria Bay for a dollar an acre and make the state rich and the people happy. He commended the developers as heroes of the state. He said they were turning wasteland into real land.

15 Frank already knew that the marsh was real enough. He also knew it was sinking and that any houses that went up on it would begin settling like a heavy book on a cushion. The money and greed were bad enough; what also angered him was the deception of wringing the marsh out like a sponge.

In the early 1960s, Frank began talking up the idea of preservation with the same fervor that the developers were exuding in their glorification of new subdivisions. Frank was alone; the developers had money and friends. But Frank did have an infectious spirit; he got himself elected to a minor political office, a space to give himself a platform. "I created my own road show to get this park idea off the ground," he tells me as he flips through his scrapbook. He spoke at schools, he wooed the local press, he gave speeches wherever he could. Poking around the would-be park, he discovered a couple of old cypress *pirogues* submerged in a bayou along with arrowheads and pottery shards. He wielded them like courtroom evidence to demonstrate to the public what would be lost if the land were allowed to succumb to dredge and bulldozer—its history, its spirit gone up in lawns and concrete slabs.

Even after he tried for years to sell the park idea, people still came up to him and wondered aloud, "Who the hell would want to visit a swamp?" The real estate developers just kept on gouging drainage canals out of the marsh. "I take defeat as an asset," Frank tells me, his voice going hoarse and his breathing, shallow. "I never give up."

His persistence paid off. In 1966, Governor John McKeithen designated the area a state park, a victory to be sure, but hollow as it turned out, for the state claimed it had no funds to administer the new holding. The publicity led former Senator Bennett Johnston to take notice, though. Frank, with Johnston's advice, wrote a proposal to create a national park. Johnston shepherded it through Congress, and in 1978, President Jimmy Carter signed the legislation into law. Another photograph on Frank's wall shows him with President Carter, the bill in front of them, Frank beaming.

I visited the park on a spring day when fields of blue irises bloomed among the cypress and spider lilies rose from pockets of black water like fairy wands. The trail I chose to hike ever so gradually descends through the remains of a cypress forest, into a brackish marsh and finally to the banks of Bayou Segnette, which connects to the Gulf. From the bayou's banks, you look west across Lake Salvador and the marshes on the opposing banks, and you can think that there is no other place so rankly primeval as right here. The bustling serenity of the exuberant growth around me struck me as the way this land was meant to be. I could sense the flow of water through the swamp, too slow to see, but feeding and filtering on its course to the sea. I could see the demarcation between swamp—where the cypress grow—and freshwater marsh with its profusion of flora, and then brackish marsh where cordgrasses predominate.

Naively, I thought that the whole coast of Louisiana should be included in this park. From time to time, proposals have been floated to try to preserve a large part of the coast along the same lines as the Jean Lafitte National Historical Park's Barataria Preserve. They have all been short-lived, as they should be. More than the Everglades, South Louisiana has always been a working coast, prolific in natural resources, industry, and local culture.

The combination of rich nature and rich human bustle is incomparable in this country. Here is South Louisiana's possibility: the melding of a working relationship between humans and nature. Developing that balance is the struggle that South Louisiana is engaged in right now. The heritage of this land is its oil men and shrimpers, fur trappers and oystermen, as much as its cypress stands and lost lakes in the marsh. Pure nature by itself, grand as it may be, is illusory in a place where human beings have for so long been implanted on the land.

Just a few miles from the preserve, the little town of Lafitte lines up its buildings along Barataria Bayou—oyster plants, fish processors, tilting houses, a couple of gas stations and delis—all pretty traditional for a bayou town, except for the recent additions of a gift shop and a bed and breakfast. The road ends just south of the town. The marsh takes over from there, and flows all the way to the Gulf, though its wholeness is severely interrupted by the crisscrossing canals of the Lafitte oil and gas fields.

The contrasting juxtaposition of the preserve and the working town nicely exemplifies the ethical impossibility of South Louisiana putting itself into a state of preservation. As lovely and peaceful as the preserve may be, its nature is compromised by the lack of human activity within its borders. On the other hand, the chewing up that the marsh has endured a few miles away under the auspices of the oil and gas fields speaks to the need for controls.

A stable relationship between people and nature in South Louisiana is still far from a reality. Movement in that direction is a slow crawl, a tedious one, as the meetings stretch on, day after day. And as the wetlands inexorably decline, day after day, the fear is palpable. Exciting to witness, however, is the growing realization among people from all walks of life along the Gulf that if they do not conduct themselves on nature's terms, all will be lost. The natural system, pushed to the limits, is rebelling. The marsh will continue to sink, the grasses die as salt water encroaches, the marine bounty vanish, and the oil and gas production remain under threat of upheaval, if compromise does not outweigh dominance as a way of life.

Compromise means that enormous quantities of water have to be allowed to flow into the wetlands from the Mississippi River, despite its diminished silt load. That's the emerging consensus, not always willingly acknowledged but in everyone's mind. Let the water flow. Let the nutrients and silt replenish the sinking land. It will cost billions of dollars, but that's what nature demands. That's what nature got before the levees and the canals went in.

The first European settlers to this country were daunted by   25
the interminable forests before them. Remnants of unease may
still run in us. Of the Pilgrims trying to survive their first winter
in this country in 1621, William Bradford, Pilgrim elder and governor of Plymouth, recorded in his journal, "They that know the
winters of that country know them to be sharp and violent, and
subject to cruel and fierce storms. Besides, what could they see
but a hideous and desolate wilderness, full of wild beasts and
wild men?" The solution was to "civilize" the new land. "Gardens
may be made [out of the wilderness] without expense," Thomas
Jefferson wrote a century and a half later. "We have only to cut
out the superabundant plants."

The debate between preservation on one hand and conservation, or "wise use," on the other, has played back and forth across
the land over the generations. John Muir, the archetypal preservationist, who founded the Sierra Club and, indirectly, the National
Park Service, believed that nature was God's temple which intem-
perate human beings had no right to alter. "The forests of America,
however slighted by man, must have been a great delight to God,"
he wrote, "for they were the best he ever planted. The whole continent was a garden, and from the beginning it seemed to be favored
above all the other wild parks and gardens of the globe."

Gifford Pinchot, founder of the U.S. Forest Service, disagreed. He argued for "wise use" of natural resources, control,
and management for the benefit of all. "The first principle of conservation is development, the use of the natural resources now existing on this continent for the benefit of the people who live here
now," he declared.

The debate continues. In 1980, then-president Jimmy Carter
signed into law the Alaska National Interest Lands Conservation
Act, which would preserve over 100 million acres—almost one-
third of the state—into ten new national parks, wildlife refuges, and
wilderness areas. Alaskans, prodded by big oil money and big politics, were outraged. They took out their anger on a Carter effigy and
hurled bottles at it. Now, they consider Carter a hero, as receipts
from tourism have topped one billion dollars a year. Even so, sentiment runs high against efforts to give national-monument status to
the 20-million-acre Arctic National Wildlife Refuge on Alaska's
north coast. The oil and business interests are lobbying hard for the
whole 20-million-acre expanse to be opened to oil drilling.

This country, so abundant in resources far beyond the
Louisiana marsh, has never shown a talent for restraint in using

them. Forests, fish stocks, water resources, topsoil, Western grazing lands, clean air, and genetic diversity—these come to mind,
for starters, as natural gifts which now run scarce from overuse
and lack of stewardship. But ask almost anyone if they are aware
of shortages of anything in this country and it's likely they'll say
"no." It's almost dead sure that urban folk don't know the meaning of being without, provided that supermarket shelves remain
stocked. Behind the abundance, we are just mustering through;
scarcity may be coming down the road.

30   Take groundwater. Not many people think about it. Half the
country gets its drinking water from wells rather than from mu-
nicipal water systems, which are apt to filter water. The United
States Geological Survey (USGS), in a survey of shallow wells
across the country, found that 15 percent are high in nitrates,
which can cause the potentially fatal "blue-baby" syndrome. In
another survey, the USGS found sixty volatile organic compounds
in both urban and rural wells. Leading in the pollutants was
methyl-butyl ether (MTBE), a compound formerly added to gasoline for the purpose, ironically, of reducing carbon monoxide in
exhaust, another pollutant. Still another sampling came up with
two or more pesticides in well water. A certain disregard has led
to this worsening situation. As links between introduced chemical
compounds in water and cancers and infertility become more
plausible, both concern and research are increasing. Somehow,
the obvious tends to get missed: stuff that is put onto or into the
ground is bound to end up in the water beneath it. The too-easy
assumption all along is that these substances, though perhaps invisible, will just go away. We can do what we want with the land;
no one will be worse off, is the assumption.

          Or fish stocks. The sardine fishery off Southern California
collapsed some years ago; the cod fishery in the North Atlantic
crashed more recently and is just showing signs of coming back;
bluefin tuna are so rare that Japanese restaurateurs are willing to
pay obscene sums for them and transport them from a Long
Island dock to Tokyo by charter jet for sushi that same evening.
One 715-pound giant sold for $83,500, or $117 per pound, to be
divided up into 2,400 servings at $75 each for a gross profit of al-
most $100,000.[2]

          Swordfish, the backyard barbecue delight, may be headed to-
ward commercial extinction due to mismanagement of the
Atlantic population since the advent of long-lining in the 1960s.
The big swordfish, the 200- to 600-pounders, are long gone.
Females do not reach sexual maturity until they grow beyond

ninety pounds. Over half the swordfish taken in recent years, however, have been immature. And the legal size limit is a mere forty-four pounds. With every small swordfish taken, fishermen are seeing their livelihood disappear.[3]

Marketing strategists have come up with a solution: get the American public used to alternative species—sharks, marlin, orange roughy, Chilean sea bass, to name a few. Now, many shark species are in trouble. Marlin are overfished. Orange roughy and Chilean sea bass, both deepwater species that mature extremely slowly, are nearing depletion.

The will to acknowledge limits appears to be lacking. But a few telling exceptions exist. Cod fishermen in the little outports that dot the rocky coast of Newfoundland, Canada, are one exception. In the 1980s, they warned that stocks were dwindling. Though cod fishing was their only income source, as it had been for their fathers and grandfathers, many volunteered to reduce their catches in hopes of reviving the species for future generations. The effort fell flat, however, as international pressure mounted to keep the offshore fishery open. The result was a severe crash, making the North Atlantic cod fishery one of the more notorious examples of poor management.

The attitude of the small fishermen is an interesting exception to the rule, one that may well have sprung out of familiarity with a resource. Such intimacy is rare today, as managers from afar determine the health of populations, whether fish or timber, and try to fulfill the demand. Late in 2000, George Barisich told me that he had been forced to lay off shrimping for a while, until "the jellies" pass through. He said he had never seen such big ones. "They just clog your nets up like big balloons." George did not know why the jellyfish were passing through his trawling grounds in such numbers.[4] He wasn't too bothered, though. He said that he had plenty of oysters to dredge in the meantime. "What with the lack of rain, they're real salty, just as good as they get," he happily reported.

Peanut Michel was happy, too. He had just heard from the Louisiana Department of Wildlife and Fisheries that his alligator quota for the fall season had been increased from sixty to seventy-five. And even better, he had been lucky enough to be a winner in an "alligator lottery" which would permit him and fourteen other hunters to kill 1,500 alligators on Marsh Island. The reason for Peanut's good fortune had to do with the wise management of the state's alligator population, so robustly revived since overhunting almost did the creatures in.

The management did not come from Washington or Baton Rouge. It came from field researchers who grew up in the marsh and cruised the same bayous as alligators. Such familiarity has allowed them to feel the reptiles' presence, know when they're around, and when they're not, know when something might be amiss.

The debate between preservation and wise use continues, but perhaps it doesn't have to, judging from the dilemma facing Louisiana. The ability to sense the land was Frank Ehret's gift. I have always been struck by the passion that South Louisianans express for their corner of the country, far more so than elsewhere. Their exuberance shows in different ways; Frank's was one way, unique and powerful. A biologist for the Army Corps of Engineers showed me another way, as did some birdwatchers on Grand Isle. The Corps biologist and I were casting for redfish and speckled trout and chatting about the coast's plight just off the Chandeleurs—the beautiful arc of barrier islands, or what's left of them, toward the Mississippi State line. "I grew up taking as much as I want," he said. "My daddy took me duck hunting when I was a kid and we shot so many we didn't know what to do with them. We have so much abundance here we couldn't conceive of not keeping what we shoot or catch."

I had heard other people in South Louisiana talk about the wetlands' seemingly endless bounty. Then the biologist added another perspective. He said that he had traveled out of South Louisiana only a few times. Each time, he couldn't wait to get back. He hoped never to have to leave. "I just don't have any interest in anyplace else. I believe right here must be the best place in the world. Maybe we are going to have to start changing the way we think about all this abundance if we want to keep it that way."

40   Louisiana's bird-watchers show a gentler side of an appreciation for nature. From April to June, the people of Grand Isle enjoy a glorious migration of neotropical birds. They arrive exhausted after their four-hundred-mile flight across the Gulf of Mexico to recuperate in the few remaining live oak thickets. On an April day that I went birding with a handful of people from assorted parts of the state, led by the Nature Conservancy, scarlet tanagers had arrived in all their showiness along with seven or eight warbler species. We did not have to look hard for them. They were resting up, actually, in a neighborhood of mobile homes and dog-patrolled bungalows shaded by a canopy of live oaks. Residents emerged from screened porches to point out different species while kids on noisy off-road vehicles crashed through the trees on

thrillingly rutted paths. The birds didn't seem to mind. One man came trotting toward us pushing a pram with a whining child in it to announce the sighting of a black-throated green warbler. He was very excited about his finding and hushed the child as he pointed out the direction. We set off and soon came to a trailer with a little clearing in front in which the owner had set up a huge bird feeder. A grand display of indigo buntings and purple grosbeaks were feeding, a sight that melted some of the purveyors. Before we left, the owner of the feeder, a retired oysterman who had allied himself with birders, made everyone sign his book. He said he was going to "take it to Washington and show those congressmen how much we care about our state down here." With birding turning into one of the most popular pastimes in this country, surpassing walking, hiking, and other outdoor recreations, it's too bad that the state does not market its living natural riches.

I keep thinking of Frank Ehret and his will to fight for the land. I keep thinking of the attachment to the wetlands that grows in people who have moved to South Louisiana from other places. And those who were born in the marshes rarely leave them; if they do, they tend to return, with a sigh of relief. Families are huge here, whole towns occupied by people with three or four last names—Arceneaux, Babineaux, Charamie, Curole, Landry, Petrie, Stelly, Voisin—like the beginning of a child's song. I think of the efforts to come to consensus to stop the coast from dying. And I think of the water lapping under the stilts that hold up bayou towns, and the worry on faces up and down the bayous. In the way people here regard their coast, with a mix of religious obsession and practical need, I see salvation. Few other places rich in nature in this country are just as rich in human activity.

That's one reality. There's another reality, or rather a possibility, that is just beginning to emerge in South Louisiana's quandary over its environment. Something that Joe Suhayda, the computer simulation hurricane forecaster, said comes back to me, about the people around here needing to know what they want to do. They have all the ingredients to set things right with the environment and still live in the environment that they have created. They have the spirit, the love of land, the desire to involve everyone in decisions, the money, but they don't have the plan. Not yet. They could learn something from those Newfoundland cod fishermen.

At all the meetings I attended during a year and a half of research, meetings at Corps headquarters, with representatives of

the Barataria-Terrebonne National Estuary Program, at universities, with oystermen and shrimpers, or with oil men, I found
myself squirming with excitement in my seat as I watched this
slow-motion struggle to find The Plan. "They're almost there," I
kept telling myself. "They're finding their way." Then I realized
they hadn't, that their direction had become mired in some bu-
reaucrat's meanderings, some oysterman's complaints that his
reefs would be buried by all the silt let in from the Mississippi,
or in just plain indecisiveness. But when the next meeting came
along, I went full of expectation that this time it was going to
happen.

The pressure is mounting to save the coast. These days, you
can feel the tension rise more quickly in meetings. People know
that an end is coming, whether by hurricane, by encroaching
salt-water, by the rapidly rising sea itself, or just by the salt
grasses giving up and dying as seemed to be happening during
the summer of 2000. They know that the cornucopia is emptying.
They also know that they all make their livelihoods here and that
while some of them work the oil rigs, their uncles and cousins
work the oyster reefs. The wetlands have brought these disparate
groups together. It is their bed and home and the entire country's
bounty, not as a park but as a working arena of life. No one can
give that up and remain true to the knowledge that we are all part
of nature.

2001

Endnotes

1. While the National Park Service does maintain other facilities and
   sites in Louisiana, the Jean Lafitte National Historic Park is its only
   extensive holding.
2. These figures were provided by Carl Safina, director of the National
   Audubon Society's Living Oceans Program.
3. Recent legislation has imposed seasonal moratoriums to long-line
   fishermen on swordfishing in nursery grounds covering over 130,000
   square miles of the Atlantic. It is expected to result in a reduction of
   juvenile swordfish catches of between 31 percent and 42 percent.
4. The burgeoning population of moon jellyfish, a species native to the
   Gulf of Mexico, is becoming an increasing threat both to the region's
   finfish species as well as to shrimp. Changes in the environment are
   responsible. First, jellyfish require hard surfaces for spawning, and
   the increase in offshore oil platforms well serves this need. Second,
   jellyfish—filter feeders—are thriving on the Gulf's rich assortment of

plankton and bacteria, a result of nitrogen pollution carried by the Mississippi, also responsible for the "dead zone." The result is that jellyfish are sweeping inland waters clean of larvae and eggs of shrimp and finfish. An exacerbating problem is the recent appearance of the Australian spotted jellyfish, a basketball-sized blob that jumped from the Pacific to the Caribbean and is slowly drifting northward.

Discussion

1. What social and economic issues have prevented the preservation of a larger segment of the wetlands than 20,000 acres?
2. Given the stated value of the wetlands' productivity, do you think the entire area should be preserved in order to maintain its productivity?
3. Explain why Frank Ehret, such an avid hunter in his younger years, has changed his point of view. What is your opinion of displaying killed game as it is described in this narrative?
4. Discuss how Hallowell's observations about economic factors in Louisiana have shaped his argument for wetlands preservation.

Thinking and Writing About Chapter 6

1. Contrast Aldo Leopold's "The Land Ethic" (p. 18) with Edward Q. Wilson's "The Environmental Ethic" (p. 198).
2. How would Edward Abbey, Leopold, and Joy Williams respond to Christopher Hallowell's "Coming to Terms" (p. 224)?
3. Compare Linda Hogan's spirituality in "Walking" (p. 207) to Henry David Thoreau's in "Walking" (p. 44) and John Muir's in "The American Forests" (p. 7). On what are they all in agreement? Where do they conflict?
4. Compare Hogan's humanistic vision of the earth's future in "Walking" (p. 207) with Wilson's scientific point of view in "The Environmental Ethic" (p. 198). Are their ideas complimentary or antithetical?
5. Compare the argument of Paul Hawken, Amory Lovins, and L. Hunter Lovins for a sustainable future in "Once Upon a Planet" (p. 210) with the anti-green argument offered by Peter Huber in "How Cities Green the Planet" (p. 53).
6. Discuss why people continue to exploit the environment even though ample evidence exists that the future will be negatively affected as a result.
7. Describe your vision of the future of the American environment.

Additional Resources

Films
A Boy and His Dog (1975), directed by L. Q. Jones
Mind Walk (1991), directed by Berndt Capra

Fiction
Ernest Callenbach. *Ecotopia: The Notebooks and Reports of William Weston* (1975)
Kurt Vonnegut, Jr. *Galápagos* (1985)
Margaret Atwood. *Oryx and Crake* (2003)

Drama
Carol Câpek. *R.U.R.* (1920)

Essay
Al Gore. *Earth in the Balance* (1992)

Hallowell, Christopher. "Coming to Terms" from *Holding Back the Sea: The Struggle for America's Natural Legacy on the Gulf Coast* by Christopher Hallowell. Copyright © 2001 by Christopher Hallowell. Reprinted by permission of HarperCollins Publishers.

Hawken, Paul, Amory Lovins, and L. Hunter Lovins. "Once Upon a Planet" from *Natural Capitalism* by Paul Hawken, Amory Lovins, and L. Hunter Lovins. Copyright © 1999 by Paul Hawken, Amory Lovins, and L. Hunter Lovins. By permission of Little, Brown and Company, Inc.

Hogan, Linda. "Walking" from *Dwellings: A Spiritual History of the Living World* by Linda Hogan. Copyright © 1990 by Linda Hogan. Used by permission of W. W. Norton & Company, Inc.

Hubbell, Sue. "Winter" from *A Country Year: Living the Questions* by Sue Hubbell. Copyright © 1983 by Sue Hubbell. Reprinted by permission of Houghton Mifflin Company. All rights reserved.

Huber, Peter. "How Cities Green the Planet" by Peter Huber. Originally published in the Manhattan Institute's *City Journal,* Winter 2000.

Hulen, Tara. "Dispatch from Toxic Town" by Tara Hulen. Originally published in *OnEarth* (www.nrdc.org/onearth). Reprinted by permission. Copyright © 2003 by NRDC Staff.

Jewett, Sarah Orne. "A White Heron" from *A White Heron and Other Stories* by Sarah Orne Jewett, Boston and New York, Houghton, Mifflin and Company, 1886.

Knox, Margaret L. "The Wilderness According to Cushman" by Margaret L. Knox. Originally published in *Wilderness,* vol. 56, no. 200, 1993. Reprinted by permission of the author.

Leopold, Aldo. "The Land Ethic" from *A Sand County Almanac and Sketches Here and There* by Aldo Leopold, pp. 201-206. Copyright 1949, 1953, 1966; renewed 1977, 1981 by Oxford University Press, Inc. Used by permission of Oxford University Press, Inc.

Lopez, Barry. "Caring For the Woods" by Barry Lopez. Originally published in *Audubon,* March-April, 1995. Copyright © 1995 by Barry Lopez. Reprinted by permission of SLL/Sterling Lord Literistic, Inc.

Muir, John. "The American Forests" by John Muir from *Our National Parks* by John Muir, Boston and New York, Houghton, Mifflin and Company, 1901. Originally published in the *Atlantic Monthly* (August 1897).